Wrong

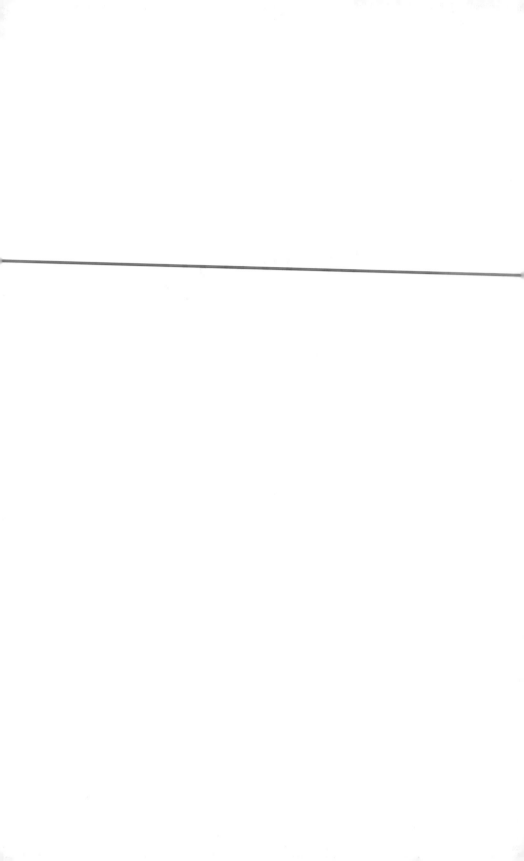

Wrong

How Media, Politics,
and Identity
Drive Our Appetite for
Misinformation

Dannagal
Goldthwaite Young

Johns Hopkins University Press

BALTIMORE

Johns Hopkins University Press

2715 North Charles Street

Baltimore, Maryland 21218

www.press.jhu.edu

Library of Congress Cataloging-in-Publication Data

Names: Young, Dannagal G., author.

Title: Wrong : how media, politics, and identity drive our appetite for
  misinformation / Dannagal Goldthwaite Young.

Description: Baltimore : Johns Hopkins University Press, 2023. | Includes
  bibliographical references and index.

Identifiers: LCCN 2023003636 | ISBN 9781421447759 (hardcover) |
  ISBN 9781421447766 (ebook)

Subjects: LCSH: Group identity—United States. | Belonging (Social
  psychology)—United States. | Truthfulness and falsehood. | Error.

Classification: LCC HM753 .Y67 2023 | DDC 305—dc23/eng/20230203

LC record available at https://lccn.loc.gov/2023003636

A catalog record for this book is available from the British Library.

Special discounts are available for bulk purchases of this book.
For more information, please contact Special Sales at specialsales@jh.edu.

Contents

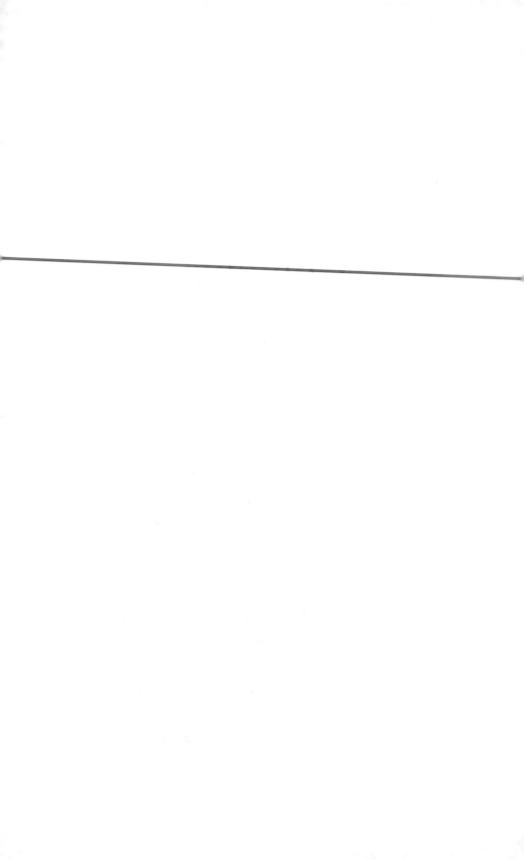

Wrong

IDENTITY DISTILLATION THROUGH OUR MEDIATED POLITICAL WORLD

⑨ SYMBIOSIS AND SYNERGY.
The behaviors of political elites, news organizations, partisan media, and social media platforms are symbiotic and synergistic. They operate in anticipation of the norms and incentives of the others to maximize attention, engagement, profit, and power.

⑧ SOCIAL MEDIA.
Social media platforms connect us to members of our team and recommend content, pages, and groups based on our prior identity-driven behaviors. Algorithms reward emotionally evocative—and hence identity-centered—content and encourage us to perform in keeping with our political mega-identities. This content becomes a part of the observations that we make of the world around *us*, while our partisan performances become a part of the observations that *others* use to make sense of the world around *them*.

⑥ NEWS NORMS.
News norms focused on conflict, drama, and nationalized culture war issues activate our political mega-identities. This content becomes a part of the observations we make of the world around us.

⑦ PARTISAN MEDIA.
Through audience segmentation and data analytics, partisan media activate political mega-identity threat to emotionally engage audiences and keep them coming back. This content becomes a part of the observations we make of the world around us.

⑤ MESSAGING BY POLITICAL ELITES.
Political elites are incentivized to appeal to our political mega-identities to emotionally engage and mobilize us. Their behaviors as elites help define and refine what a perfect partisan prototype looks like. Their identity-centered messaging becomes a part of the observations we make of the world around us.

⑩ IDENTITY DISTILLATION.
As socially sorted Americans, we look to our mediated world to help make sense of events, issues, and crises. In doing so, we encounter communication from political elites, news organizations, partisan media, and social media that repeatedly activates and refines our sense of who we are as a member of our team. This constant distillation of our political mega-identities encourages us to make observations of the world based on how prototypical team members engage in the three Cs: comprehend the world, seek to control the world, and create community in the world, thus fueling identity-driven wrongness.

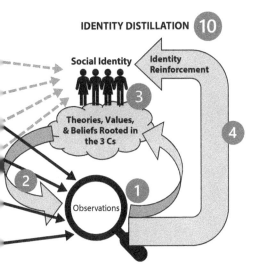

❶ WHAT WE SEE SHAPES WHAT WE KNOW.
Our observations of the world inform our values, theories, and beliefs.

❷ WHAT WE KNOW SHAPES WHAT WE SEE.
Our values, theories, and beliefs inform our observations of the world. These observations are thus theory laden and operate in service of our needs for comprehension, control, and community.

❸ OUR SOCIAL IDENTITY SHAPES WHAT WE KNOW AND WHAT WE SEE.
Since salient social identities help define our values, theories, and beliefs, our observations of the world are also identity laden. We are motivated to comprehend the world in keeping with our team, control the world in ways that serve our team, and experience community by connecting with and belonging to our team.

❹ IDENTITY REINFORCEMENT.
The interplay between these identity-laden values, theories, and beliefs and our identity-laden observations of the world reinforces our political mega-identities.

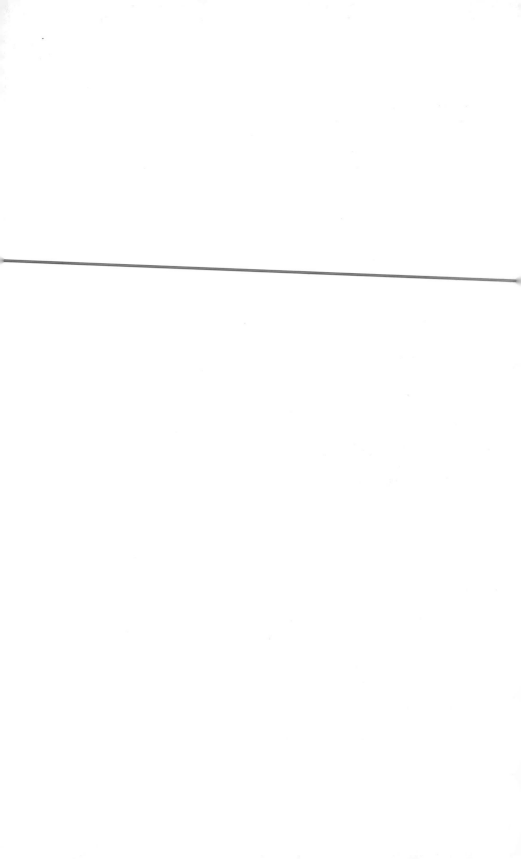

Prologue

IN MAY 2020, two months into the COVID-19 pandemic, I wrote a personal essay that was published on *Vox*. The piece, titled "I Was a Conspiracy Theorist, Too," details how I had fallen down a rabbit hole of conspiratorial thinking when my late husband, Mike, was hospitalized with a brain tumor in 2006.* In it, I describe how the confusion and fear I felt from Mike's diagnosis left me grappling for comprehension and control. I simply could not fathom how our baby boy and I could live without him.

Over the course of seven months in 2005 and 2006, Mike had 13 brain surgeries and lost his vision, his short-term memory, and control over his bodily functions. That time has become one of the defining periods of my life. It has also become an interpretive frame through which I think about human behavior. As a social scientist, I think about human behavior a lot.

Although I fell into a thousand pieces from the moment of Mike's diagnosis, Mike did not. He reminded me regularly that "events of life don't define us. It's how we respond to those events that defines us." While I demanded an

---

* Young, D. G. (2020, May 15). I was a conspiracy theorist, too. *Vox*, https://www.vox.com /first-person/2020/5/15/21258855/coronavirus-covid-19-conspiracy-theories-cancer.

x 5 x

off-ramp to return to our old life, Mike took each day as it came. I often reference Mike Young's uniquely high tolerance for ambiguity. As an artist and im-
proviser, he used the concept of "yes, and" to inform his approach to the
events of his life. He accepted the offer (event), built on it, and found a way to
move the "scene" forward. In the early days of his diagnosis, his high tolerance
for ambiguity was especially valuable. It allowed him to be at least somewhat at
peace in the moment and open to the fact that we wouldn't (couldn't) know his
fate until we encountered it.

Meanwhile, I was spending my days spinning out every scenario, and all of
them were horrifying. The lack of control and constant uncertainty were too
much to bear. I wanted a direction to move in, and I had none.

His first surgery, in November 2005, offered me some sense of control.
The tumor was the enemy, and Mike's doctors were taking it out. But within
weeks it grew back. This meant another holding pattern and more surgeries before we could begin radiation treatment. I was directionless once again. After
several weeks adrift and out of control, I discovered the comfort of anger and
assigning blame. I began to consider who or what might have caused the tumor in the first place. Perhaps it was something at his office? A local industry
site? (The answer was likely a genetic abnormality.) Then I started to question
why the tumor grew back. Was it suboptimal care? Something the doctors did
wrong? (The answer is that that's just what craniopharyngiomas do.) I spent
hours online, looking at websites that offered alternative explanations for the
origins of brain tumors. I searched publicly available environmental documents
to learn the locations of local Superfund sites. I looked for patterns: Did our
neighbors suffer similar or related illnesses? What about his coworkers?

I did my own "research," all with the goal of finding someone to blame. It
gave me a renewed sense of energy and optimism. Instead of being adrift and
out of control, I had agency and direction. Fueled by anger at forces working

against me, I became unyielding and defiant. This anger gave me energy and direction, but as the weeks passed, I began to feel a mismatch between my increasingly paranoid online searches and Mike's spirit of openness and acceptance. He would have hated my going down these rabbit holes. "For what? How is that going to help?" he would have said.

I say "would have said" because by the time I had become "conspiracy curious," Mike was not able to engage in these conversations with me. But because I was his best friend and partner for six years, Mike's identity—who he was and how he approached life—very much informed my own. We also had a circle of friends—artists, musicians, academics, and comics—people whose days were spent exploring, playing, and creating. For our friends, Mike's illness was not about identifying who to be angry with or how to get revenge. It was about spending time with their friend Mike—being playful with him, loving him, and keeping him comfortable.

Being a part of that community, tapping into their social norms of practicing gratitude, openness, and playfulness, helped to stop my dysfunctional spiral. Mike offered the perfect prototype to model how to play that role. Even when he didn't know where he was or what day it was or even that he was sick, he pleasantly greeted friends and loved ones as they came in the door. He joked with us and laughed as we laughed. He bobbed his head to the music playing on the stereo and remarked at how delicious the food was. All Mike had was the present moment, and for him that was enough.

Witnessing the spirit and approach of Mike and our community of friends, I began to see anger and conspiracy theories as a violation of our group norms. And as fast as I had fallen down the rabbit hole, I pulled myself out of it. I stopped thinking about where the tumor came from or who was to blame. Instead, to satisfy my need for comprehension, I began thinking about what I might be learning through the process of Mike's illness. The experience was teaching me about qualities I never knew I had: patience, unconditional love, and a willingness to put someone else's needs before my own. To satisfy my need for control, my friends and I organized a calendar where people could sign up for meal shifts at the hospital so that I could be home with the baby for dinner. People signed up to visit in the evening to read books to Mike, and I took comfort in knowing that he was rarely alone. And to satisfy my need for community, I embraced the gratitude, openness, and playfulness of our friends and loved ones and allowed them to guide me. At night, I would fall asleep picturing Mike, me, and our baby boy being carried by a sea of our friends and family.

In the spring of 2020, as the world wrestled with the uncertainty, chaos, and isolation of COVID-19, I witnessed in friends and loved ones the very same inclinations that I had succumbed to in 2006. My social media feed became home to conspiracy theories and false narratives, with people sharing their doubts about the origins of the coronavirus, the severity of COVID, and the efficacy of face masks. In early May 2020, several friends shared a misinformation-filled documentary that falsely claims that the director of the National Institute of Allergy and Infectious Diseases, Dr. Anthony Fauci, was concealing information about COVID. The film presented conspiracy theories, including the claim that wearing face masks "activates" COVID and makes people sick, and that vaccines have killed millions of people. Importantly, the friends and acquaintances who were sharing these posts were *not* unintelligent people. They were *not* foolish people. These were people feeling confused and scared, looking for comprehension and control. And they were sharing these false narratives with members of their community to say "Hey, have you seen this? Do we believe this? Is this possible?," as if to say, "How do people like us process something as confusing and difficult as this?"

Recognizing the parallels between my psychological needs during the chaos of Mike's illness and the psychological needs of many loved ones during COVID, I decided to share my story and discuss it in terms of the psychology of misinformation. My thought was that through vulnerability and humility, I might be able to encourage people to reconsider their decision to embrace COVID-related conspiracy theories—or, perhaps, help people understand why their loved ones were entertaining these ideas. Understanding the underlying mechanisms of these inclinations, I believed, might help people connect in ways that facilitated trust and discussion. So I wrote the online piece "I Was a Conspiracy Theorist, Too." The emails I received in response to my published essay told me that I was right. I heard from folks who developed empathy for their conspiracy-curious loved ones. I heard from people who suddenly recognized their own impulse to believe COVID misinformation because it had helped them feel less frightened.

It may seem odd that a social scientist is willing to share such a personal story, especially one that reveals that I embraced conspiracy theory beliefs. As a scholar, I'm supposed to be rational. I'm supposed to make observations based on data and logic. Educated people do not entertain unfounded claims, right? Wrong. We all have inclinations from time to time to believe information that is untrue. Not always for long. Not in all domains. Not always in ways that have harmful effects on us or others. But we are all motivated to comprehend our world, feel in control, and be part of a community. Sometimes these motivations lead us to believe things that are demonstrably false.

This book is an exploration of how the ways that we satisfy those needs—our need for *comprehension*, *control*, and *community*—are shaped by our social identities: how we think of ourselves in relation to others, and how we believe members of our group think and act. Just as I looked to Mike and our close friends to inform my approach to the chaos and trauma of his illness, so do we all look to our social groups to help guide us. One of the defining questions of human behavior is, How do people like me deal with situations like this? Which means that our conceptualization of "people like me" becomes very important.

The conundrum here (and why this gets complicated) is that "people like me" does not comprise just my best friends or family. "People like me" is a social construction that is intentionally—and incidentally—shaped by synergistic forces related to politics, journalism, media technologies, and media economics. And what about our understanding of how these socially constructed groups think and act? This, too, is shaped both intentionally and incidentally by those same political, cultural, and media-related forces.

The goal of this book is to help us think broadly about the interdependence of these complex features of our political, media, and social worlds. Sometimes the social identities we consult to understand how "people like me deal with situations like this" encourage us to seek out, embrace, and even share information that is demonstrably false. Our social identities are both constructed by *and anticipated by* political and media entities. If we can find ways to disrupt these dynamics, we might reduce our own attraction to—even demand for—misinformation.

Outline of the Book

This book chronicles how belief in misinformation doesn't start with false content or specific conspiracy theories themselves. Humans are not clean slates. We already hold values, theories, and beliefs that help us comprehend the world, have control over it, and form a sense of community—all tied to our team. Humans are also agentic: we are goal directed as we observe the world. We engage with information. We seek out information. We use information. We even create information. And when we do, we do so to comprehend, to control, and to find and create community—in service of our team. This means that when our team identity is salient in our minds, it guides this entire process, from the values we hold to the observations we make.

In the US context, social identities tied to our politics are notably salient and thus especially powerful. Many Americans' political identities don't necessarily capture a specific slate of policy positions as much as they capture an entire way of life. Republicans and Democrats have become increasingly distinct from one another in their members' racial, ethnic, geographic, and cultural characteristics.[1] This is especially true on the political right, where Republican Party identification has come to overlap with more *homogeneous* primal identity categories including race (white), religion (Christian), geography (rural), and culture (traditional and conservative). The sorting of these distinct American political identities along primal sociodemographic and cultural lines means that our "political mega-identities" become an efficient sensemaking shortcut in American politics and American culture.[2] And the fact that this social sorting has led to a more racially, religiously, culturally, and geographically homogeneous *Republican* party means that the consequences of social sorting are asymmetrical—more pronounced on America's political right than on the left.[3]

These political mega-identities shape how we comprehend the world, what we want to control, and how we enact our need for community. Meanwhile, powerful entities have realized the influence of American political mega-identities and use them to their advantage every day. Political elites tap into and reinforce them to mobilize voters. Mainstream news outlets emphasize culture war issues and frame stories in terms of the Right versus the Left, reinforcing our membership in our political team. Partisan media tap into and reinforce our political mega-identities to attract audiences. And social media platforms reward content that taps into and reinforces these identities because it engages users, elicits user data, and activates consumers. This results in what I call the identity distillation apparatus, consisting of political elites, news organizations, partisan media, and social media—all of which tap into and offer up content that reinforces our political mega-identities. As our distilled political mega-identities come to dominate how we think and what we see, identity-reinforcing information that is *empirically inaccurate* can satisfy our needs for comprehension, control, and community quite well.

Rather than focusing on misinformation (the supply of inaccurate information), I concentrate instead on "wrongness," or, the quality on the part of individuals to be in error, to believe things that are inaccurate. This book is thus divided into two sections. The first half (chapters 1–5) explores the social psychology and political roots of American wrongness. The second half (chapters 6–9) tackles the mediatization of wrongness. We first explore how we make sense of the world and the roles that false beliefs can play for us in service of our needs for comprehension, control, and community (chapter 2). Next, we move to the American political context to explore political polarization and research from political science showing how the two major parties have become "socially sorted," resulting in a wide partisan gap in racial, religious, and cultural identities and a Republican Party that is made up of people who are more sociodemographically the same (chapter 3). We'll then unpack how social identity shapes our perceptions of the world and tie this back to the social sorting of America's political parties (chapter 4).[4] I will then draw on my own research as I illustrate how the two parties have become epistemically sorted; that is, even the very way we come to know what we know is tied to our political identities, with the gut-guided "intuitionists" and the evidence-based "rationalists" on opposite sides of a wide gulf (chapter 5).[5]

The second half of the book considers how the interactions between political elites, journalists, partisan media, and social media platforms tap into and reinforce our political mega-identities. Chapter 6 explores how news economics and journalistic norms reinforce political mega-identities and reward dramatic displays of "identity ownership" by lawmakers.[6] Chapter 7 investigates partisan media and how outlets like Fox News seek to engage viewers efficiently and emotionally through the activation of identity threat. Chapter 8 considers how social media outlets incentivize content to get us to *do things* on their platforms to help advertisers target us and sell to us. The content best suited to get us to do things online is content that is emotionally evocative. Such content often taps into our salient political mega-identities. While these mediated political spaces are giving us what they think we want, they are also actively constructing and distilling who we think we are. Finally, in chapter 9, I detail some of the ways we might work toward dismantling the machinery of wrongness.

While the book discourages us from thinking simplistically about the direct effects of misinformation on individuals, it does offer a mechanism through which our political and media environments encourage and reward the "performance of politics and identity" in ways that perpetuate this harmful cycle.[7] This process of identity distillation (yes, an analogy drawing from whiskey production) is cyclical, as media and political forces draw on, and then contribute to, those constructed social identities. And since our political and media institutions themselves anticipate and respond to the political, social, and cultural climate, America's distilled political identities become embedded in the communication, content, and rhetoric of American political media.

So, while others tackle the supply side of misinformation, let us travel upstream on the demand side, to identify factors that encourage people to be attracted to misinformation, to *demand* misinformation. People are always going to be wrong. But we don't need to reinforce identity-driven social categories through our media economics or incentivize wrongness through political and media institutions. And at the individual level, we don't need to privilege confidence over humility or prioritize fabricated group memberships over authentic connections. Finally, part of the disruption of wrongness can come from simply embracing the possibility that we might not be right.

Maybe this book will help us figure out how.

Of course, I could be wrong.

Part I
The People

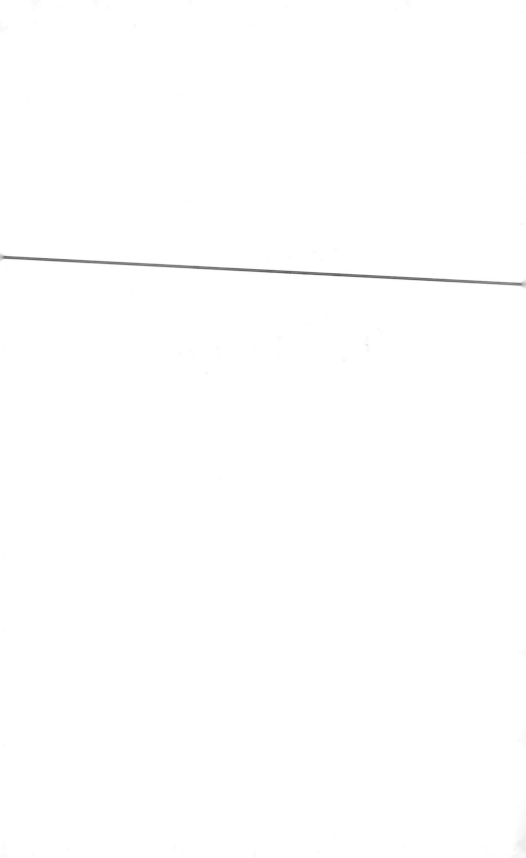

Chapter 1

People Like Us
Believe These Things

ON THE EVENING OF JANUARY 6, 2021, relaxing at her Washington, DC, hotel in the aftermath of the insurrection at the US Capitol building, rioter Jenny Cudd from Midland, Texas, recorded a video reflecting on her feelings about the day: "Fuck yes, I am proud of my actions. I fucking charged the Capitol today with patriots today. Hell yes, I am proud of my actions."[1]

Jenny Cudd was one of thousands of supporters of President Donald J. Trump who traveled to Washington, DC, on January 6 to protest the certification of a presidential election they wrongly believed had been stolen from Trump. They listened as President Trump reinforced the "Big Lie," asserting that their "election victory [was] stolen by emboldened radical left Democrats."[2] The group of rioters then marched down Pennsylvania Avenue and confronted police officers at the Capitol building, pushed through police barriers, broke windows, and beat police officers with hockey sticks and American flags. After gaining access to the building, they wandered the halls chanting "Execute the traitors" and "Hang Mike Pence." They were intent on disrupting the routine congressional electoral vote certification and stopping Joseph R. Biden from becoming the next president. The insurrectionists' actions that day resulted in several deaths, including those of officer Brian Sicknick and rioter Ashli Babbitt, all because these thousands of people believed in an identity-reinforcing fiction. The fiction of the "Big Lie" did what all identity-based fictions do: it allowed the rioters to *comprehend* the incomprehensible (how their team could have lost the election), *control* the uncontrollable (offering a path forward where their team ends up in the White House), and have a sense of *community* (connection and belonging to a social group of individuals like them). These mechanisms all centered on the rioters' sense of who they were and what team they were a part of.

The January insurrection played out against the backdrop of another misinformation-fueled tragedy: the COVID-19 pandemic. Like the insurrection, the pandemic illustrated the lethal consequences of inaccurate beliefs, but on a far grander scale. With over a million Americans dead in a little more than two years, the virus's impact was overwhelming. So, too, was the political divide in Americans' beliefs, attitudes, and behaviors related to the deadly virus.

Scholars define misinformation as information that is inconsistent with "clear evidence and expert opinion,"[3] or information that contradicts "expert consensus contemporaneous with the time period [under] study."[4] Based on these definitions, in the early days of the pandemic in the United States, President Trump was a purveyor of COVID-related misinformation. While scientists emphasized the high mortality rate from COVID and how little they knew about prevention, treatment, or the origins of the virus, President Trump compared it to the common flu, and touted unfounded remedies, even suggesting that doctors look into the injection of disinfectants as a possible way to clean the body of the virus.[5] As early as April 2020, a partisan divide in Americans' beliefs about COVID had emerged. Belief in COVID-related misinformation (regarding its severity and its origins) was higher among Republicans than Democrats.[6] Researchers found that the more people believed COVID-related misinformation, the less likely they were to wear masks or practice social distancing.[7] That summer, data pointed to a partisan gap in Americans' beliefs about the efficacy of masks, with Republicans less likely to see masks as an effective way to slow the spread of COVID.[8] Republicans were also less likely than Democrats to engage in preventive behaviors like masking, social distancing, and limiting travel. A YouGov poll from October 2020 indicated that Biden supporters were twice as likely as Trump supporters to wear a mask outside of their home.[9]

At the beginning of the pandemic, the United States saw Democratic-leaning locations, which tended to be cities high in population density and mobility, bearing the brunt of the virus's negative impact.[10] But by the fall of 2020, when medical experts recommended masks and social distancing to slow the spread of the virus, the partisan divide in COVID's impact had reversed. By then, death rates in Republican-leaning counties were significantly higher than in Democratic ones. As COVID cases surged in November 2020, the hot spots with the highest COVID numbers were overwhelmingly counties that voted for Donald Trump.[11]

As vaccines rolled out across the country in the spring and summer of 2021, counties where Trump won during the 2020 election lagged in vaccine uptake compared with those counties where Biden had won. Throughout 2021, this gap in COVID deaths grew wider. The emergence of highly contagious COVID variants like Delta put the efficacy of COVID vaccines to the test. The good news was that the vaccines were exceptionally effective at preventing serious illness and death from the virus. The bad news was that Republicans were disproportionately more likely to remain *un*vaccinated. In the fall of

2021, about 10 months after the rollout of the vaccine, the Kaiser Family Foundation reported that of the quarter of Americans who remained unvaccinated, only 10 percent identified as Democrats.[12]

Over the course of the pandemic, we heard countless stories of people who believed things about COVID, masks, and vaccines that were inconsistent with evidence and expert consensus. These include the 56-year-old truck driver from Missouri who told the *Guardian*, "It's a hoax. There's no pandemic. As Trump said, how many millions die of flu?" and the West Palm Beach, Florida, woman who testified at her local commissioners meeting that it was not COVID-19 but rather *masks* that gave people COVID.[13] We saw footage of anti-mask rallies where participants argued everything from masks not adequately protecting people from the virus to COVID being a hoax.[14] And we heard vaccine-related conspiracy theories, such as Bill Gates using the vaccine to track people with microchips and the vaccines causing people to become magnetic.[15] Even a year and a half into the pandemic, belief in misinformation about COVID was shockingly high, with over a third of Americans reporting the belief that the US government was exaggerating the number of COVID deaths.[16]

Meanwhile, long after the 2020 presidential election, a surprisingly large number of Americans continued to believe the Big Lie. A year into President Biden's first term in office, about one-third of Americans reported the belief that Biden was not the legitimate winner of the 2020 election. Among Republican respondents, two-thirds reported the belief that Biden's win was illegitimate.[17]

When we talk about the people who believe misinformation about COVID and the people who believe misinformation about the 2020 election, in many cases we are talking about the *same* people. Many of these misinformation beliefs hang together, even those that would seem to have little to do with each other—for example, vaccines containing microchips and dead people voting in

Pennsylvania. Consider the "health conference" held in Nashville, Tennessee, in 2021, which was billed as a truth-seeking social event where people would "discuss the truth about cancer, vaccines, and many other aspects of natural health."[18] Although described as a health conference, the gathering served as a place where conspiracy theorists and the "conspiracy curious" could come together to discuss everything from cancer to COVID to the 2020 election. And while the slate of speakers for the event included natural health advocates, it also included longtime Trump associate Roger Stone and Trump's son Eric. As misinformation psychologist Lisa Fazio observed, it seemed that conference attendees were forming a "community of belief"—that is, people who think "people like us believe these things."[19]

The 3 Cs: Comprehension, Control, and Community

The overlap between belief in misinformation about COVID and belief in misinformation about the 2020 election highlights the social nature of human knowledge. We do not come to knowledge of the world randomly or objectively. The things we "know" are not just "accurate neutral facts" that we arbitrarily acquire from logic and analysis, on the one hand, or observations of the world, on the other. Rather, the things we "know" are the result of a complex interaction between our values, needs, and beliefs and our observations of the world, which operate together in service of our social identity—our sense of what team we identify with. These social identities inform what we value and believe (inside our minds) and what we see (our observations of the world) by shaping our needs for *comprehension*, *control*, and *community* (the three Cs). Human beings are motivated to understand their world (comprehension), have agency (control), and be socially connected with a sense of belonging (community). What shape these motivations take depends on what shape they take for members of our team.

While the specific form that these three Cs take varies from person to person, among members of a shared social category we will tend to find shared understanding, shared mechanisms of control, and shared social norms. This is because members of the same team come up with the same answers to questions like, How do people like me comprehend things like this? or How do people like me control things like this? or How do people like me have community in times like this? The result is members of a shared social identity sharing an understanding of the world, even if it might be wrong.

From Misinformation Supply to Misinformation Demand?

In 2021, data scientist Jevin West and biologist Carl Bergstrom warned that "misinformation has reached crisis proportions. It poses a risk to international peace, interferes with democratic decision making, endangers the well-being of the planet, and threatens public health."[20] Scholars around the globe have been working to address the misinformation problem. They're testing the effectiveness of content moderation (flagging or removing misinformation from social media platforms) and designing online interventions to slow users down and have them think twice before believing or sharing questionable content. These scholars are also identifying promising fact-checking and belief-correcting techniques, and they are mapping the ecology of the misinformation environment—identifying networks of people, organizations, and social media accounts that spread misinformation.[21] All of these measures are necessary to reduce the spread of misinformation, especially given the complexity of the digital media landscape. But focusing only, or even primarily, on the side of misinformation supply is not going to solve the problem of identity-driven wrongness.

I would like this book to help turn the misinformation problem upside down, to offer what communication scholar Zeynep Tufekci describes as "study[ing] the people end of [misinformation],"[22] or what I call the "demand" side of wrongness. In the US today, the all-encompassing nature of political identity overwhelms our desire to be empirically accurate in our understanding of the world. Instead of being motivated by accuracy, we are motivated by identity-based needs for comprehension, control, and community. I propose that we understand wrongness as a complex set of dynamics fueled by a political and media environment that draws on and actively constructs our social identities, thus leaving us with more culturally resonant and distilled political identities every single day.

Being wrong is about who we think we are, who we want to be, and who we want to be like. It's about how people like us comprehend the world, seek to control it, and find community within it. Remember how Jenny Cudd reported being proud of storming the Capitol? How she talked about her actions that day? She said she "fucking charged the Capitol with patriots."[23] Seeing the election as stolen allowed her to comprehend how her team could have lost. Believing that Vice President Pence could simply overturn the election results and declare President Trump the winner offered her and her team a sense of control. And as prominent in her mind as the false allegations of voter fraud was how she thought of herself as a part of a community of patriots.

This is the essence of identity-driven wrongness.

Chapter 2

How Do We Know What We Know?

IMAGINE YOU VISIT A GROCERY STORE on a sunny spring day, and there, in the produce section, you see a flowering houseplant with beautiful yellow blooms. On a whim, you put the plant into your cart and bring it home along with your groceries. When you get home, where do you put that plant? You probably put it in the window, or some location that receives nice sunlight. But why do you do that? You do it because you know the plant needs sunlight to thrive.

But, how do you know *that*?

Perhaps you've had other plants that thrived in the sunlight. Or perhaps you inadvertently killed a plant by keeping it too far from a window. But what if you had never owned a houseplant before? Would you still know that you need to put the plant in the window? Probably. You likely know that all plants need sunlight to survive. You learned about photosynthesis in school, and you recall that plants undergo a chemical process in which they use sunlight to help convert water and carbon dioxide into food. Or maybe you simply recall that all plants need sunlight to survive. Thus, if all plants need sunlight to survive, and what you have purchased at the grocery store is indeed a plant—and not an animal (let's hope)—then you can deduce that this little houseplant needs sunlight and should be placed in the window.

This example illustrates two very different ways of knowing. One way draws on our observations of the outside world; the other way is based on the theories already in our minds. For the first way, you recalled your observations of how plants responded in the past and then generalized from those observations to conclude that plants need sunlight. In the philosophy of science, we call this induction. Your observations and lived experience suggested a pattern to you, and you used that pattern to come to a general proposition: plants need sunlight.

The other process of knowing is deduction. With deduction, we start with a broad theory—like photosynthesis—and then logically deduce a specific claim from that theory. Photosynthesis is what keeps plants alive. Photosynthesis requires sunlight. Therefore, plants need sunlight. This thing I bought at the store is a plant. Hence, it needs sunlight.

These issues are at the heart of what is called epistemology, the centuries-old pursuit of the question, How do we know the things we know? For empiricists, who prioritize observation and experience (induction) over logic and reason (deduction), understanding human perception is paramount. If we are going to base our knowledge on what we observe in our world, we need to be able to trust our observations. But we know our senses can lead us astray, such as when we see an animal out of the corner of our eye only to realize it's just a leaf blowing in the wind or hear someone call our name and say "Hi!" to a stranger who clearly wasn't talking to us. The trouble is, if we believe that observations of the world are the pathway to objective knowledge and we acknowledge that our senses are fallible, then we need some standards to hold ourselves accountable whenever we're drawing conclusions from our observations of the world.

For a while, philosophers relied on a concept known as verification; that is, can you confirm a claim with observations of the world? Can you verify that plants need sunlight? If I put my houseplant in the window and it thrives, and then I move it to a dark corner and it gets pale and stops flowering, this would be verification of my claim that this houseplant needs sunlight. But what if I want to conclude that *all* living houseplants need exposure to sunlight? Is this accurate? What about indoor lights for plants (known as grow lights) that mimic sunlight indoors? The existence of grow lights means that plants do *not* need exposure to the sun to survive. Generalizing from our observations of the world can lead us to incorrect conclusions. The eighteenth-century Scottish philosopher David Hume called this the problem of induction. We can't possibly know that what we're observing here and now will be true in other contexts. We cannot know if it is going to happen again tomorrow or the next day or somewhere else.

This is the problem of induction.

But if we do not allow ourselves to generalize from our observations of the world around us, what can we even say? I suppose I could conclude that when *this* plant is in *this* window on *this* day it seems green and healthy. Congratulations. I have developed a useless theory.

If we can't generalize to a broader theory after verifying a claim through observations, then how will we ever decide whether a broader theory is true? According to scientific philosopher Karl Popper, we don't. He turns the whole question upside down and suggests that instead of trying to prove whether something is *true*, we should do our best to see if it's not *wrong*. This is the concept of falsification.[1]

Maybe I buy 100 of those houseplants. I randomly place half of the houseplants in various windows around the house and place the other half in various darker spots in my house, away from the window. I give all 100 plants the same amount of water. After a few weeks, if the plants in the dark look about as healthy as the plants in the windows, I reject my theory about plants needing light. If the plants in the dark died and the ones in the windows are thriving, then, following Popper, I can say that we have observed evidence consistent with the theory that plants need sunlight, but I *cannot* say that the theory has been proved. The falsifiability principle says we never remove ourselves from doubt. This is one of the many reasons the life of a scientist is frustrating: we are never totally right; we are just varying levels of "not wrong."

Seeing What We Want to See

Now imagine that on the same day you bought that plant, your friend Judy also bought a plant. Judy also has the idea to place the plant on a sunny windowsill in her home. Judy has witnessed that when she has placed plants on the windowsills next to her cats' favorite spots, the plants have thrived. But Judy doesn't know about photosynthesis or the relationship between sunshine and plant health. Instead, Judy has observed that when she has placed plants next to her beloved cats, the plants stayed green and healthy. Judy has induced that the cats' breath produces a special cat-specific substance that is key to the health of her plants. Her empirical observations have verified to her that this is true.

You urge Judy to run an experiment in the hopes it will expose her false perception that her cats are improving the health of her plants. Judy conducts the same experiment that you did, placing 50 plants on the windowsill and 50 in the dark. After a few weeks, the plants on the windowsills are thriving and the ones in the dark are dead. She concludes that the cats' breath is the key to the health of her plants. Judy's cats spend most of their time sleeping in sunny spots near the windows, and so the plants that have been placed in the sunshine *also* happen to be next to her cats. To Judy, the causal factor that is helping the plants survive is not the sun but the cats.

Obviously, Judy's experiment has a fatal flaw. She introduced what we call a confounding variable by tying the presence of a cat to the sunshine. But that fatal flaw, and Judy's conclusion from this experiment, brings me to one of my favorite concepts from the philosophy of science: observations are theory laden.

Can we ever objectively "see" the world absent our interpretation of it? Philosophers like Norwood Russell Hanson argue that all observations are theory laden.[2] There are no objective perceptions of the world absent our interpretations of them. There is no "sensing" something separate from "interpreting what we sense." Judy observes the cats helping her plants. She knows the cats are helping her plants. She sees it with her own eyes. It is the essence of her observation.

If observations are theory laden, shaped by our own theories and ideas about the world, then our observations are unlikely to get us to the objective truth. The tests we run, the measures we use, the questions we ask—Hanson argues that these are *all* designed with theoretical assumptions behind them. Our underlying values and beliefs about the world are inseparable from the things we "see." So, Judy "saw" that her cats' breath helped her plants grow.

Take also the example from the early twentieth century, in which social scientists in the United States and Britain were influenced by the study of eugenics. Eugenics sought to "improve" the human species through selective reproduction.[3] Among British and US social scientists, eugenics provided a useful biological defense for racist and anti-Semitic ideologies, including Naziism. Eugenics researchers pointed to "empirical evidence" in support of the racial superiority of white Anglo-Saxon Protestants. They pointed to the fact that immigrants and ethnic minority populations displayed characteristics that were deemed less desirable than those displayed by whites: higher rates of poverty, lower education, and higher rates of imprisonment. Eugenics researchers also cited the results of intelligence tests, which purportedly showed lower rates of intelligence among ethnic and racial minority populations.

What the eugenics researchers had *not* done, however, is consider the social, cultural, economic, and political context that contributed to the observed differences in socioeconomic status by race. They also failed to see that their measures of "intelligence" captured a kind of knowledge that was closely tied to socioeconomic status—for example, questions asked respondents the color of an emerald or in which city a particular brand of car was made.[4]

What eugenics researchers saw as clear empirical evidence of biological, or even genetic, differences between the races, contemporary social scientists see as artifacts of social, cultural, and political context. Whereas the eugenics researchers of the 1920s were operating from the assumption of white racial superiority, most social scientists in the 2020s operate from the assumption of systemic racial inequities—in schooling, professional opportunities, and treatment within the criminal justice system—that contribute to poverty rates, imprisonment, and test performance. This is what we mean when we say that all observations are theory laden. The same data sets viewed by these two different groups of researchers hold two opposing sets of meaning. The former views the observations as evidence that whites are inherently superior to racial and ethnic minorities. The latter views the observations as evidence that racial and ethnic minorities have been systematically disadvantaged by political, economic, and cultural institutions.

The psychological phenomenon responsible for the "theory-ladenness of our observations" is the concept of confirmation bias, the human tendency to pay more attention to information that confirms our preexisting theories and beliefs.[5] Not only do we pay more attention to information that agrees with us, but we also look for it. We also interpret the world around us in a manner consistent with those beliefs and resulting expectations. As psychologist Raymond Nickerson writes, "If one were to attempt to identify a single problematic aspect of human reasoning that deserves attention above all others, the confirmation bias would have to be among the candidates for consideration."[6] The related concept of motivated reasoning captures the notion that our cognitive processes are rarely carried out objectively with the goal of learning what is empirically true. Rather, we have skin in the game; we are motivated to land on a particular answer, often the one that favors us in some way.[7]

Popper's principle of falsifiability is intended in part to help us push back against the theory ladenness of observations, against confirmation bias. Scientists design tests to try to prove a claim *wrong*. After they gather data and analyze patterns, they find that their hypothesis is either confirmed in the data or not. If it is confirmed, they don't say their theory is right. They simply say it's not wrong . . . yet. Over time they revise and expand the theory and derive a new testable hypothesis, and the process goes on and on. This is the day-in and day-out of scientific inquiry: coming to an understanding of the world through a never-ending process of elimination.

While this might make sense for scientists, for the rest of us this practice would be ridiculous. For nonscientists, as soon as we realize that we bought a

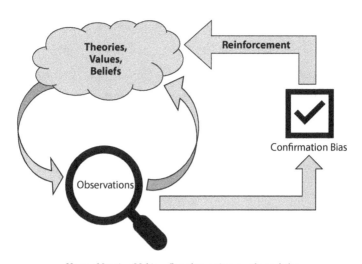

Human Meaning-Making. Our observations are theory laden.

live plant, we also realize that it obviously needs sun. And with that, we're done. Our process of knowing ends here. We derived a claim based on prior knowledge, and we "know" it's true.

Because, in daily life, our goal in observing the world is *not* to get closer to truth.

What is our goal, then?

Is our goal to understand what's happening around us? Or maybe not to actually understand it but to "feel" like we understand it? (comprehension motivations).

Maybe our goal is to feel like we have control over things that seem chaotic or random (control motivations). Maybe our goal is to feel loved, respected, or connected to others as we make sense of the world around us (community motivations). Importantly, *all* of these goals (comprehension, control, and community) are rational. They are all directly related to survival and to our psychological and sociological well-being. But these goals also lead us to conclude things or be attracted to things that are not true.

Lies We Tell Ourselves

I have been, and continue to be, wrong about a great many things.

For years living in Philadelphia, I was convinced that there were two different mail systems: one (still operative) that used the big blue boxes bolted down on street corners, and a second, older mail system (now defunct) that used big green mailboxes, also bolted to street corners. I observed that the green mailboxes had no slot for depositing a letter, and I decided that the slots had been welded shut. This observation, combined with my prior knowledge and beliefs about the government being slow to act, led me to conclude that the government had simply failed to remove the old mail system after introducing the newer, blue mailbox system.

Mailboxes and Relay Boxes (a.k.a. Danna's old Pony Express mailboxes)
Photo by Elliott R. Plack, Own work, CC0,
https://commons.wikimedia.org/w/index.php?curid=113397578.

When my husband and our friends learned of my belief, they were beyond amused. They explained that the green boxes were called relay boxes—storage boxes where postal workers could leave large bags of mail that they would then deliver throughout the neighborhood. The relay boxes relieved the mail carriers of having to carry tons of mail around the city all day. My husband started calling the relay boxes "Danna's old Pony Express mailboxes." And I'll be honest: to this day, when I see the green relay storage boxes, I have a fleeting moment of "Wow, I can't believe they *still* haven't removed those old boxes."

Also in the early 2000s, our dear friends started to have families. Within a year, we knew five couples who had given birth to baby boys. At that point, I deduced that since the distribution of sex is about 50/50 in the population, if my husband and I got pregnant, we *had* to have a baby girl because our friends had "taken up all the boy slots." So, when we learned we were having a baby in 2004 and the ultrasound revealed a baby boy, I thought there was a good chance the doctor had read it wrong. Lo and behold, in December 2004 we had a healthy baby boy.

In high school, my friends and I loved going to the boys' basketball games on Friday nights. When the referee called a foul against our team, and a player from the other team approached the foul line to take a shot, all the fans from my school would boo and holler to try to distract the player. One night my friend randomly—and loudly—yelled the word "raisins." The opposing team's player missed the basket. He tried another shot, she yelled "raisins" again, and he missed again. Soon we were all yelling "raisins" and the other team kept missing the foul shots. We observed, with our own eyes, that yelling "raisins" caused them to miss. For the entire season, my friends and I yelled "raisins" when the other team was at the foul line. It filled us with glee, and even if the player made the shot, we were convinced we were successfully sabotaging the opposing team.

We—all of us—are wrong about lots of things. And although my misperceptions about mailboxes, the sex of my baby, and the magic powers of the word "raisins" might seem arbitrary, they're not. They are all motivated by my psychological needs and desires. I wanted to comprehend why these big green mailboxes had no mail slots, so my brain came up with an answer for me. I wanted to feel like I had some control over my pregnancy by knowing the sex of the baby before the doctors were able to tell me, so my brain came up with an answer for me. I wanted to feel like I was part of a community with my high school friends and classmates, united in opposition to our out-group (the rival team), so my brain (and my friends) came up with an answer for me. Observations are theory laden—and my observations of the world, and the theories that informed them, served my own needs and desires for comprehension, control, and community.[8]

Comprehension motives (also called epistemic motives) capture our desire to feel as though the world makes sense to us. These motivations encourage us to identify cause and effect relationships and to see patterns in events, even when those relationships and patterns aren't there.[9] This tendency is functional and adaptive. It helps us live more efficiently and helps us survive. An inability to recognize cause and effect relationships would be an absolute hindrance to our survival. Imagine if we could not predict that touching fire would cause us to get burned or that animals baring their teeth are likely poised to attack. The human species might be extinct in just a few generations. But while these tendencies are adaptive, they can also lead us to identify causal relationships where they don't exist. This is because these motivations are more about feeling as though we comprehend things than they are about actually being accurate in what we comprehend. It is enough for us to feel like we "get it," without having to verify that our understanding is correct. So when I concocted the story that the green mailboxes didn't have slots because they were from an outdated postal system, that answer—even though it was wrong—was good enough for me.

While we are motivated to feel like we comprehend the world, we are also motivated to feel like we have control over our worlds. Control motives (also called existential motives) concern our desire to feel as though we are safe or in control—again, not necessarily to *be safe* or *have control*. After my friends had all given birth to baby boys, my belief that they had used up all the boy slots offered me a sense of control over something that was clearly out of my hands. That feeling of control was good enough for me.

Finally, we have a desire for community. By sharing beliefs with members of our social group, we feel closer to them and feel like we are being good mem-

The three Cs

COMPREHENSION	CONTROL	COMMUNITY
We want to make sense of our world.	We want to have some control over our world.	We want to be a part of a social group.

bers of our group. Once my friends and I were yelling "raisins" to sabotage the other basketball team, why would I *ever* have challenged that misperception? It felt good to share that with my friends. Socially motivated misperceptions like this typically operate in service of both in-group bonding and intergroup conflict, like believing that yelling "raisins" would sabotage our rival team. Did it actually sabotage our rival team? No. But it felt like it did, and that was good enough for me.

Notice that these examples are not about my belief in false information that has been *shared* with me. My false beliefs about mailboxes, babies, and basketball foul shots were not the result of "misinformation"—that is, false information shared by people unaware that the information is false. Nor were they the result of "disinformation"—that is, false information shared intentionally and strategically by people trying to deceive.[10] Instead, the examples I just offered are falsehoods that I have told myself—to help me make sense, feel in control, and feel a part of my group.

While I will spend significant time in later chapters exploring belief in mis- and disinformation that is shared *with* us, it's important to recognize just how much of our "wrongness" can come *from* us. In fact, even when we believe misinformation that has been shared with us, or disinformation designed to deceive us, the resulting misperceptions—our beliefs in the things that aren't true—largely stem from us. In later chapters we will learn how our needs for comprehension, control, and community are informed by our social identity. We will also learn how our identity-based needs are often deliberately cultivated and exploited by political and media elites. But by starting out with a consideration of how much of the misinformation problem stems from *us*, we might later recognize that we have the agency to disrupt these dynamics.

Comprehension

Our motivation to feel like we understand the world around us drives us to quickly and efficiently draw conclusions based on the information available to us. Misperceptions that come from these epistemic or sense-making motivations are closely tied to how carefully we are thinking. My conclusion about the green mailboxes was just a shortcut that my brain created to account for the lack of a slot on the mailboxes. It wasn't the result of research or investigation. These kinds of errors in understanding come from our tendency to make judgments quickly and efficiently, using as little mental energy as possible. This makes sense. Thinking long and hard about everything in our world would leave us unable to function. We would be stymied—and therefore vulnerable to threats. Now, in the context of my hasty conclusion about the weird green mailboxes, if I had stood at the street corner for a while, examining the mailbox, and asked some passersby what it was, I probably wouldn't have experienced any severe threats. I would have been late to wherever I was going, and I likely would have annoyed people who found me strange. But otherwise, thinking long and hard about why this mailbox looked the way it did wouldn't have affected much.

But now imagine it was thousands of years ago, and instead of mailing a letter, I was out picking berries. And instead of a mailbox that didn't look like any mailbox I had ever seen before, it was a weird-looking large cat that didn't look like any cat I had ever seen before. As I stand there, examining the animal, I look for a passerby to whom I might inquire, "Excuse me, dear sir. Do you happen to know what this large cat is? I have examined his sharp teeth and fur standing on end and he appears to be poised for attack. But before I do anything rash, I want to be sure I have properly identified him."

Speed and efficiency are essential to survival in the wild, but they also increase our likelihood of being wrong.[11] Importantly, not all human beings are equally likely to prioritize speed and efficiency when making decisions. Some people take their time and think long and hard before forming a judgment or decision. This is true for people with high levels of a psychological trait called "need for cognition," a trait that captures how much people enjoy—or get satisfaction from—thinking hard and solving problems.[12] People who are high in "need for cognition" are more likely to evaluate and reevaluate information before updating their beliefs, and so are less susceptible to mis- and disinformation.[13] Another trait associated with careful thinking is cognitive reflection.[14] But before I say too much about cognitive reflection, humor me for a moment. Consider how you might answer the following questions from Shane Frederick's Cognitive Reflection Test:[15]

- A bat and a ball cost $1.10 in total. The bat costs $1.00 more than the ball. How much does the ball cost? _____ cents
- If it takes 5 machines 5 minutes to make 5 widgets, how long would it take 100 machines to make 100 widgets? _____ minutes
- In a lake, there is a patch of lily pads. Every day, the patch doubles in size. If it takes 48 days for the patch to cover the entire lake, how long would it take for the patch to cover half of the lake? _____ days

This three-question test measures whether an individual will arrive at an intuitive, but inaccurate, conclusion or whether they will engage in the kind of thoughtful reflection required to come to a cognitively taxing, but correct, response. If you're answering quickly and efficiently, chances are you'll answer (1) 10 cents, (2) 100 minutes, and (3) 24 days.

And you would be wrong.

But if you engage in careful analytical reasoning, you might get to the correct answers: (1) 5 cents, (2) 5 minutes, and (3) 47 days. Or, if you're like me and you're impatient and prone to efficiency over reflection, you can be fully aware that your intuitive response is incorrect, try to come to a less intuitive *correct* response, think for 15 minutes, and still answer all three items incorrectly. This is probably bad. Researchers have found that people who score lower in cognitive reflection are more likely to believe false information shared online.[16] They also tend to follow sources on social media that are less reputable than the sources that people with higher scores follow.[17]

In general, studies point to meaningful variation in the way that people interact with and understand their worlds. While all of us are somewhat motivated by efficiency and use cognitive shortcuts (called heuristics) for guidance, some rely on heuristics more than others. Individuals who have a high level of the trait "need for closure," for example, tend to prioritize efficiency over accuracy, especially under conditions of urgency.[18] These individuals are uncomfortable with uncertainty and ambiguity and prefer to have answers sooner rather than later. People who are high in need for closure and low in need for cognition tend to use their emotions to guide their beliefs and behaviors—for example, angry: attack, happy: relax, fearful: run, aroused: approach. While those who need closure tend to form judgments more efficiently, this approach is also more likely to result in errors in judgment and recall.[19]

Control

When I was a high school freshman, I concocted all kinds of falsehoods to make me feel like I had agency. I believed that brushing my hair would make it grow faster and that I could tan more quickly by lying on top of my picnic table (rather than on the ground) because I'd be closer to the sun (it was the early 1990s; tanning was still a thing). As a teen consumed with self-image, who felt little of her life was *in* her control, I felt a sense of agency from these ego-driven lies.

Needing a sense of control is central to many of the lies we tell ourselves. While we may outgrow the distinct challenges of adolescence, the salience of other things, such as our own mortality, can take their place. In 1973, cultural anthropologist Ernest Becker proposed a sweeping account of contemporary society, based on the idea that just about everything we do here—from commerce to war to art to religion—is designed to manage our fears of, and lack of control over, our own death.[20] His book *The Denial of Death* inspired social scientists to develop terror management theory (TMT).[21] TMT posits that humans are uniquely capable of thinking abstractly about the inevitability of their own death. But, to avoid perseverating on our own death and ruminating ourselves into oblivion, TMT suggests that we engage in various protective strategies, including maintaining a cultural worldview, developing self-esteem and theories of immortality (like religion), and investing in close attachments with loved ones.[22] But, as scientists Ajit Varki and Danny Brower argue, some of the strategies we use to avoid thoughts of death involve self-deception: "It is important to note that denial of mortality is part of a much broader concept about our human ability to deny many other aspects of reality, especially when such realities are not to our liking. . . . We go further in our denial of reality, holding completely false beliefs about many things even in the face of the cold, hard facts."[23]

Rituals and superstitions, for example, may help us feel like we can prevent bad things from happening, including death.[24] Underestimating our likelihood of contracting a contagious disease makes us feel safe and in control.[25]

These beliefs do not make us safer. They do not increase our agency. But they do increase our perceptions of safety and agency.

For example, religion is a faith-based belief system that is unable to be empirically verified or falsified.[26] Regardless of its ultimate truth value, it is a framework that humans use to manage their terror about death, largely through the proposition of a powerful deity who influences events on earth, and some form of life after death. Research has shown that religion manages our fear of death quite well. Religiosity mitigates the negative effects of mortality salience (death thoughts) on well-being, especially when the religious beliefs are firmly held.[27]

In rare but extreme cases, individuals' need for control over an uncontrollable world may contribute to false beliefs that cause them to engage in pathological behaviors. In the case of obsessive-compulsive disorder, for example, people are made so anxious by their lack of control, they may believe that the performance of certain ritualistic behaviors will help them impose order on their worlds.[28] In other words, their misperception is that by performing the ritual (counting, washing hands, etc.), bad things will not happen. These invasive—and false—beliefs can be debilitating, as the behaviors fail to alleviate the fears and anxieties.

It turns out that people often believe things that aren't true because those falsehoods can provide them a kind of hope that reality doesn't. As my friend and colleague Dr. Brian Southwell explains about belief in medical misinformation, "Sometimes misinformation offers hope in the face of a devastating disease or dire condition and that's why it gains traction among people."[29] It turns out, people really need hope.

Community

Community, the *social* dimension of wrongness, is a central tenet of this book. Falsehoods can bring us closer to the people we want to feel closer to (our in-group) while distancing us from people we want to feel farther from (our out-group). We might come to hold false beliefs because we believe that "people like me believe this," and so the false beliefs make us feel close to our group, or because we want to actively engage in social interactions that stem from a given belief–as when people talk to members of their in-group about how they all believe the earth is flat.

Depending on the nature of the falsehood, the content of that false belief might help me and my group feel good about ourselves while justifying our sense of moral superiority toward members of the out-group. This explains the existence of false beliefs held to justify and maintain divisions in social status, wealth, and power that might be disproportionately distributed across different social groups. The false belief that different races or ethnicities are inherently intellectually inferior, for example, is something that people use to justify harmful racial and social hierarchies (remember eugenics?).[30] The psychological and social appeal of racially motivated falsehoods accounts in part for the prevalence and influence of mis- and disinformation that reinforces racial hierarchies and racial conflict.[31]

Such socially motivated falsehoods can also justify feelings of disgust and dehumanization toward out-groups–like the 16 percent of Americans polled in 2021 who agreed that "the government, media, and financial worlds in the US are controlled by a group of Satan-worshipping pedophiles who run a global child sex-trafficking operation."[32] If you believe that powerful people are doing criminal, horrible things, then being disgusted by them, seeing them as less than human, and even engaging in violence to stop them might be seen as justified moral responses.

Conspiracy Theories: A Special Kind of Fiction

That last example–believing that the government, media, and financial worlds in the United States are controlled by a group of Satan-worshipping pedophiles who run a global child sex-trafficking operation—is one of a host of beliefs tied to the conspiracy theory known as QAnon. And while actual conspiracies do exist, as they did during the Watergate cover-up or when researchers failed to provide lifesaving care to Black study participants in the Tuskegee syphilis study in the 1950s, *conspiracy theories* are allegations of conspiracy that remain unsubstantiated. They "attempt to explain the ultimate causes of significant social and political events and circumstances with claims of secret plots by two or more powerful actors."[33] They also assume that powerful people operating in the shadows are bad actors deliberately keeping the public in the dark.[34]

In the QAnon conspiracy theory, Q is an anonymous internet poster who is said to have inside knowledge of criminal activity among powerful liberal leaders—Democrats and media celebrities—involving crimes against children. Q would post premonitions and allegations cloaked in mystery and coded language. Over time, Q's following grew. The QAnon conspiracy theory soon evolved into a "big tent conspiracy theory" that included references to countless elites, various historical figures, and world events.[35] According to some QAnon supporters, Donald Trump's presidency was orchestrated by military leaders to help expose child sexual abuse among Democratic elites and to break up their criminal conspiracy ring. Some QAnon supporters also believed that, after his electoral loss in 2020, President Trump would appear in Dallas, Texas, in November 2021, where he would be reinstated as president and would announce the late John F. Kennedy Jr. as his vice president.[36]

The "Big Lie" was built on conspiracy theories and was embraced by many groups, far beyond just QAnon supporters. The rally in front of the White House that preceded the storming of the Capitol building was called "Stop the Steal"—an expression that had circulated on right-wing social media for months before the election.[37] The phrase "Stop the Steal" is efficient shorthand for the conspiracy theory that argued Democrats had illegitimately stolen the election from President Trump. In the weeks just after the election, a Reuters poll found that 68 percent of Republicans (versus 16 percent of Democrats) reported the belief that the election was rigged—specifically that state vote counters had unfairly handed the election to Biden.[38] Meanwhile, 77 percent of Trump voters, versus 26 percent of Biden voters, reported that voting in the United States was prone to fraud.[39]

This last study, conducted by social psychologists Gordon Pennycook and David Rand in the week immediately following the 2020 election, also examined what events or evidence might alter Trump voters' beliefs about the election outcome. What would change their minds? If Trump conceded, would they change their minds? If Trump lost all his legal challenges, would they change their minds? One would imagine that just one of these would convince Republicans that President Biden had been legitimately elected and that the election was free and fair. But Pennycook and Rand found that 40 percent of Trump voters reported that *neither* Trump's concession nor his loss of every legal challenge would convince them that he really did lose the election. As depressing as this finding is, the reality was even worse. By December 2021, long after Trump had conceded the election to President Biden, long after Trump had lost all his legal challenges in courts across the country, a whopping 71 percent of Republicans still reported the belief that Biden's win was illegitimate.[40] And this belief persisted despite the fact that the reasons they had previously cited for disbelieving Biden's victory (false claims about votes from dead people, votes from noncitizens, and fraudulent ballots) had all been debunked and thrown out of courts across the country. For many Republicans, the Big Lie had generated what scholar Emily Thorson calls a "belief echo." Their broader attitudes toward Trump and the legitimacy of the election results persisted even after the specific false claims had been discredited with evidence.[41]

Using the language of epistemology, what 71 percent of Republicans were engaging in was nonfalsifiable reasoning. They were not updating their perception of truth in the face of new evidence. Instead, they doubted the credibility of the institutions providing that evidence, allowing them to ignore it altogether.[42] The *nonfalsifiability* of the Big Lie is what makes it so powerful. No matter what evidence one might bring to bear on the lie, in the minds of the believers, there is always a reason to throw that evidence out. By refusing to trust the institutions and people charged with safeguarding election outcomes (courts and local election officials), by questioning the motives of journalists covering the election, they can dismiss contradictory evidence as "fake news." Conspiracy theories are unable to be falsified *by design*. Their inability to be "disproved" is what makes them especially sticky. Legal scholars Adrian Vermeule and Cass Sunstein describe conspiracy theories as "self-sealing," which makes them "particularly immune to challenge."[43] Put simply, any evidence you might introduce to disprove the theory is reframed by the conspiracy theorist as more evidence of the depth and genius of the conspiracy plot.

When confronted with disconfirming evidence, the conspiracy theorist can simply say, "See? They're all in on it."

Like the Big Lie about the 2020 election, much of the misinformation related to COVID-19 was also rooted in conspiracy-theory narratives, typically involving beliefs about political figures or other elites operating in the shadows to make money, acquire power, and undermine the will of, or cause harm to, the public. In 2020, this included the following beliefs: the pharmaceutical industry created COVID to make more money, the US government exaggerated the risk of COVID to hurt President Trump, and the government covered up the fact that wearing face masks actually makes you sicker.[44] As the vaccines were rolled out in 2021, new COVID conspiracy theories emerged. These theories focused on unsubstantiated risks of the vaccine, including the proposition that the vaccine would implant a microchip inside your body so Bill Gates could track you through his surveillance system.[45] Other vaccine conspiracy theories peddled false information about the harms posed by the vaccine and claims of a deliberate cover-up of information about those harms by scientists and the government. Among these false claims were vaccinated people "shedding the virus" to others, as well as the vaccine causing infertility, causing many deaths, or making people magnetic.[46]

Conspiracy Theories: All Three Cs

While the most well-known conspiracy theories are those spread by citizens or political leaders, the internal logic of conspiracy theories is so attractive that we may even come up with conspiracy theories on our own. A few days after Russia attacked Ukraine in 2022 and the United States placed sanctions on Russia in retaliation, I was watching the news on television when suddenly our power went out. Having just learned about the economic sanctions that the United States had placed on Russia and that Russia might retaliate with a cyberattack, I confidently said, "It's probably a Russian cyberattack." Within a few minutes, though, the lights came back on, power was restored, and we learned that it was just a temporary short circuit limited to our block. Not the Russians. Soon thereafter, I got a call from my 82-year-old mother complaining that her email wasn't working and that it was "probably the Russians." The conspiracy theorist doesn't fall far from the tree, it seems.

Conspiratorial thinking is attractive because it satisfies *all three* needs and urges that typically drive our sense-making—the trifecta of meaning-making: comprehension, control, and community.

Comprehension through Conspiracy Theories

Conspiracy theories allow us to "connect the dots" and feel like we comprehend things that are otherwise inexplicable. Conspiracy theories are thus more likely to be held by people who are prone to "pattern-seeking,"[47] including people high in "need for closure," who dislike ambiguity and prefer predictability and clear, fixed answers.[48] Human beings are also generally biased in favor of "agency detection," meaning we generally see events as the outcomes of someone's or something's actions, rather than as random chaos.[49] As social scientists Jan-Willem Van Prooijen and Karen Douglas explain, "People tend to perceive events as caused by intentional agents."[50] However, whereas some people are higher in need for closure than others, some people are higher in agency detection than others. I, admittedly, am high in agency detection.

I also ascribe intentionality to individuals, animals, and objects. Work by Karen Douglas has shown that *anthropomorphism*—the tendency to attribute human characteristics to anything other than a human being—is a form of agency detection that is positively associated with conspiracy theory beliefs.[51] My natural state is to anthropomorphize all things: plants, trees, flowers, and even cutlery. I once wrote a college French essay about how, when looking at a table setting, it is evident that the fork is the husband, the spoon is the wife, and the knife is the aggressive male lover who has separated the fork and the spoon with a plate. It seems my psychological traits accurately predict that I am the person who would explain a brief neighborhood power outage with a story of a secret Russian plot.

Control through Conspiracy Theories

"Connecting the dots" and concocting human-centered stories to account for chaotic events might also—at least temporarily—serve our need for control. Control motives help explain why we find greater belief in conspiracy theories among people who feel powerless.[52] Even when a person's sense of control has been manipulated, as in a study by experimental researchers, this can affect conspiracy theory belief.[53] In a reassuring set of findings from Jan-Willem van Prooijen and Michele Acker, just getting respondents to recall a situation in which "something happened, and they were in complete control of the situation" was enough to reduce their conspiracy theory beliefs.[54]

Part of the control function offered by conspiracy theories may stem from their ability to generate a feeling of anger.[55] Anger is a mobilizing emotion that we tend to experience when we perceive a threat and have some sense of certainty about the nature of the threat and what to do about it.[56] Unlike fear, which we experience in the face of threat combined with uncertainty (and which may leave us feeling pessimistic), anger provides agency and optimism.[57] By giving us a target to which we can direct our anger—the bad people operating in the shadows—conspiracy theories can make us feel hopeful and provide a logical course of action: get the bad guys.[58]

Among groups who feel that they are lower status or somehow losing, conspiracy theories can allow them to save face by blaming their losing status on an orchestrated plot against them.[59] This explains why people who vote for the losing political candidate are more likely to believe conspiracy theories related to an election,[60] like Jenny Cudd from Midland, Texas, who stormed the Capitol. This also accounts for the appeal of the racist right-wing conspiracy theory known as replacement theory, which argues that liberals and elites are deliberately encouraging immigration from nonwhite, non-Christian countries to "replace" whites and Christians and dilute their political and cultural power.[61] Following the mass shooting in a Black neighborhood grocery store in Buffalo, New York, by a white supremacist who embraced "great replacement theory," the *New York Times*'s Nick Confessore explained, "Like all conspiracy theories, the 'great replacement' provides, for some people, a comforting and also angering explanation for changes that they see around them."[62]

The desire for control and safety also explains why conspiracy theories arise in response to horrifying, unthinkable events, like the attacks on September 11, 2001, or the mass shooting at Sandy Hook Elementary School in 2012. Large mass casualty events—terrorist attacks, mass shootings, and natural disasters—make us feel afraid, uncertain, and insecure. We have trouble processing their horror. We want to assume they didn't really happen. And if we *are* willing to admit to ourselves that the events did occur, we are governed by the adage "Major events have major causes."[63] In the face of events like these, sweeping conspiracy theories seem more plausible than the notion that just one or two people (or nature) could cause such vast devastation. Narratives that offer alternative explanations for these terrifying moments, especially narratives that propose the events were either preventable or staged, promise to make us feel safer. To the listeners of InfoWars propagandist Alex Jones, this was part of the appeal of his Sandy Hook conspiracy theories. For years after the horrific event, Jones alleged that the shooting never really happened and that the victims' families were "crisis actors" hired to perform the role of grieving family members.[64] For people unable or unwilling to face the prospect of twenty kindergartners being massacred in their classroom, Jones's fiction provided an escape hatch.

It is clear from the literature on conspiracy theory beliefs that fear, threat, and uncertainty are associated with a higher likelihood of conspiratorial thinking. As van Prooijen writes, "Feelings of uncertainty and fear . . . cause an activation—and frequently, an overactivation—of the human tendencies to perceive patterns and detect agency."[65] Faced with uncertainty and threat, we crave comprehension and control even more than usual. And when these urges are on overdrive, they encourage us to grab on to whatever story fits the bill.

The uncertainty and sense of threat in the early days of the coronavirus pandemic provided the perfect storm for conspiracy theory beliefs to thrive.[66] Two conspiracy theories suggested we didn't need to worry so much about the virus: the belief that the coronavirus was fake and that the medical community was exaggerating COVID death rates. Some COVID beliefs also suggested simple solutions. If people believed that 5G cell phone towers were somehow amplifying or spreading COVID, which some people did, then the solution was simple: burn down the cell phone towers. Which some people did.[67]

Given that social isolation has been found to be associated with various superstitions and conspiracy beliefs,[68] it seems the isolating experience of quarantines and lockdowns may have contributed to COVID conspiracy theory beliefs as well, either through a lack of interpersonal interaction or through increased time spent online, where coronavirus misinformation thrived.[69]

Community through Conspiracy Theories

While conspiracy theories may offer us a promise of comprehension and control, they serve our need for community as well. Remember how proud the insurrectionist Jenny Cudd was because she had "fucking charged the Capitol with patriots"? The human desire to connect with members of a group and monitor intergroup hostilities is central to the function of conspiracy theories. Van Prooijen explains that conspiracy theory beliefs involve the perception that "hostile coalitions" are working against the interest of other groups.[70] Conspiracy theories increase in-group cohesion while emphasizing the threat posed by an out-group (bad actors operating in the shadows). Conspiracy theories also efficiently reinforce social identity and mobilize the in-group toward action. According to Van Prooijen, "Conspiracy theories have a clear social dimension. A conspiracy by definition is a hostile outgroup, and most conspiracy theories specify how the suspected conspiracy harms or deceives a larger collective of people."[71]

In a fascinating evolutionary psychological account of the social functions of misinformation and conspiracy theories, political scientist Michael Bang Petersen proposes that false beliefs among the public—especially those associated with elite-spread disinformation—are more about taking action than they are about "believing things."[72] He suggests that fringe beliefs held within the group help solve what he calls "the coordination problem," the difficult task of coordinating the behaviors of large numbers of individuals all at once. It's not that people have been manipulated into suddenly believing something that is false, but that the belief (which tends to complement existing intergroup conflict) signals group membership and mobilizes group action. Writes Petersen, "The psychology of coordination helps explain why people happily believe preposterous things without a need to resort to notions of manipulation. From a coordination perspective, the primary function of fringe beliefs is thus not epistemic but social: They serve as a signal to others about your allegiances."[73] Viewed this way, false conspiratorial beliefs like "the election was rigged" or "Bill Gates is implanting a microchip through the vaccine" are about what team you're on, who you're opposed to, and what you're going to do about it (e.g., storm the Capitol and not get vaccinated). Conspiracy theories are quite good at "solving the coordination problem." Political scientist Yongkwang Kim found that not only were individuals who believed in conspiracy theories the same people with high rates of participation in the 2012 election (including attending rallies, wearing campaign buttons, or signing petitions), but after experimental participants saw election-related conspiracy theories, they became more likely to participate, even more than people exposed to similar but nonconspiratorial election information.[74]

A Matter of Trust

The social roots of conspiracy theory beliefs also help explain the close relationship between conspiracy theory beliefs and trust. Conspiracy theory beliefs are higher among both those who do not trust other people[75] and those who don't trust institutions like government and media.[76] Given that most conspiracy theories are about deception by elites working within our existing institutions, the latter of these associations is quite intuitive. If you believe that people working in government, media, science, or medicine are in it for themselves or power hungry, it's not a huge leap to believe they are coordinating in secret to harm the public and help themselves. In the very early days of the COVID pandemic, psychologist Daniel Freeman and his colleagues studied COVID-19 conspiracy theory beliefs among citizens in the UK. They found that these beliefs were most prevalent among people with low levels of trust in government, military, doctors, scientists, the World Health Organization, and even the United Nations.[77]

As described by media scholar Ethan Zuckerman, a lack of institutional trust fosters "the loss of a single collective reality."[78] Without trust in the institutions and experts charged with creating and disseminating information, members of the public will look elsewhere to fill in the gaps of their understanding—perhaps to friends, social media, or partisan political leaders. Given that over the last half century America has experienced a vast erosion of trust in government,[79] media,[80] and education, it follows that information from these institutions is increasingly likely to be met by a skeptical public, leaving us more susceptible to mis- and disinformation.

The role of trust in shaping our belief in false information highlights how much of our understanding of the world is derived from knowledge communicated to us by experts and official sources. Most of us do not have access to specialized knowledge in all things. Our direct observations of the world certainly don't get us there. We rely on experts and institutions to provide it for us. In *A Lot of People Are Saying: The New Conspiracism and the Assault on Democracy*, political science professors Russell Muirhead and Nancy Rosenblum put it plainly: "Much of what we know, or think we know, we take on trust."[81] We are not the ones conducting scientific experiments on the safety of the COVID vaccines or counting mail-in ballots on election day. We know COVID vaccines are safe and the 2020 election was conducted properly because we trust what members of our key institutions say on these matters. And if we don't trust what these key institutions say, we may well come to believe that microchips are being implanted through vaccines or that bad people rigged the election—or both.

American Political Asymmetry

As troubling as the erosion of institutional trust among the public is the asymmetry in institutional trust between America's two major political parties. Republicans report having significantly less trust in science, higher education, media, and the federal government than Democrats do.[82] And along with lower levels of trust, some researchers have found greater belief in conspiracy theories and misinformation on America's political right.[83] In cross-cultural studies of the relationship between political ideology and conspiracy theory beliefs across the globe, researchers have found that conspiracy theory beliefs are more prevalent among political extremists on both the political left and the political right.[84] Given that our needs for comprehension, control, and community (needs that contribute to conspiracy theory beliefs) also likely contribute to the strength of people's political beliefs, the notion that political extremists on both sides of the political spectrum would be more likely to believe conspiracy theories makes sense on its face. However, while cross-cultural studies suggest that conspiracy theory beliefs are the domain of the Far Right *and* the Far Left, the American context may tell a different story.[85]

Some research suggests that, compared with liberals, American conservatives are more likely to believe in conspiracy theories and score higher in their general tendency to engage in conspiratorial thinking.[86] While American liberals are more likely to believe conspiracy theories related to Republican presidents Trump and Bush,[87] American conservatives are more likely to hold empirically false beliefs on everything from President Obama's birthplace[88] to the origins of COVID and climate change.[89] Conservatives are also more likely to share false information online than are liberals.[90] Communication scholars R. Kelly Garrett and Robert Bond found that American conservatives are less adept at "discriminating between political truths and falsehoods," largely because a greater proportion of the false claims circulating in the information environment benefited conservatives.[91] Garrett and Bond found that "socially engaging truthful claims tended to favor the left, while engaging falsehoods disproportionately favored the right." In other words, there was an ideological asymmetry in the supply of misinformation, with more false claims favorable to the Right than to the Left circulating online. And because humans are generally not very good at identifying false information that is biased in our favor, this asymmetry in misinformation *supply* contributed to an asymmetry in misinformation *beliefs*.

In various studies of Russian disinformation efforts in the 2016 election, scholars found evidence of an ideological asymmetry in the supply of disinformation as well, with the majority of Russian-led efforts to undermine American democracy targeted toward conservatives.[92] As Deen Freelon and his team concluded, "The rightward skew of the ideological asymmetry is consistent with the inference that the [Russian propaganda agency] IRA considers the American right wing to be especially vulnerable to disinformation attacks."[93]

Although it is certainly not a foregone conclusion that belief in conspiracy theories and misinformation are necessarily the domain of conservatism, there may be something going on in the United States that is making it so.[94]

To explore potential asymmetries in American "wrongness," we must first understand America's unique and evolving political context. In the next two chapters, we will explore how America's two political parties became ideologically polarized and sociodemographically distinct, especially on the political right. We will then explore how partisan identity shapes our needs for comprehension, control, and community, thus affecting what we "know" and what we "see."

Chapter 3

How Did We Get So Far Apart?

IF I TOLD YOU there was a man named John and asked you whether he was a Republican or a Democrat, you'd likely say "How would I know?" But if you learned that John is a 40-year-old African American male with a college degree and lives in a medium-size city, you might start to make some guesses about his political party. And if I told you I know a man named Frank who is white, lives in rural Texas, and is an evangelical Christian, you'd probably make some guesses about his political party as well. Chances are you'd say John is a Democrat and Frank is a Republican.

Is this stereotyping? Yes it is. Is it possible our assumptions about John's and Frank's political parties are completely wrong? Absolutely. It's unlikely, but it is *possible* these extrapolations would be incorrect. To return to the language of how we know what we know, you probably reached these conclusions using the process of deduction. You guessed that John is a Democrat because you have a sense that people who live in medium to large cities and who are African American are more likely to be Democrats. And you probably guessed that Frank is a Republican because you are aware that people who live in rural

Texas and who are evangelical Christians are more likely to be Republicans. Based on the empirical reality across today's America, your two conclusions are more likely to be true than not true. According to work by political scientists, these probabilities–that John is a Democrat and Frank is a Republican–are more likely now than at any point in the past 70 years.[1]

Political scientist Lilliana Mason and others have chronicled how, starting in the latter half of the twentieth century, the two major political parties in the United States have become more different from each other in terms of sociodemographic characteristics, like race, religion, and even culture.[2] The Republican Party became more conservative, white, rural, and Christian while the Democratic Party became more liberal, secular and agnostic, and racially diverse. The people within the parties did not change in their gender, race, religiosity, or political ideology. But over time people within these different sociodemographic categories became more likely to identify with one party over the other.[3]

This "social sorting" of political parties is bad for democracy.[4] From the increasing animus that everyday partisans hold against members of the other party, to encouraging party leaders to refuse compromise of any kind, to the many downstream consequences we will explore in the pages that follow, having two political parties that are distinct along dimensions of race, religion, geography, and culture is a bad thing.[5] But while political scientists today are concerned that American political parties are too distinct, back in 1950 political scientists were concerned that the two political parties were not distinct enough. Political scientists at that time urged that the American political party system be revamped to increase opposition between the parties and increase party loyalty. Their report, *Towards a More Responsible Two-Party System*, emphasized the importance of contrasting party platforms and distinct issue positions informed by two opposing ideological orientations.[6]

Remember, it was 1950. The United States was busy celebrating its victory of democracy over fascism, enjoying the fruits of its economic boom, and making lots of babies. Compared with today, it was a moment of relatively high trust in government, high trust in journalism, and broad economic growth. The two political parties in the United States were not ideologically distinct at that time, meaning there was a lot of overlap of liberal and conservative issue positions between the two parties. The parties were most accurately described as "two loose associations of state and local organizations, with very little national machinery and very little national cohesion."[7] Political scientists suggested that without ideological anchors (liberal and conservative) to signal meaningful policy differences to voters, the two parties were doing voters a disservice. As a proposed solution, they urged the parties to realign along the lines of ideology.

Importantly, though, that lack of clear ideological distinction in the mid-1900s stemmed from a strategic compromise on the part of the Democratic Party, in which it would embrace the racist policies of the Jim Crow South for purposes of legislative victories. It wasn't until millions of Black southerners migrated north and west in the early 1900s that northern Democrats began prioritizing civil rights, and thus the great "racial partisan realignment" began.[8]

This new emphasis on civil rights among northern Democrats in the mid-1900s triggered a backlash among southern conservatives, on which the Republican Party soon capitalized. The 1964 campaign of staunch conservative Barry Goldwater is an early example of such efforts. Goldwater ran an explicitly ideologically conservative campaign: strong national defense, anti-Communist, small government, and anti-tax. He opposed civil rights legislation on the grounds that it violated states' rights, a position that invigorated a white supremacist push from local party leaders in the southern states.[9] And although Goldwater suffered a massive defeat in the 1964 general election, his campaign had done something profound. By placing conservatism front and center—tying party to conservatism, and conservatism to race (states' rights = conservative values = white values)—he helped usher in (or perhaps just sped up) the shift toward "a responsible two-party system" that political scientists had advocated 14 years before.

Goldwater's loss left a sting, and the Republican Party didn't immediately adopt his ideologically conservative covenant. He was defeated on election day, after all. But by the mid-1970s, Republican Party leaders realized the electoral benefits of culturally conservative issue positions, and through the 1980s and '90s, the two parties began drifting further apart on policy platforms, a drift that was more pronounced among Republican legislators than Democratic ones.[10] As summarized by Pew Research Center's Drew DeSilver. "What's happened? In large part, the disappearance of moderate-to-liberal Republicans (mainly in the Northeast) and conservative Democrats (primarily in the South). Since the 1970s, the congressional parties have sorted themselves both ideologically and geographically."[11]

And while political change usually takes a while, it can sometimes happen quickly, as it did in 1994, the year of the Republican revolution. Following Democrat Bill Clinton's presidential victory in 1992, House Speaker Newt Gingrich crafted the Contract with America—a 200-page document outlining ideologically rooted issue positions that would serve as the cornerstone for the Republican Party. Gingrich called for smaller government, balanced budgets, tax cuts, term limits, and reforms to various social programs from social security to welfare. Three hundred and sixty-seven Republican candidates for the House of Representatives publicly signed the contract and placed its conservative policy positions at the forefront of their campaigns for the 1994 midterm elections. At a public signing on September 27, 1994, the Republican candidates stood on the steps of the US Capitol building and swore an oath:

"If we break this contract, throw us out."[12] The Republican victories over the Democrats in November 1994 were staggering. The Republicans gained 54 seats in the House and 9 seats in the Senate, thus regaining majority control of both houses of Congress. They had also shown that nationalizing congressional races by focusing on federal (rather than local) policy could be a winning strategy. And so, America bid adieu to the loosely affiliated, nonideological, local political coalitions that made up the parties of the past. Party leaders became slightly more ideological in the votes they cast through the 1970s and 80s, with Republicans supporting conservative policies and opposing liberal ones and Democrats supporting more liberal policies and opposing conservative ones. Importantly, until 1994, there was still an overlap in congressional votes. After Contract with America, that kind of cross-party cooperation became increasingly rare.[13]

Political Polarization and Partisan Animus

Several overlapping concepts are at play here and need to be cleared up before we go much further. The first is the concept of political polarization or ideological polarization, referring to the shift in the two major political parties toward more ideologically extreme issue positions. These include both "elite polarization" (ideological polarization in the votes cast by elected lawmakers) and "mass polarization" (ideological polarization in the issue positions of regular people in the electorate). Elite polarization means that Democratic lawmakers support liberal policies and legislation (expanded social programs, tax increases, regulation on industry) and Republican lawmakers support more conservative policies and legislation (smaller government, lower taxes, fewer regulations on industry). It also means that lawmakers rarely, if ever, cross party lines to support legislation from the other party. These votes are informed not only by lawmakers' beliefs on the issues but also by the political calculus they are making: "Is it worth it for me to vote against my party?" "Will I suffer in the next election if I vote against my party?" And here, on elite polarization, we have seen striking shifts over the past 50 years.[14] Fewer lawmakers are working with the opposing party on legislation or breaking ranks to support legislation proposed by a member of the other party. This means less legislation gets passed, as well as significant legislative delays—all affectionately known as gridlock.[15]

Mass polarization is when regular Democrats and Republicans—your neighbors and family members—move further apart on which policies they support. While evidence of elite polarization among lawmakers is clear, evidence of mass polarization (in the form of people's positions on public policy) has proved more elusive.[16] As lawmakers became more ideologically distinct and extreme, most Americans continued to support policies that were a mix of liberal and conservative.[17] Over the past several decades, however, ticket-splitting—voting for members of both the Democratic Party and the Republican Party—has just about disappeared.[18] Today most voters are straight-ticket voters, either all red or all blue.

And yet, lots of Americans with mixed policy positions (a little bit liberal and a little bit conservative) certainly exist. Work by Matthew Levendusky and Neil Malhotra shows that Americans tend to overestimate the extent of ideological polarization among the public, especially when judging the policy positions of the "other side."[19] They suggest that this "false polarization" might result from party stereotypes that come through media or from our propensity to overestimate differences between us and our "out-group."

Perhaps more concerning than mass ideological polarization has been a phenomenon political scientists call affective polarization.[20] Here, "affect" (synonymous with "emotions" or "feelings") captures the notion that we feel negatively about the other party and the people who identify with it. Both Republicans and Democrats rate the other party and its members more unfavorably than at any time in the past 40 years.[21] In 2019, Pew reported that 75 percent of Democrats and 64 percent of Republicans described the other side as "closed minded." And about half of Republicans and Democrats would describe the other side as "immoral."[22] A 2014 study by Pew found that a quarter of consistent liberals and about a third of consistent conservatives reported being unhappy at the thought of an immediate family member marrying someone from another political party.[23] Using property deed records combined with data from voter rolls, a team of scholars studied the behaviors of homeowners when members of the other party move close by. The results show that people are more likely to sell their homes when members of the other party move in—especially when those party members are strong partisans and when they move especially close by (like immediately next door).[24] Some research even points to Americans feeling a sense of physical disgust just from looking at a picture of someone described as having voted for the opposing political party.[25]

While the ideological polarization among lawmakers in Washington might be partially responsible for Americans' high levels of affective polarization,[26] political science research points to a host of other factors.[27] Shanto Iyengar and his colleagues highlight the role played by the social sorting of the parties described earlier, a process that fuels the construction of in-groups and out-groups.[28] They also explain how our "high choice media environment"— where people can choose media programming that confirms their worldview— reinforces party identification and deepens the political divide, and how negative political campaigns exacerbate interparty contempt. Finally, they propose that Americans increasingly dislike members of the other party because we have become less likely to interact (both on- and offline) with friends, neighbors, and coworkers who are politically different from us. This increasing isolation of Americans from folks with contrasting political preferences widens the gulf between the Left and the Right.[29]

Yet at the same time, political scientists are warning of a devastating spiral that may be triggered by the overestimation and mischaracterization of political polarization.[30] On average, voters—regular Democrats and Republicans—perceive that members of the other party are far more extreme in their ideology than they really are. Americans also assume that members of the other party are far more politically engaged than they really are. This is a bad combination. The more I think members of the other party are ideologically extreme and politically engaged, the less I like them. However, when my misperceptions are corrected to reflect the ideology and engagement of "average" out-party members (rather than hyperpartisans on the margins), my dislike of the other party drops. This means that the way we talk about political polarization, and our decisions about what kinds of partisans we (scholars, journalists, and citizens) center in our discussions, affects how regular party members feel about the other side.

When partisans dislike members of the other party, they are less likely to support democratic norms and principles that might disadvantage their own party. For example, Americans who most strongly dislike the out-party are also the most supportive of restrictions to the other side's speech and voting rights. These same people are also the most open to the idea of weakening the system of checks and balances among the branches of government and concentrating executive power if it serves their own side.[31] But, just getting Americans to *like* members of the other party might not be enough to increase our desire to protect democratic processes. Studies show that getting partisans to like each other doesn't necessarily translate into increased protection of democratic norms. It does result in some interpersonal outcomes, like an increased willingness to engage with members of the other party and less aversion to the idea of being friends with members of the other party. But it does not lead to core democracy-protective attitudes. In experimental research, even those whose affinity toward the other party had been increased through an experimental manipulation were just as likely as the control group to oppose the right of the out-group to peacefully protest, oppose investigations into corruption in their own party, and be amenable to their own party's overturning an election in their favor.[32] As much as we might hate to embrace these norms when they are "bad" for our side, they are essential to democratic health. So, if increasing bipartisan affinities isn't enough to strengthen Americans' support for democratic institutions and practices, where does this leave us?

Well, what if it's not just about liking people from the other party but about identifying with them and sharing things in common with them? Because, on that front, America is in a bad spot too. In addition to finding negative attitudes toward members of the other party, the Pew Research Center has also documented countless social and cultural differences between the parties. Almost half the liberals in Pew's 2014 study reported that if they could live anywhere, they would choose to live in a city, and only 4 percent of conservatives said the same. Instead, just about half of conservatives would choose a rural area, compared with only 11 percent of liberals. These distinctions go on and on, including conservatives wanting to live in communities with people who share their religious affiliation, and liberals wanting racially and ethnically diverse neighborhoods—where they are close to cultural hubs like museums and theaters.[33] In 2020, Pew published an article with the headline "Voters Say Those on the Other Side 'Don't Get' Them." The article described how only 2 percent of Biden and Trump supporters said that supporters of the other candidate "understood them very well."[34]

Race and Populism

While affective polarization is harmful to democracy, what's worse is political sectarianism—in which people perceive their political party to be morally good and opposing parties to be morally bad. In the US context, such moral identification with our political parties has been driven by the social sorting described earlier, especially by the sorting of racial and religious groups into separate political parties.[35] In his book *Why We're Polarized*, journalist Ezra Klein highlights the crucial role of race in America's political divide.[36] From the party realignment over civil rights in the 1960s, to the "racialization" of conservative politics as a backlash against Obama, to Trump's successful exploitation of the perceived "demographic threat" among the conservative base, Klein ties America's political divide directly to the country's ongoing journey with race. And there is ample evidence that Klein is correct.

Take, for example, Americans' beliefs about whether it is more difficult to be Black than white in the United States. In 2020, the Pew Research Center found that 95 percent of Biden supporters agreed with this statement, compared with half of Trump supporters.[37] The same trend is found when voters are asked whether white people have societal advantages that Black people don't have. And although Americans' attitudes toward immigrants have improved overall, the Pew data still point to a giant partisan gap, with 84 percent of Biden supporters in 2020 agreeing that "newcomers strengthen American society," compared with a third of Trump supporters.

Which brings us to the unique case (or maybe not) of President Trump. Countless political scientists have worked to trace the origins of support for Republican presidential candidate Donald Trump in 2016. Using surveys and longitudinal studies to measure people's attitudes at various points in time and analyzing how those beliefs relate to vote choice, these researchers found that support for Trump was largely driven by racial resentment. In their data-driven account of the 2016 election, *Identity Crisis*, political scientists John Sides, Michael Tesler, and Lynn Vavreck conclude that "attitudes concerning race, ethnicity, and religion were more strongly related to how Americans voted in 2016 than in recent elections."[38] They also show that the centrality of racial and ethnic identity and attitudes in the election outcome was not a direct result of demographic changes in the United States or even a result of hugely shifting attitudes on race. Instead, it was about the words and behaviors of the candidates themselves in choosing to highlight certain issues (related to race and ethnicity) over other issues (anything else). By putting race and ethnicity front and center, Trump succeeded in unearthing starkly contrasting racial views among America's cultural conservatives and cultural liberals.

With his "America First" and "Make America Great Again" slogans, President Trump ran a nationalist, culturally conservative campaign, one focused on tightening border security, reducing immigration, and pushing back against "political correctness."[39] Even in his declaration of his bid for the presidency in June 2015, the former real estate mogul and reality television star stated that the Mexicans immigrating to the United States were drug dealers and rapists (with the caveat that "some, [he] assumed, were good people").[40] Back in 2011, after appearing at the Conservative Political Action Conference, Trump began making appearances on cable news programs, where he publicly challenged the authenticity of Democratic president Barack Obama's birth certificate and demanded that Obama prove his US citizenship—a thinly veiled (if that) racial attack.[41] "Birtherism" as it was called, was also tied up with false rumors suggesting that President Obama was a Muslim and was born in Kenya.[42] Even back in 2011, people who believed in Birtherism were more likely to see Trump as a "potentially good or great president" than to see Mitt Romney, the actual GOP nominee at the time, as such.[43]

Trump is emblematic of a populist politician. Populism, as described by expert Cas Mudde, is a "thin ideology" that is "malleable."[44] It's less about policy positions and more about a generic opposition between the "pure people" and the "corrupt elite."[45] Populist leaders construct an idea of the "real people," typically a mythologized subpopulation of "common people," whose pure heart ought to (according to populist rhetoric) dictate the direction of the country. In lieu of policy, it is the identity-centered rhetoric of populism, with its adulation of "the people," their homogeneity, and their moral distance from the "corrupt elites," that is its defining characteristic.[46] Populism flatters people by contrasting the morality of these competing social categories. Populism is accessible and attractive because of its emotional, common-sense appeals. It mobilizes people by appealing to their sense of resentment and disenfranchisement, using the construction of out-group threats to do so.[47]

In their book *Cultural Backlash*, democracy experts Pippa Norris and Ronald Inglehart explore the global rise in support for populist authoritarian leaders like Donald Trump.[48] They test various competing explanations for the rise of populist authoritarian leaders, including the often-suggested "economic anxiety hypothesis" (which states that populist leaders are elected when people are concerned about the state of the economy).[49] Norris and Inglehart land not on economic anxiety but instead on cultural backlash as the reason for populist authoritarians' success. That is, changing racial and cultural aspects of postmodern society have provoked uncertainty and fear in those who feel that traditional values are being eroded. This has prompted a backlash steeped in resentment and a desire to reclaim a "traditional" way of life, especially among older, white, male, less educated, lower-skilled citizens (the "pure people"), whose perceived displacement "generates resentment, anger, and a sense of loss."[50]

Support for Trump in the United States followed this very pattern. Trump facilitated this support through rhetoric that "peddle[d] a mélange of xenophobic fear tactics (against Mexicans and Muslims), deep-seated misogyny, paranoid conspiracy theories about his rivals, and isolationist 'America First' policies abroad."[51] And through these appeals to xenophobia and racism, Trump offered up himself as a solution to their resentment, fear, and anger. It was no accident that support for Trump in 2016 was highest among those who indicated that immigration was the number-one problem facing the country.[52]

These findings are consistent with work by Lilliana Mason, Julie Wronski, and John Kane exploring the predictors of support for Trump in 2016. Using data gathered over time, they trace the social and political attitudes most predictive of later support for President Trump. Again, the answer is racial and cultural animus. Animus toward African Americans, Hispanics, gays and lesbians, and Muslims measured in 2011 was a strong, significant predictor of people's favorability toward President Trump in 2016 and even 2018. The authors write that "Trump support is uniquely predicted by animosity toward marginalized groups in the United States" and warn that, "given Trump's success, future candidates may attempt to create a winning coalition based on activating group-based animosities through the explicit use of anti-out-group rhetoric."[53] And here we are.

Culture Wars and Christianity

While race is certainly at the center of the American partisan political chasm, that divide is accompanied by divides on human rights issues related to gender, LGBTQ rights, and abortion. The Pew Research Center identified a growing partisan divide on gender attitudes between 2016 and 2020. In 2016, almost three-quarters of Hillary Clinton supporters and only one-third of Trump supporters agreed that, when it comes to getting ahead, women face significantly more obstacles than men do. By 2020, this gap had grown even larger between supporters of Biden and those of Trump. Similar gaps are found between Democrats and Republicans on whether the country has "not gone far enough" or has "gone too far" on giving women the same rights as men.[54]

The American public's view of same-sex marriage has grown increasingly favorable over the past two decades, with a 30-point increase from 2004 to

2019 in the percentage of Americans favoring same-sex couples being legally allowed to wed (from 31 to 61 percent). However, this trend looks quite different when we break it down by party, where 75 percent of Democrats and less than half of Republicans currently support gay marriage.[55] Turning to transgender rights, in 2022 Pew reported a similar partisan divide with over half of Republicans saying that "greater social acceptance of people who are transgender is generally very or somewhat bad for society," compared with 13 percent of Democrats.[56] And on abortion, in 2022 Gallup reported 57 percent of Democrats supporting legal abortions under any circumstances, compared with only 10 percent of Republicans.[57]

When it comes to the increasing partisan divide on these "culture war" issues (related to gender, sexuality, and abortion), scholars point to the central role of religion. Using 20 years of data from the American National Election Studies, political scientist Geoffrey Layman documented the changing religious makeup of the parties from 1972 to 1992, a shift that resulted in a Republican Party dominated by active, vocal evangelical Protestants, and a Democratic Party dominated by active, vocal secular liberals.[58] Layman proposed that this divide was triggered by strategic actions of Republican Party leaders who appealed to traditional, culturally conservative value systems, thereby "creating" new Republicans out of already morally conservative evangelicals. Indeed, among Republicans, his work shows a steep rise in self-reported church attendance and in the number of people who reported getting "a great deal of guidance" from their faith over that 20-year period—most notably among first-time Republican voters. Central to Layman's argument about the implications of this religious shift for the so-called culture wars, his work documents a growing gap between Democrats' and Republicans' views on abortion, women's rights, and gay rights over that same 20-year period, especially on the issue of abortion.

The fact that these patterns have unfolded as the parties have sorted along religious and racial lines—with Republicans becoming more homogeneously white and Christian, and Democrats becoming more racially and ethnically diverse, secular, and agnostic—is unlikely a coincidence. The historian Randall Balmer documents how evangelical leaders capitalized on the issue of race in their early mobilization efforts in the 1960s.[59] Balmer points to white Christian resentment over the 1970 governmental order to revoke the tax-exempt status of private, racially segregated Christian schools. Conservative Christian activists like Paul Weyrich leveraged the school issue to mobilize the cultural Right. He also cofounded the conservative think tank the Heritage Foundation and coined the term "moral majority" to refer to these new, politically awakened, Christian conservative voters. In other words, racial resentment has long been tied to the mobilization of the Christian coalition.[60]

Divides in Trust, Education, and Geography

As we witness the sociodemographic sorting of the parties along the lines of race and religion, we are witnessing a growing partisan gap in trust, with Republicans less likely than Democrats to trust media, higher education, or science. According to Gallup, in 2022, 70 percent of Democrats reported having a great deal or a fair amount of trust in the media, compared with only 14 percent of Republicans.[61] In 2019, when asked if they believed colleges and universities had a positive effect on the way things are going in the country, two-thirds of Democrats said yes, compared with one-third of Republicans.[62] And data from the 2021 General Social Survey suggest a larger gap in trust in science than any time in the survey's 50-year history, with 64 percent of Democrats reporting a great deal of faith in the scientific community, compared with only 34 percent of Republicans.[63]

While some are concerned about the partisan divide in trust, others are worried about the accompanying—and growing—partisan education gap, where the Democratic Party is overwhelmingly the party of the college educated.[64] In 2016, Pew found that among those with a college degree, one-quarter reported consistently liberal political values, compared with only 5 percent of those with a high school degree or less.[65] Data from 2017 show a sharp contrast, especially among Americans with postgraduate experience, with 41 percent reporting a Democratic Party affiliation, and only 19 percent reporting a Republican one.[66]

The rural-urban political divide is yet another vivid manifestation of social sorting. As described in Bill Bishop's book *The Big Sort*, the separation of Americans into urban and rural communities overlaps with all kinds of individual characteristics, from educational attainment to religion, hobbies to cuisine, diversity to, of course, politics. As the *New York Times*'s Emily Badger writes, "Today the urban party is also the party of gay marriage and gun control. The more rural party is also the party of stricter immigration and abortion restrictions." Badger highlights the dangers of one category of membership serving as a proxy for another: "We keep adding more reasons to double down on geography as our central fault line, and to view our policy disagreements as conflicts between fundamentally different ways of living."[67]

When you start digging into these dynamics, you quickly find that there is a synergy between them. Take, for example, work by Jay Hmielowski and his colleagues exploring over time trends in media trust among urban- and rural-dwelling Americans. Using over 40 years of data from the General Social Survey, Hmielowski and his coauthors find decreases in media trust across the population, but more among conservatives than among liberals. They also find a greater drop in media trust among Americans living in rural areas compared with those in urban ones. The most interesting finding is that these characteristics—political ideology and geography—interact, such that the steepest drops in media trust were found among conservatives living in rural areas.[68] In other words, the steepest drops in trust were found among Republicans whose sociodemographic categorizations were well aligned.

Polarized or Lopsided?

While it's tempting to view these dynamics as happening on both sides, it's apparent to political scientists that these phenomena are not symmetrical. Democrats and Republicans do not mirror each other's attitudes, knowledge, behaviors, and politics. We are not two parties drifting at the same pace in opposite directions. Rather, these trends are more pronounced in the Republican Party than in the Democratic Party. As political scientists William Galston and Thomas Mann wrote in 2010, "These developments have not produced two mirror-image political parties. We have, instead, asymmetrical polarization."[69]

In their book *Asymmetric Politics*, Matt Grossman and David Hopkins propose that this asymmetry results from differences in the central function of each of the parties.[70] While the Republican Party prioritizes conservatism and "ideological purity," the Democratic Party is a party of coalitions—groups of voters who want "concrete government action."[71] This gap in what the parties are *for* then informs what they *do*. The consequence is a Republican Party increasingly committed to ideological purity in their votes in a way that the Democratic Party is not. This is demonstrated by the increasingly conservative votes of Republican legislators over the past 40 years, a trend that has not been matched by a comparable liberal shift in Democratic congressional votes.[72] As political scientists Thomas Mann and Norm Ornstein put it, "Let's just say it: The Republicans are the problem."[73] According to Mann and Ornstein, "The GOP has become an insurgent outlier in American politics. It is ideologically extreme; scornful of compromise; unmoved by conventional understanding of facts, evidence and science; and dismissive of the legitimacy of its political opposition."[74]

On the one hand, this asymmetry is the result of the behavior of Republican lawmakers and party leaders, not only through their embrace of ideological purity but also through their failure to constrain the more fringe elements of their party. In 2010, for example, the conservative Tea Party wing of the GOP scored electoral victories and helped the party reclaim control of the House of Representatives. Their dedication to "ideological purity" meant little to no willingness to compromise; this value system not only made it difficult to pass legislation but even led to a 16-day government shutdown in 2013. This impasse created substantial headaches for Republican Party leaders, especially for House Speaker John Boehner, who opted to resign his position in 2015 rather than deal with the intransigence of his own party members. It was also vividly illustrated by the failure of the Republican Party leaders to sideline the candidacy of authoritarian populist candidate Donald Trump. The latter of these failures is what political scientists Steven Levitsky and Daniel Ziblatt refer to as "the great Republican abdication"—resignation of democratic responsibility; in other words, party members shirked their responsibility to gatekeep party leadership and keep out a populist autocrat.[75]

On the other hand, though, this asymmetry is also an artifact of the social sorting discussed throughout this chapter. The sorting process itself has been asymmetric, with the Republican Party becoming more homogeneously white and evangelical Christian, and the Democratic Party becoming more racially diverse, secular, and religiously unaffiliated.[76] Even the geographic sorting is asymmetrical, with almost half of Republicans living in rural areas but only a third of Democrats living in urban areas.[77] As described by Ezra Klein, "Sorting has made the Democrats into a coalition of difference and driven Republicans further into sameness."[78]

As bad as it seems for a political party to fit a distinct and homogeneous racial, religious, geographic, and cultural profile, in terms of social psychology, it's even worse. When we perceive ourselves as members of a readily identifiable team operating in opposition to another team, fundamental aspects of human psychology are activated. In the next chapter, we will explore how aligned sociodemographic and cultural categories increase the efficiency of the construction of "otherness" based on synergistic primal categorizations. These aligned social identity categories also affect how we arrive at truth. When it comes to how we comprehend the world, seek to control it, and connect to our communities, the power and influence of these aligned and salient social identity categories are paramount.

Chapter 4

What Does My
Team Think?

WHILE WE MAY TECHNICALLY be the same people today that we were yesterday, the *way* we think of ourselves changes from day to day—or even from minute to minute. Sometimes I think of myself as extroverted and idealistic; other times I think of myself as a professor or as a native of New Hampshire. Sometimes I think of myself as a University of Delaware Blue Hen (since I'm on faculty there) or as a University of New Hampshire Wildcat (where I completed my undergraduate degree). These are all aspects of my identity, or what it means to be who I am.

When we think about who we are, we might think about the ways in which we're distinct from other individuals. This is where we might use words like "confident," "optimistic," or "thoughtful." Thinking of ourselves in terms of qualities, traits, and beliefs helps establish our mental schemas—cognitive representations—of self that feature our "most centrally-defining attributes."[1] But we also think of ourselves as members of social groups. When I think about how I identify with college faculty or with people from New Hampshire, I am tapping into a social identity rather than a personal identity.[2]

One of These Things Is Not Like the Other

When Polish social psychologist Henri Tajfel developed the concept of social identity in the late 1960s, it was a result of his quest to understand the roots of intergroup prejudice, or, what causes one group of people to look down on another group of people. Tajfel was a Polish Jew whose entire family was murdered by the Nazis while he was held as a prisoner of war by the Germans during World War II. This trauma led to a passion for understanding group dynamics and the causes of intergroup prejudice. His research in these areas was also influenced by the work of psychologist Gordon Allport, who in the 1950s considered discrimination and prejudice not just as social phenomena related to power and status but as by-products of human cognition. As we seek to understand and make sense of our world, we find ways to simplify what we observe.

One such method of simplification is through categories that we create to separate different kinds of things, such as objects, ideas, and even people. In his book *The Nature of Prejudice*, Allport argues that "the human mind must think with the aid of categories. . . . Once formed, categories are the basis for normal prejudgment. We cannot possibly avoid this process. Orderly living depends upon it."[3] Remember the old *Sesame Street* song "One of These Things Is Not Like the Other"? On our television screens we would see, for example, an apple, an ice cream cone, a hamburger, and a mitten. The child viewing the show would need to recognize that three of those are food items and one is a piece of clothing. And since you can't eat a mitten, the mitten "doesn't belong." Henri Tajfel built on Allport's premise that humans simplify their worlds through processes of categorization. He began to consider how putting things into categories erases differences where they do exist and creates differences where they don't.

For example, imagine you have a list of distinct things, like porcupines, lake trout, blue jays, daffodils, hydrangeas, and roses. Wouldn't it be easier to just have an animal category and a flower category? This would certainly simplify this list and make it easier to remember. It's efficient. But notice that by grouping together porcupines, lake trout, and blue jays, we ignore very real differences between these distinct animals—like the fact that some swim, some fly, and some attack with quills. Meanwhile, putting daffodils, hydrangeas, and roses in a separate category from the animals erases qualities that they might have in common. For instance, both blue jays and hydrangeas can be the color blue. And a porcupine's quills and a rose's thorns can both prick your skin and make you bleed. This is what the process of categorization does. As Tajfel writes, categories "transmute fuzzy differences into clear ones" and "create new differences where none existed."[4]

Categorizing people does the same thing: it erases some differences while exaggerating others. As social psychologist Nils Karl Reimer and his colleagues explain, "Self-categorization is the cognitive grouping of oneself and other members of a category as similar ('us'), in contrast to the members of another category ('them')."[5] This process of self-categorization thus involves social comparisons, comparisons between ourselves and members of our own social groups (intragroup comparisons), and comparisons between ourselves and people from other groups (intergroup comparisons). When we engage in these social comparisons and categorizations, we have two goals: first, we want to reduce our uncertainty; and second, we want to feel good about ourselves.[6] Because we are motivated to protect our self-concept, we tend to perceive "us" as more desirable than "them." We are also motivated to be more like those who share our in-group, and so we downplay the differences that might exist between us.

If you've ever been a fan at a sporting event, you've probably felt this happen in real time. You see fans of your team (your in-group) in the parking lot or in line entering the stadium, and you feel a connection to them. You feel like you share something, and so you are "like" them. You're not thinking about how you have vastly different occupations, life experiences, or politics. You're thinking about how you are all clad in your team colors and are united in your scorn for the other team—and the other team's fans.

To protect our self-concept, we also tend to exaggerate the differences we perceive between us and members of our out-groups, sometimes even manufacturing differences to justify our cognitive separation from them. As you see fans of the opposing team entering the stadium, you might tell yourself how they are different from you, maybe even morally inferior. In our rational minds, we may know that—outside of geography—most football fans are comparable. (I would argue that fans of various NFL teams are probably similar—unless you're talking about fans of the Philadelphia Eagles, who infamously threw snowballs at Santa Claus in 1968.) And yet, simply by being fans of different teams, we perceive our fellow fans as "like us" and fans of the opposing team as "different from us." We also see our fellow fans as "better," and fans of the opposing team as "worse."

Why Groups? Why Not Individuals?

Although we may consider ourselves as individuals distinct from other individuals, we think, feel, and act—by definition—in a social context. As social psychologists John Turner and Penelope Oakes write, "Individuals are society and society is the natural form of being of human individuals."[7] Sociologists Peter Berger and Thomas Luckmann make a similarly emphatic case for the social essence of man, writing, "As soon as one observes phenomena that are specifically human, one enters the realm of the social. Man's specific humanity and his society are inextricably intertwined."[8] This is a provocative proposition as it suggests that our thoughts, feelings, and actions, as well as aspects of self that we think of as highly autonomous, are socially informed. But, as psychologists Jay Van Bavel and Dominic Packer state plainly, "The fact is that individual aspects of identity are hard to separate from social aspects of identity."[9]

From an evolutionary standpoint, the explanatory mechanism to account for "human as social animal" is simple. We survive better together than we do alone. According to social psychologist Jonathan Haidt, "Once human groups had some minimal ability to band together and compete with other groups, then group-level selection came into play and the most groupish groups had an advantage over groups of selfish individualists."[10] If you've ever watched the television show *Survivor*, where one of the episodes features a contestant who has to spend a night away from their tribe alone on Exile Island, this probably doesn't come as a shock. Unable to capitalize on the skills of others in their group—like the guy who can make fire, the girl who is great at catching fish, or the dude who can get a papaya from a tree—the person alone on Exile Island must do it all by themselves, often with limited success. It frequently results in no fire, no fish, no papaya, and lots of tears.

Those of our ancestors who were fortunate enough to be members of "groupish" groups had a greater chance of surviving and contributing to the gene pool than did the individualists. Fast-forward to millions of years later and here we are: We like being in groups. We like our group and want to be accepted by our group. We want to be good members of our group. As a result of these primal forces, social identity has an efficient and powerful influence on our attitudes and behaviors. Without much reflection or critical thought, our individual beliefs, feelings, and actions are shaped by the beliefs, feelings, and actions of our group. Even in the United States, where research suggests European Americans in particular score high on "individualism" and low on "collectivism,"[11] our group norms and social dynamics are integral to our attitudes and behaviors. In fact, in a piece aptly titled "We're All Individuals," social psychologist Jolanda Jetten and her colleagues illustrate that the very concept of "American individualism" is itself a group norm.[12] That's right—we think of ourselves as "individualistic" because everyone else does too. Oh, the irony.

This brief account explains why we want to be good members of our in-group, but it doesn't necessarily explain why we might come to dislike our out-group. Here Tajfel emphasizes the importance of societal context, real-world factors relating to the distribution of power and wealth—scarce resources for which various groups compete. When scarce resources are unequally distributed across social groups, we find "pervasive ethnocentrism and out-group antagonism between the over- and underprivileged groups."[13] Societies with histories of racially determined social strata provide vivid examples of such intergroup conflict. Social identity theory also points to "social competition" as a source of intergroup conflict—that is, conflict over reputation, status, and social self-esteem.[14] Here, the conflict is not about an unequal distribution of wealth, per se, but about an unequal distribution of power.[15] And of course, when both resources and power are unequally distributed and *also* correlate with readily available cues like race or ethnicity, the potential for social conflict is huge.

Because these intergroup conflicts center on power and social status, they tend to play out as battles over social change, where groups are looking to either "create social change or preserve the status quo."[16] In fact, our social identity is so closely tied to our motivation to push for—or resist—social change that social psychologist John Jost drew on social identity theory in his development of system justification theory,[17] a theory to account for things like, Why do people who would benefit from government assistance programs oppose them? Or why do people whose health is negatively affected by nearby industrial pollutants oppose environmental regulations that would reduce industrial harm? Jost's work explains why so many people are driven to protect the existing social order and power hierarchies, even if the existing system may harm them personally. As it turns out, much of our inclination to keep things the same—to favor tradition over change—is borne of our psychological needs related to our social identity.

Are Social Identities Changeable?

Our primal human need to be a part of a group is so strong that even random group constructions can trigger feelings of favoritism toward in-group members. In the 1960s, Henri Tajfel tested whether randomly constructed groups could trigger the same in-group favoritism that we witness when groups occur organically—through shared interests, values, or activities. In a series of experiments, he examined what happens when people are randomly assigned to groups and how that affects their behavior toward people described as part of their team compared with those described as part of a different team. The results consistently revealed that participants favored in-group members over out-group members, even though those groups were arbitrary and brand new. As Tajfel concludes, "Perhaps the most important principle of the subjective social order we construct for ourselves is the classification of groups as 'we' and 'they' as ingroups and outgroups."[18]

The fact that social identities can be artificially constructed through experiments shows that they are affected by context. What group we identify with changes based on what is happening around us, what we're thinking about—or, in the language of cognitive psychology, what is cognitively accessible or *salient*. If I am at the stadium watching the Philadelphia Eagles play, I am thinking of myself as a fan of the Eagles. My Eagles fan identity is accessible and salient. The same is true when we find our category in the minority—for example, where you look around and find that you are the mitten in a room of food items. Being in one social category when most people around you are in a different one likely makes you feel distinct, and this increases the salience of that social identity in your mind. If you have ever been an Eagles Fan in a sea of Patriots fans, you might be familiar with this kind of identity salience. The same is true if you are the only man in a room full of women, or vice versa.

But social identity is also informed by how well we feel we "fit" in our category. I may be a fan of the Philadelphia Eagles, but I don't really think of myself as an Eagles fan, because I don't do the things Eagles fans do. I don't attend the games. I don't wear the gear. I've never thrown snowballs at Santa. I don't even watch all the games on TV. "Categorical fit" also concerns whether I see myself as more like my in-group members than my out-group members. If I went to a football game and the opposing team's fans sitting next to me were grading college midterm exams in the parking lot, it would make my Eagles fan identity less salient because I'd see similarities between myself and the opposing team's fans.[19] Those same two criteria—accessibility and fit—inform how we categorize others too. We place other people in social categories based on what is on our minds and on how well we think they "fit" into that category.[20]

While context shapes what social identities are salient in our minds, some social categorizations—ones we use all the time—become "chronically accessible" to us. These are social categories that we use regularly, for ourselves and others, and so having them readily available makes decision-making more efficient. For example, gender and race, social categories that may be accompanied by identifiable visual characteristics, tend to be chronically accessible in our minds. Not only do we use these categories frequently, but others also may use these categories for us, hence reminding us of where they see *us* fitting.

As one of our social identities becomes more prominent—owing to accessibility or fit—our other identities will tend to be less accessible to us in that moment. For example, when I am at home in New Jersey, I don't think too much about my identity as "someone from New Jersey." But in the summer, when I spend time in my home state of New Hampshire, and our car is one of the few cars with New Jersey license plates, my New Jersey identity becomes very accessible to me. Family members joke about the way we pronounce words like "water" (wooder) or "crayon" (crown). In New Hampshire, I remind my kids that we need to use our "New Hampshire" voices at the beach, because "New Jersey" voices are too loud and will be considered impolite.

Even though my New Jersey identity is made salient by being in New Hampshire, I find that I don't want to be in the out-group when I'm up there. I want to be in the in-group with the people we interact with at the beach and in the grocery store. So, I try to tap into my New Hampshire identity. Having grown up there, I know that people from Massachusetts—or, heaven forbid, south of there—are considered "flatlandahs" (flatlanders), and with that comes judgment (playful, of course, but judgment all the same). Flatlandahs have soft hands. They don't know how to work the land. They are spoiled, drive too fast, and are rude and always in a rush. If they are from Massachusetts, we affectionately refer to them as "Massholes."

So, when I'm in New Hampshire, I try to perform my New Hampshire identity, explaining that "I grew up heah" and that my parents "still live heah." I throw in specific references to businesses that used to exist in the community back in the '80s, like "Frosty's Ice Cream Corn-ah . . . Remembah that?" And when I see license plates from Massachusetts—or *even from New Jersey*—I feel myself internally scoff at these "outsidahs."

I find it interesting that the "flatlandah" resentment is also related to Tajfel's proposition that intergroup conflicts stem from the unequal distribution of wealth and social status. People who vacation in rural areas have enough money and leisure time to do so. They may have free time and disposable income that local residents may not have—or at least be perceived as such. This is the same sort of social conflict we find between "townies" and tourists in beach towns or between "townies" and college students in university towns. Unequal distribution of power, resources, and status causes intergroup conflict.

Once we identify with a social group and begin to see our in-group as good and our out-groups as bad, we're motivated to think, feel, and act how "people like me" think, feel, and act. But when we look to our in-group to inform our thoughts and actions, we're not trying to figure out what is normal group behavior. Rather, we're looking for the *best* examples of our group—the shining star that represents what our group's all about. This shining star is called a group prototype. It's a stereotyped, idealized group member. This group member may or may not actually exist. Social psychologist Michael Hogg and his colleagues explain that these "prototypes" are "fuzzy sets" of descriptions, "often in the form of representations of exemplary members (actual group members who embody the group) . . . or ideal types (a relatively nebulous abstraction of group features)."[21] These prototypes are the poster children for our social categories— mythical versions of ideal group members who look, think, feel, and act the way that we feel is most desirable for our group.

For example, my prototype of a Philadelphia Eagles fan is a middle-aged male, decked out in face paint, draped head to toe in Eagles gear, attending every game, tailgating in the parking lot, yelling passionately at the refs, or even throwing snowballs at Santa Claus. Never mind that the average Eagles fan may just try to catch most of the games on TV and is disappointed when they lose. My mental image of an Eagles fan isn't a person who tries to catch some of the game on Sunday. It's a dude in face paint swearing at Santa Claus.

What Do People Like Me Think, Feel, and Do?

We not only learn the appropriate attitudes and behaviors of our group from these group prototypes, but we begin to incorporate and embody them as well.[22] As I mentioned, I identify as a native of New Hampshire. More precisely, I identify as someone from a rural New Hampshire community, where my family still lives. It is a beautifully pristine lake and mountain region that is largely untouched by developers. I also consider myself to be someone who cares about the environment. We own a hybrid car, recycle, and use reusable grocery bags. I would consider both of these identities—New Hampshirite and environmentalist—to be among my social identities.

In New Hampshire, several renewable energy companies have constructed large wind farms along the surrounding mountaintops near my family's home. These farms are home to dozens of wind turbines that use the power of the wind to generate electricity that is exported south. These wind farms have changed the appearance of the landscape. Many local folks from the area don't like the windmills. Some find them to be unsightly or invasive. Others feel that they might hurt the local economy if tourists decide to stop visiting because they find the windmills too industrial-looking. Along the backroads, residents have put up signs making it known that they oppose the wind turbines. One particularly popular sign features a picture of a windmill with the colorful pun: "I am NOT a FAN."

So where do I stand on the wind turbine issue?

It depends on which of my social identities is salient—which hat I'm wearing. A good environmentalist supports policies that reduce our reliance on fossil fuels. Wind energy is clean energy. So, when I wear my environmentalist hat, I celebrate the windmills. But, when I put on my rural New Hampshirite hat, I am not a fan. I feel like they ruin the view, make the hillside look like an industrial park, and rob the landscape of its natural beauty. What's wild is how easily I can tap into either one of these identities. When I'm chatting with locals, people I've known since I was a kid, I see those turbines as the product of outsiders, as invasive and unsightly. But once at a distance, chatting with my environmentally minded friends, I see those same windmills as a symbol of progress. I feel critical of the "not in my back yard" attitude and judge wind-turbine opponents as short-sighted, even small-minded.

And here is the most disconcerting part: the wind turbines even *look* different to me when I tap into the two different identities. Depending on what team I feel like I'm on that day, either they look monstrous and industrial, or they look like clean air and progress. It all varies based on which identity is most salient in my mind. And because I'm not a full-time resident of New Hampshire, the competition between these two social identities causes my ambivalence on the issue.

Can priming one social identity over another change not only how we think, feel, and act but even what we see? Work from social psychology says yes. Take, for example, studies described by Jay Van Bavel and Dominic Packer in their book, *The Power of Us*.[23] The authors recount a study led by their colleague Leor Hackel exploring how activating a social identity affects how people rate the deliciousness of various foods.[24] After researchers primed participants' southern identity (by having them write about things southerners typically do), the participants rated foods they considered to be southern (like collard greens and grits) tastier than did those participants who did not participate in the writing assignment. In other words, priming their southern identity changed how they anticipated southern foods would taste. The same effect was found among Canadians in their ratings of Canadian maple syrup. When their Canadian identity was made salient, Canadian maple syrup tasted better to them. So yes, it is very possible that how my brain perceived those wind turbines—as friend or foe—varied according to who I felt I was: a proud New Hampshirite or a progressive flatlandah.

Van Bavel and Packer describe these processes in terms of attention.[25] They explain that our social identities change what we pay attention to, thereby altering which information is processed in our minds. This changes what we think about, thus changing what we "see"—and "taste," apparently. Van Bavel and Packer equate social identities to a pair of glasses that shape our view of the world by winnowing down the information that we let in: "Identity helps you grapple with the vast amount of information continually bombarding your senses. It tells you what is important, where to look, when to listen, and perhaps even what to taste."[26] Voilà. Here we are back at chapter 2, where we learned that observations are theory laden. Or perhaps I should say: observations are *identity laden.*

Recall that we make sense of the world through the use of observations and the theories, knowledge, and beliefs we already have in our minds. That is, what we *know and believe* is shaped by what we *see*; and conversely, what we *see* is shaped by what we *know and believe.* Social identities shape both of these. Social identities shape our theories, values, and beliefs. We tend to value and believe what we feel that good members of our team value and believe. Social identities also influence what we see—like seeing the wind turbines as monsters when I think of myself as a New Hampshire local.

But our social identities are also informed by our observations of and interactions with in- and out-group members, like when my conversations with New Hampshire locals teach me that the group norm in my hometown is to view wind turbines as negative. Our social identities also shape how we engage with in- and out-group members in the first place—and how we view them, their values, and beliefs. These interactions and observations influence our own theories, values, and beliefs as well. All these processes result in our salient social

Social identities and the three Cs

SOCIAL-IDENTITY-BASED COMPREHENSION	SOCIAL-IDENTITY-BASED CONTROL	SOCIAL-IDENTITY-BASED COMMUNITY
Making sense of the world in keeping with our team	Controlling the world in ways that are good for our team	Connecting with and being a good member of our team

identities influencing how we comprehend the world, how we seek to control it, and how we think about and connect with our communities (see table above).

"It's a Good Fit": American Politics and Aligned Social Categories

If social identities are powerful enough to affect what I believe and even what I see, then understanding what makes a given social identity salient will help me understand the origins of my knowledge and beliefs. Recall that the more I think about my group membership, the more accessible that social identity will be in my mind. And the closer I feel I am to my group prototype, the better the fit with that social identity. When I'm in New Hampshire, wearing my New Hampshire flannel, breaking out my NH accent, and referencing landmarks from days gone by, I am activating my NH social identity and making it accessible in my mind. But I am also illustrating how well I fit. By wearing the clothes, using the accent, and sharing relevant cultural history, I'm approaching my sense of the group prototype. Then, once my identity is both accessible and a good fit, that identity is salient. And once salient, it shapes my perceptions and judgment formation. Translation: I start to see cars from Massachusetts as interlopers and wind turbines as eyesores.

In the US political context, the concepts of accessibility and fit are working to tear us apart. Recall that because of social sorting, America's political parties serve as efficient proxies for racial, religious, geographic, and cultural categorizations. One's political party in the United States has come to serve as a mega-identity that envelops all these sociodemographic and cultural categorizations. In fact, Lily Mason's work shows that as these identities are aligned, partisans identify more with these related groups.[27] The fit of America's parties extends not only to cultural differences in how Democrats and Republicans tend to spend their free time and raise their children but even to their aesthetic preferences—for art, music, and entertainment.[28] These differences allow our group prototypes (star examples of our team and our opposing team) to be observed and reinforced in the world around us all the time.

Republicans in particular have exceptionally good fit. Working-class conservative white evangelicals who live in rural places fit very well into the Republican category; they embody the group prototype. But liberal Americans from ethnically diverse urban or suburban neighborhoods who might question the existence of God fit fairly well into the Democratic category, where they are approaching a group prototype—albeit a more ambiguous one than we find on the political right. Thus, the social sorting of the parties, and the fit of party members, is asymmetrical (see figures below and on facing page).

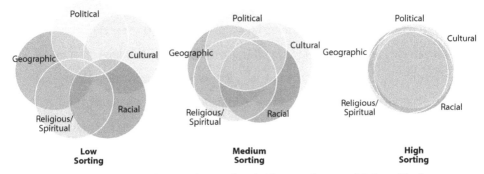

Social Sorting. As our social identities become aligned with one another, our political party identity efficiently captures our racial, religious, geographic, and cultural identities as well.

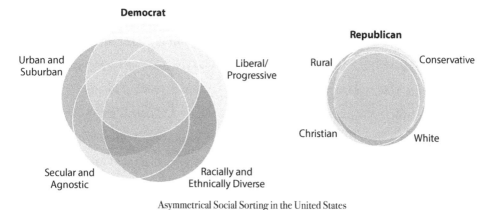

Asymmetrical Social Sorting in the United States

It should go without saying, but I'll say it anyway: there is nothing inherently bad about occupying "aligned" sociodemographic and cultural categories. Simply being conservative, white, Christian, and rural-dwelling doesn't make someone a bad person, nor does being liberal, from a racial or ethnic minority group, secular, and city-dwelling. However, having aligned categories makes our corresponding political identities salient by giving us good fit. Good fit means we are more likely to think of ourselves in terms of our partisan identities. And thinking of ourselves in this way means our attitudes and behaviors can be readily "guided" by prominent group prototypes (like politicians or media elites) and constantly reinforced (or strengthened) through our political and media environments. Ezra Klein summarizes it this way: "Since these mega-identities stretch across so many aspects of our society, they are constantly being activated, and that means they are constantly being reinforced."[29]

Expressive Approaches to Partisanship

The identity-based approach to political partisanship—also referred to as an expressive approach—considers political party to be a stable characteristic and thus largely unaffected by policy considerations or ideology.[30] Instead of being about the issues, expressive approaches to partisanship suggest that my party identification is about my identification with my team. In *Partisan Hearts and Minds: Political Parties and the Social Identities of Voters*, political scientist Donald Green and his coauthors compare political identity with religion—where the team identity comes first and related beliefs and feelings about other religions come later.[31] For example, you're born into a Catholic family, so you don't believe in abortion or sex before marriage, and you feel an opposition to Protestants. This picture of partisanship operates in stark contrast to more "rational" or "instrumental" models that see party identification as the thoughtful result of policy preferences, which would change as my policy positions change.[32] I find the parallels between party and religion quite helpful, but maybe that's just because I have a whole lot of loved ones who identify as Catholic and yet are pro-choice and open to premarital sex. Their religious social identity stays the same, regardless of their specific beliefs.

For decades, political scientists have traced the ideological sorting of America's political parties, in which the Republican Party has become more conservative and the Democratic Party more liberal.[33] It was then that experts began to consider that these increasingly overlapping aspects of partisan and ideological identities might facilitate a more "expressive" (less policy-based) approach to party identification.[34] Researchers found that political participation was driven more by strength of partisan identity and less by concerns about political policies. Instead of just measuring party identification on a scale from "strong Democrat" to "strong Republican," scholars began examining the "identity" part of party identification. Through questions like, "When talking about [Republicans/Democrats/Independents] how much do you use 'we' instead of 'they'?" they learned that strong party identification was associated with heightened emotional responses to party-based threats and reassurances.[35]

All of these findings were consistent with partisanship functioning more as a social identity and less as an outcome of rational policy deliberations.

As our various identity categories become more associated with our political parties, and as our categorical fit improves, the salience of our political party mega-identity grows too. In fact, political scientists Lily Mason and Julie Wronski found that Democrats and Republicans with highly aligned racial, religious, and political categories—and thus highly salient partisan identities—report feeling closer to members of their party than those whose categories are less aligned.[36] If I am an agnostic Democrat from a diverse Boston neighborhood, I will feel closer to the Democratic Party than if I am a churchgoing Democrat from rural Iowa, regardless of my opinions about government policy. And party members whose identities aligned were also more likely to identify as strong Democrats and strong Republicans compared with other party members.[37] So the agnostic Democrat who lives in the diverse Hyde Park neighborhood of Boston will tend to feel more strongly like a Democrat than the churchgoing one in rural Elk Horn, Iowa. All this makes sense when you consider how these political cleavages facilitate group prototypes. As our categories align, we get closer and closer to our sense of what an idealized group member looks and acts like.

Does thinking of ourselves in terms of our political party or identifying strongly with our party matter? Well, if tapping into one's southern identity makes southern food taste better, and if connecting with my rural New Hampshire identity transforms environmentally friendly windmills into industrial eyesores, then yes. Thinking of ourselves in terms of our political party matters. It matters for a host of reasons I'll summarize here, but let's start with this one: partisan identity salience matters because observations are theory—*and identity*—laden. Salient partisan identities shape what we see.

Take, for example, the much-studied phenomenon of partisans changing their evaluation of America's economic performance on the basis of which party holds the presidency. When asked how well they feel the economy is doing before and after important elections, partisans will change their economic evaluations seemingly overnight to reflect whether their party is in control. When my party is in control, I think the economy is strong. When the other party is in control, I think it's in the toilet.[38] These partisan effects on perception extend to how partisans experience news events and media content as well. Partisans selectively perceive their party's candidate to have performed better in presidential debates.[39] They are more likely to perceive news show hosts who critically cover their political side as being unfairly "biased" against them, and they are less likely to see actual bias in opinion programming that supports their political side.[40]

Not only does political identity influence what we see and how we see it, but it also influences what we feel.[41] When a salient social identity is threatened, we experience heightened anger.[42] In the context of political identity, then, having aligned social, political, and cultural identities facilitates deep emotional and ego-driven responses in the realm of politics. Partisans with aligned identity categories experience more anger at the opposing party's candidate and greater pride in their own party's candidate.[43] They are made angrier and more enthusiastic by exposure to emotionally charged political content and tend to participate more in politics.[44] While category-aligned people are more likely to hold slightly more extreme issue positions than those with less aligned social and political categories, the real difference between aligned and non-aligned groups is in the emotional and social aspects of their polarization: their anger, their political participation, and their perception of the other side.[45]

Crucially, these hyperemotional responses to partisan identities contribute to the dehumanization of the other side.[46] Political psychologist Erin

Cassese finds that the more partisans identify with their party, the lower they place members of the other political party on the Ascent of Man visual scale—the graphic that shows various stages in the evolution of humans, from apes to Neanderthals to *Homo sapiens*. In other words, the more people identify with their own party, the more they rate the other side as less evolved, and hence less human.[47]

Partisan Identity Salience Shapes Belief in Misinformation

Not only does partisan identity salience affect what we see and feel, but it also shapes what we know—or at least what we *think* we know. In my work with my colleagues at the University of Delaware, we studied how partisan identity salience relates to belief in misinformation about COVID-19 and the 2020 election. Recall that in late 2020, President Trump both downplayed the severity of COVID-19 and falsely alleged that the 2020 election had been rigged and was riddled with fraud. Thus, it would have been consistent with the Trump-guided Republican Party prototype for Republicans high in partisan identity salience to hold beliefs consistent with these propositions.

Because our research team was studying health-related attitudes and beliefs among at-risk groups, our data are split into two samples: ages 18–49 and ages 50 and older, surveyed in November–December 2020. First, we identified Democrats and Republicans as low, medium, or high in partisan identity salience on the basis of their agreement with the following statements: "My identity as a (Democrat/Republican) is important to me" and "Being a (Democrat/Republican) is a big part of who I am." These two items were averaged and used to separate respondents into low, medium, and high partisan identity salience.[48]

We then looked at the percentages of Democrats and Republicans who somewhat to strongly agreed with three pieces of COVID misinformation as a function of their levels of partisan identity salience. Those three pieces of misinformation were (a) "The coronavirus is a hoax," (b) "The coronavirus vaccine will be used to implant people with microchips," and (c) "The flu is more lethal than coronavirus."

Our results tell a simple story. Among Republicans, the more central that partisanship was to their identity, the more likely they were to report believing that COVID was a hoax, microchips would be implanted through the vaccines, and the flu was more lethal than COVID. Note, however, that belief in misinformation about COVID was lower in the older sample than in the younger one. This should give us some peace of mind, as it shows how the population most at risk from the harmful effects of COVID (older individuals) was less likely to believe false information about COVID than were younger folks. When I look at these graphs, my concern is about what happens to perceptions of reality on issues that are *distant* from us (which COVID may have seemed for younger people). The extent of misperceptions reported among Republicans ages 18–49 who said their political party was a big part of how they think of themselves is staggering, with about half of the 18- to 49-year-old Republicans high in partisan identity salience reporting that COVID was "a hoax."

We conducted a similar analysis of misperceptions related to the 2020 election in the weeks immediately following the presidential election.[49] Here we looked at the percentage of respondents with varying levels of partisan identity salience who somewhat to strongly agreed with the following: (a) "The fact that Trump lost means that the election was rigged," (b) "There was widespread voter fraud in the 2020 Presidential election," and (c) "We can never be sure that Biden's win was legitimate." The story is similar. Across both age groups, Republicans who reported that their political party affiliation was a central part of their identity were the most likely to report believing party-serving misin-

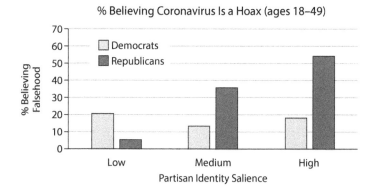

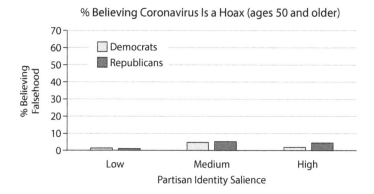

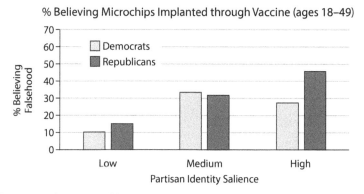

Democrats and Republicans Who Report Believing COVID Misinformation by Their Partisan Identity Salience   (*continued*)

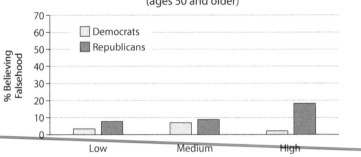

% Believing Microchips Implanted through Vaccine (ages 50 and older)

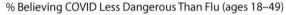

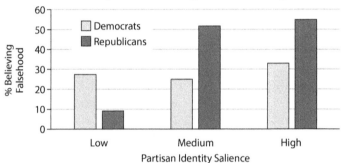

% Believing COVID Less Dangerous Than Flu (ages 18–49)

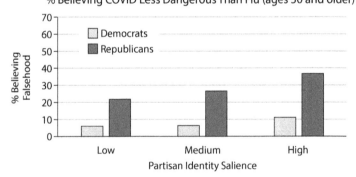

% Believing COVID Less Dangerous Than Flu (ages 50 and older)

(*continued*)   Democrats and Republicans Who Report Believing COVID Misinformation by Their Partisan Identity Salience

formation. Among Democrats, election misinformation beliefs were higher among the younger population than among the older one.

These findings are consistent with the results of a CNN poll conducted almost 10 months after the 2020 election that found that 59 percent of self-identified Republicans reported that "believing that Donald Trump won the 2020 election" was "very" or "somewhat important" to what being a Republican meant to them. Belief in the Big Lie had become a central part of their partisan identity.[50]

Partisan Identity Salience Shapes Our Actions

As our partisan identities shape what we *see* and how we *feel*, they also shape what we *do*. Political scientist Marc Hetherington traced increases in Americans' political participation from 1996 to 2004.[51] Following 30 years of decreased voter turnout, in 1996 American voter turnout began to rise, a trend that Hetherington connects to the increased political polarization among elites starting at that time. (Remember the 1994 Republican revolution and Republican candidates taking the oath to uphold the Contract with America on the steps of the Capitol building?) His analyses show that it was then that Americans became more interested in elections and started to care a whole lot more about who won. They became more likely to express their political opinions through bumper stickers, buttons, campaign donations, and efforts to influence the votes of others. While some of these increases in voter turnout appeared to be the outcomes of more active outreach efforts on the part of campaigns, partisan identity researchers point to intensifying political group *identities* and resulting partisan *emotions* as the pivotal factors driving Americans' increased political action.

In a study of 30 years of survey data from the American National Election Survey, political scientists Shanto Iyengar and Masha Krupenkin tracked

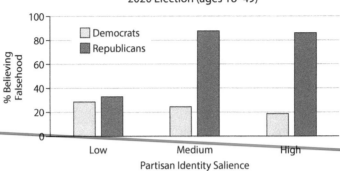

% Believing There Was Widespread Voter Fraud in 2020 Election (ages 18–49)

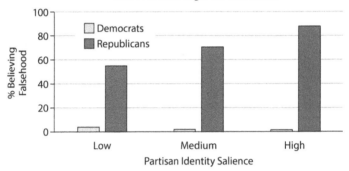

% Believing There Was Widespread Voter Fraud in 2020 Election (ages 50 and older)

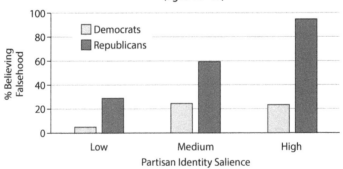

% Believing Trump's Loss Proves Election Was Rigged (ages 18–49)

Democrats and Republicans Who Report Believing Election Misinformation by Their Partisan Identity Salience

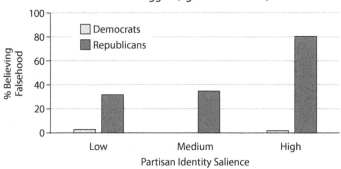

% Believing Trump's Loss Proves Election
Was Rigged (ages 50 and older)

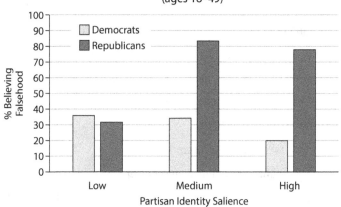

% Believing Biden's Win May Not Be Legitimate
(ages 18–49)

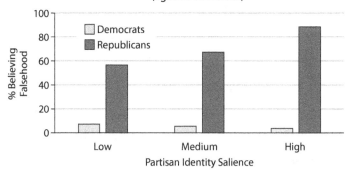

% Believing Biden's Win May Not Be Legitimate
(ages 50 and older)

(*continued*)   Democrats and Republicans Who Report Believing Election Misinformation
by Their Partisan Identity Salience

changes in partisans' evaluations of—and emotional responses to—the opposing party and how these trends contributed to increases in political participation.[52] Not only did they find increasingly negative evaluations of the opposing party, but starting in the mid-1990s (again, the year 1994 seems important here) the relationships between out-group evaluations and emotions increased. Meaning, now more than ever, the more you dislike the opposing party's candidate, the more you also dislike members of the other party, evaluate the other party's candidate more negatively on key traits, and report more negative emotions in response to the other party. All this negativity focused on the out-group is increasingly being experienced as part of one big cohesive partisan package.[53] And all these negative evaluations are increasingly associated with political participation. To me, the most alarming finding is that prior to 1994, voting and political participation were driven by Americans' positive feelings toward their own party more than they were by negative feelings toward the other party. But today, we participate more because we hate the other side. So, in 1984, someone might wear a button and put up a yard sign because she loves Ronald Reagan. Today, she attends a rally and donates money because she hates Joe Biden.

The Problems for Democracy

To be clear, the concern here is not that Americans are participating too much in politics but rather that the forces driving that participation are corrosive and dangerous. Political communication scholars Nathan Kalmoe and Lily Mason explore the distinction between benign partisanship anchored in party pride (e.g., wearing a button because you love Reagan) and malign partisanship tethered to out-group animus (e.g., attending a rally because you hate Biden).[54] Their analyses suggest that as party identity gets stronger and more salient, partisans are more likely to endorse a kind of partisanship that is open to aggressive attacks—or even violence—against the other side. Considering that we look to the "best" members of our social categories for a sense of how to think and act, this is bad news. Today when we look to those who identify most strongly with our party, we find partisans who are more likely to hate the other side, participate in politics driven by hate, see the other side as less than human, morally disengage from them, and be open to the idea of threats and violence in service of our opposition to them. Note that this is not what we see when we look at the "average" party member (who is less affectively polarized, less participatory, and less morally disengaged), but rather what we see when we look at prominent partisan prototypes.

There are so many reasons why these dynamics are bad for democratic health that it's hard to know where to begin. I find it helpful to think more broadly about the criteria necessary for democracies to thrive and how each of the developments discussed here complicates those criteria. Steven Levitsky and Daniel Ziblatt, authors of *How Democracies Die*, explain that a key criterion for democratic health is support for democratic *norms* among political elites—that is, the unwritten rules that allow for democracy to function. Chief among them, they argue, are "mutual toleration" and "forbearance." Mutual toleration is described as "the idea that as long as our rivals play by constitutional rules, we accept that they have an equal right to exist, compete for power, and govern."[55] Forbearance is the democratic proposition that "politicians should exercise restraint in deploying their institutional prerogatives."[56] When members of the two opposing political parties have deep animus for one another or begin to see the other side as a threat to their way of life or as less than human, the prospect of mutual toleration becomes grim. Such hostilities discourage legislators (and regular citizens) from recognizing the other side's views as remotely acceptable—or even legitimate. These conditions easily morph into an "ends justify the means" mentality in which people fighting for their side feel justified in using any means necessary to stop the other side, hence violating the norm of "forbearance."

So, what do Levitsky and Ziblatt see as the chief contributors to the erosion of these two democratic norms? Like many political scientists studying the state of American democracy, the authors point to the social sorting of the parties as a central factor: "The social, ethnic, and cultural bases of partisanship have also changed dramatically, giving rise to parties that represent not just different policy approaches, but different communities, cultures, and values."[57] As a possible solution, they suggest a "reshuffling" of the parties to undo the racial and religious alignment that has occurred over the past 50 years.

The authors also warn of the ability of populist leaders to take advantage of these fertile conditions for democratic erosion, stating simply, "When populists win elections, they often assault democratic institutions." Recall that populist leaders like Donald Trump are antiestablishment figures who promise to rid politics of "corrupt elites" (e.g., "Drain the swamp") through identity-based appeals to the good, pure, moral people.[58] Polarization and social sorting increase the effectiveness of such "us/them" appeals. And in places where the population has become ideologically polarized and parties have become sorted along the lines of race and religion, populist authoritarians have thrived.[59]

In the next chapter we will unpack another by-product of social sorting: the epistemic sorting of America's political parties. As the two parties have sorted in terms of race, religion, and culture, they seem to have also sorted in the very ways that they come to understand their worlds. And because of the nature of the sorting process—especially the sorting of evangelical Christians into the Republican Party—the asymmetrical way Americans make sense of their worlds may be contributing to asymmetrical wrongness, potentially contributing to a greater belief in misinformation and conspiracy theories on the right than on the left.

Chapter 5

What Guides My Team, Intuition or Evidence?

IN AUGUST 2021, scrolling my Twitter feed, I came across a tweet from Nathan Vickers, a reporter at KCTV5 in Kansas. He was covering the Johnson County Board of Commissioners meeting where community members were speaking out about face mask mandates and COVID-19 vaccines. Vickers highlighted one mother's public comment: "I have a bachelor's degree in logic, a master's in motherhood, and I'm board certified in American freedom."[1] I messaged Vickers to confirm that this statement was real, and he kindly forwarded the link to the Johnson County Facebook page so that I could hear the resident for myself: "Bachelor's degree in logic, a master's in motherhood, and board certified in being a freedom loving American." A few words off from the original quote, but, yes, it was real.

Recall that we understand our world through two pathways: the theories, values, and beliefs we hold in our minds, and our observations of the world. These two paths are intertwined, as our theories and beliefs are updated by our observations, while our observations of the world are both theory laden and identity laden. The willingness to allow observations and evidence—even disconfirming observations and evidence—to inform our theories, values, and beliefs is central to the pursuit of empirical truth: truth as it exists not in our minds but in the world. Relying only on the theories, values, and belief we already hold in our minds will inevitably lead us to reinforce what we already believe to be true, even if it's not. Without the incentive to integrate disconfirming observations and challenge our preexisting theories, it's difficult to imagine how we would ever get closer to empirical truth.

Countless psychological theorists have recognized that humans form judgments in wildly different ways under different conditions. We have the capacity to make decisions quickly, based on gut instinct and emotional responses; and we also have the capacity to make decisions more slowly, based on reflection and thoughtful integration of new information with existing knowledge and beliefs. As described by the late Seymour Epstein, these are "two kinds of processing [that] are not opposite equivalents but represent two kinds of information processing that are independent."[2] In other words, it's not an either-or situation. Most of us are regularly using both. The research and theorizing on these two systems are vast.[3] Perhaps best known is Nobel Prize winner Daniel Kahneman's book *Thinking Fast and Slow*. In it, Kahneman characterizes two systems of thought: System 1 is the more efficient system that uses emotions and instinct to form judgments quickly, and System 2 is the more thoughtful system that takes time to reflect and even challenge the judgments derived through System 1.

While all of us rely on both systems to survive, some tend to rely on one more than the other. Individuals who place faith in their own intuition and emotions tend to feel as though their automatic responses to the world—informed by their preexisting theories, values, and beliefs—are sound, even though they may sometimes be wrong.[4] Individuals who prefer to deliberate and evaluate evidence may take longer to arrive at their beliefs about the world.[5] They will tend to engage in more cognitive reflection as they consider how their observations of the world ought to update their theories, values, and beliefs.

Political psychologists Kevin Arceneaux and Ryan J. Vander Wielen use individual psychological traits to identify the kinds of people who will tend to use one system over the other. They propose that people who are less inclined to enjoy thinking and problem solving (people who score lower in the trait "need for cognition" [NFC]) and people who enjoy and prefer to experience intense emotions (people who score higher in "need for affect" [NFA]) are more likely to engage with the world through intuition and emotions (System 1), while those *high* in need for cognition and *low* in need for affect are more likely to engage in deliberate thoughtful reflection (System 2). Their research shows that those more prone to thoughtful reflection (high in NFC and low in NFA) are more likely to "tame their intuition," adjusting their immediate reflexive responses through a more thoughtful process. Meanwhile, those prone to emotional responses (low in NFC and high in NFA) are more likely to go with their gut—and are also more likely to be wrong.[6]

We can also think about these different decision-making systems in terms of "epistemic motivations" related to our "beliefs about the nature of knowledge and how one comes to know."[7] On the one hand is how much an individual trusts intuition and emotion as a pathway to truth, and on the other is how important it is that one's beliefs match and are updated by empirical evidence and data. For obvious reasons, epistemic beliefs have become a centerpiece of the study of misinformation and conspiracy theory beliefs. People who are guided by intuition over evidence are more likely to believe misinformation. And people who value evidence and data as a pathway to judgment formation are less likely to believe misinformation.

Political communication scholars R. Kelly Garrett and Brian Weeks examined how these different ways of knowing are correlated with beliefs in conspiracy theories. They assessed "faith in intuition for facts" by asking respondents how much they "trust their gut to tell them what's true and what's not," "trust their initial feelings about the facts," and "can usually feel when a claim is true or false even if they can't explain how they know." They then measured "need for evidence" by asking respondents if they agreed with statements like "Evidence is more important than whether something feels true," "A hunch needs to be confirmed with data," and "I trust the facts, not my instincts, to tell me what is true."[8] Their findings show that valuing intuition is associated with greater belief in conspiracy theories, while "needing evidence" is associated with less belief in conspiracy theories. Because intuition is about coming to conclusions efficiently and "feeling" what's true, this way of knowing emphasizes what we already value and believe over observations or evidence to the contrary. Individuals who place their faith in intuition are more likely to observe or "see" the world in keeping with their preexisting theories and social identities—and so sometimes those observations are wrong.

Actively Open-Minded Thinking, Intuition, and Religion

In contrast to intuition or gut-guided thinking is "actively open-minded thinking" (AOT), which reflects the extent to which we allow new information, settings, and stimuli to influence our knowledge and beliefs.[9] When we measure AOT, we ask people how much they agree with statements like "A person should always consider new possibilities" and "People should always take into consideration evidence that goes against their beliefs." It also includes the reversed-coded items "It is important to persevere in your beliefs even when evidence is brought to bear against them" and "One should disregard evidence that conflicts with your established beliefs." Professor Gordon Pennycook and his colleagues have conducted extensive research of how these individual "thinking styles" affect one's susceptibility to false information.[10] While they have used many different measures to assess how individuals come to truth (including Frederick's dreaded Cognitive Reflection Test involving lily pads and the cost of baseball bats, covered in chapter 2[11]), Pennycook has focused extensively on AOT. His studies consistently show that when people place value on the role of evidence as a means of updating their beliefs, they are less likely to believe misinformation and conspiracy theories.[12]

In an interview with Pennycook and his frequent collaborator David Rand, I asked about these psychological measures, and their thoughts about the importance of actively open-minded thinking in particular. Pennycook explained AOT this way:

> [AOT] is not about how much you care about the truth, because everyone cares about the truth. . . . To exist in the world, you have to rely on things being true. What the AOT is about is the way that you approach evidence and problems, whether you're questioning yourself. Do you *care* enough? . . . Are you obsessed with knowing what is actually true? How much are you motivated to put *that* first rather than how you're feeling about something?[13]

Pennycook's research points to relationships between AOT and countless psychological, political, and informational constructs. People who score higher on AOT score higher on acceptance of science and tend to be more politically liberal, while those who score lower on AOT are more likely to embrace traditional moral values and religious fundamentalism.[14]

In our discussion of AOT, Rand highlighted an important distinction between people who come to truth based on faith and those who prefer evidence:

Yes, people want to know the truth. But at the same time, work that you [Pennycook] and I have both done suggests that there also is—with religion as the dominant example—big variation in the extent to which people are happy to take things on faith, rather than wanting evidence. These are separate dimensions, right? Like how much I need evidence to believe a thing versus "Am I down to believe it on faith?"[15]

One cannot study the psychology of misinformation without being overwhelmed by the amount of empirical evidence regarding the relationships between religiosity, cognitive style, and belief in misinformation. As Michael Bronstein and his colleagues (including Pennycook) conclude, "Delusion-prone and dogmatic individuals, as well as religious fundamentalists, are more likely than others to believe fake news, and that this may be in part because they exhibit reduced analytic and actively open-minded thinking."[16] Notice that this lack of open-minded thinking does not mean that fundamentalists are pigheaded or prejudiced, but rather that they simply prioritize faith in what they *already* believe over any evidence to the contrary.

When I first encountered research on the social sorting of the political parties in the United States, I was struck by the potential dangers inherent in racially and religiously sorted political parties simply because of their capacity to fuel the identity-based divides we've discussed so far. These dynamics *are* dangerous, and democracy experts warn that these aligned political mega-identities are contributing to political sectarianism, which threatens democratic health.[17] But through the social-identity-driven dynamics of wrongness, social sorting may have another insidious downstream effect: the *epistemic* sorting of the parties. Because of the ideological, religious, and cultural sorting of our parties, partisanship also signals a divide between different ways of comprehending the world.

For reasons related to biology, physiology, and genetics, individuals have interpersonal threat-monitoring systems on varying levels of alert.[18] These systems then shape our psychological needs that contribute both to our social and cultural attitudes and beliefs *and* to our preferred ways of engaging with the world.[19] This process creates asymmetries in the needs and urges that shape how liberals and conservatives think and behave, in terms of both existential needs related to threat management and epistemic needs related to how they come to know the things they know.[20]

Social and cultural conservatives are more likely to be monitoring for interpersonal and physical threat. As a result, they are more likely than liberals to be motivated by efficiency and to form judgments based on emotions and intuition.[21] In contrast, those who are less concerned about physical threats feel less pressure to make decisions quickly; instead, they have the luxury of being comfortable with uncertainty, ambiguity, and unpredictability. Liberals thus have a higher tolerance for ambiguity and engage in more cognitive reflection when faced with new information. These same underlying predispositions likely contribute to more socially liberal attitudes, especially on issues relating to race, sexuality, and crime.[22]

This association—between ways of coming to truth, on the one hand, and political ideology, on the other—might help account for some of the political asymmetry researchers find in belief in and spread of misinformation and conspiracy theories.[23] In the US context, for example, we know that Republicans were more likely than Democrats to believe COVID misinformation and conspiracy theories and more likely to share false information about COVID online.[24] Studies of rumor-sharing online show a sizable asymmetry in the sharing of false information (this time related to the 2013 Boston Marathon bombings and the 2020 death of sex trafficker Jeffrey Epstein in prison), with conservatives far more likely to share rumors than liberals.[25]

But not all studies show that belief in misinformation and conspiracy theories is higher among conservatives than among liberals. In a massive cross-national study of conspiracy theory beliefs, a team of researchers found that the association of conservatism with conspiracy theory beliefs depended on context, like which political side was favored by the conspiracy theory and which political and cultural elites were sharing it.[26]

Additionally, the relationship between conservatism and conspiracy theory beliefs depends largely on what kind of political conservatism we're talking about. These relationships between psychological traits, on the one hand, and political ideology, on the other, don't really show up in the context of fiscal conservatism (our positions on taxes, regulation, and welfare). Instead, they are most pronounced in the context of social and cultural ideology—that is, issues related to gender, sexuality, race, and crime.[27] This same ideological dimension is central to the sorting of America's political parties discussed in chapter 3.[28] This is the divide that captures everything from debates over critical race theory to transgender rights, LGBTQ rights, abortion, immigration reform, and policing issues. With conservative beliefs on these social and cultural issues, come more efficient, emotion-based, and intuitive forms of information processing. And with liberal views on these issues come a higher tolerance for ambiguous situations and experiences, a higher need for cognition, and more careful information processing. No, these relationships are not necessarily true for every individual conservative or every individual liberal, but on average, these associations between thinking styles and social/cultural political ideology do exist.

There's an additional angle to this "epistemic sorting" story that I find compelling as well. Recall that as the Republican Party deliberately began courting the vote of white evangelical Christians, the party grew more conservative in its views on everything from abortion to women's rights to LGBTQ issues.[29]

As the number of evangelical Protestants in the Republican Party grew throughout the 1980s and '90s, the frequency of church attendance and the importance
of religious faith in the lives of Republican Party members steadily increased.
And with that shift toward Evangelicalism in the Republican Party came a shift
in how Republicans—and Republican Party leadership—came to value different ways of coming to "truth."

In their book *Enchanted America: How Intuition and Reason Divide Our
Politics*, political scientists J. Eric Oliver and Thomas Wood argue that the most
significant consequence of this religious shift in American partisanship is how
it changed the ways in which the two major parties come to know the things
they know.[30] As the Republican Party became the home to evangelical and fun-
damentalist Christians, it also became home to a way of understanding the
world rooted in faith and intuition—as opposed to empirical evidence and data.
Explain the authors, "Conservatives are far more likely than liberals to be
Intuitionists. Partly this is because so many of them are conservative Christians. And it is precisely the conflation of ideology, intuition, and religion that is
causing much of the confusion about the role of ideology in US politics."[31]

While Oliver and Wood acknowledge that we *all* use intuition to navigate
the world to some extent, people vary in how they prioritize intuition and emotions over evidence and data. Intuitionists display what the authors refer to as
"magical thinking," a way of interpreting the world that is designed *not* to bring
them closer to truth but to "validate their feelings and placate their anxieties."
Using a fascinating series of items, the authors measure people's preferences
for situations that involve symbolic harm (those that can't harm you but that feel
harmful) over situations that involve real harm (such as physical harm)—for example, a preference for the symbolic harm of "stabbing a photograph of one's
family six times" over the real harm of "sticking one's hands in a bowl of cock-
roaches," or for "yelling 'I hope I die tomorrow' six times out loud" over "riding

in a speeding car without a seat belt." The authors then integrate these responses with people's scores on "apprehension" and "pessimism" scales to create a full "magical thinking" measure. Their results show that the "magical thinkers"—those who are more afraid of symbolic harm than situations that pose real harm—are more religious and attend church more frequently. They are also more likely to believe in angels, ghosts, and the paranormal and are more likely to believe that "everything happens for a reason." These highly religious intuitionists are also more likely to believe conspiracy theories. As Oliver and Wood write, "The most important thing that conspiracy theories share with religion is that they both attempt to order an ambiguous reality."[32]

The work of sociologist and media scholar Francesca Tripodi illustrates that some of the relationship between conservative Christianity and pathways to truth is reflected in the evangelical practice of individualized scriptural inference. She describes how evangelical Christianity encourages "close readings undertaken to find truth in the words of sacred documents like the Bible or the Constitution."[33] Rather than relying on higher-status religious leaders to serve as arbiters of truth, evangelical Christianity empowers members of the congregation to find their own meaning in sacred texts. Although "encouraging conservative voters to do their own research is not necessarily nefarious," argues Tripodi, "it is a key component of conservative propaganda."[34] "Doing our own research" inevitably emphasizes what we already believe (and what people like us believe) as we make sense of the world, leaving us with observations that are highly theory laden and highly identity laden.

Do Ways of Coming to Truth Come First?

Most of these political psychological models assume that people hold underlying propensities (originating from their threat-monitoring systems) related to ways of knowing—favoring System 1 (intuition and emotions) or System 2 (reflection and evidence)—and that it is the influence of these traits on inter-personal threat-related beliefs as well as the *sorting* of different kinds of people into the different parties that has exacerbated these political divides. But there is another possibility that I find provocative and compelling—one that has the causal arrow moving in the opposite direction.

What if psychological traits related to epistemology are not fixed but malleable? What if our need for cognition, need for affect, tolerance for ambiguity, value placed in intuition, and value placed in evidence are contingent on what is happening around us—on what is made salient? What if the very way we comprehend the world is informed by "how people on my team understand things like this"?

In survey research conducted in 2008, Chris Federico and Pierce Ekstrom found evidence consistent with this. They explored how the link between certain psychological traits and political issue positions varied with the partisan identity salience of the individual.[35] They found that the link between people's issue positions and their need for cognitive closure (a trait that captures a discomfort with ambiguity and a need for clear, final answers) was higher among those whose partisan identity was more salient. While need for cognitive closure was higher among issue-based conservatives than among liberals (consistent with prior work), the need for cognitive closure was *especially* high among issue-based conservatives who reported that "political attitudes are an important part of my self-image." And among issue-based liberals who reported high partisan identity salience, need for cognitive closure was *especially* low. If your partisan identity is important to you, your epistemic traits will look a lot like those shared by members of your team. Admittedly, these are correlational data that do not show that identity salience *causes* these associations to get stronger. It is still possible that people who hold those traits are just higher in political identity salience.

Fortunately, political psychologists Bert N. Bakker, Yphtach Lelkes, and Ariel Malka were on the case with experiments and panel studies that allowed them to examine changes in psychological traits over time.[36] In studies conducted in the Netherlands, Germany, and the United States, they found that the personality traits most characteristic of an epistemically "closed" personality (high in need for cognitive closure and authoritarianism) did predict more right-wing issue positions at later points in time. But they also found evidence that people's politics affected how they *later* comprehended the world, with conservative issue positions at one point in time associated with more "closed" personality traits later on. Notably, given the religious sorting of the parties described above, this was most pronounced in the US sample in the context of attitudes toward abortion and LGBTQ issues. Here, conservative attitudes at Time 1 predicted authoritarian personality traits at Times 2 and 3. These results support a model in which people have a partisan identity that then increases their likelihood of reporting personality traits that are in line with those of their political team.

The researchers then conducted an experiment in which they hypothesized that just getting people to think about themselves politically would cause them to report psychological traits that are most valued by their political team. In other words, how people think of themselves as part of their political team would affect how they comprehended the world around them. The researchers told a random half of the participants that the survey was about politics and asked them political questions, including what they disliked about the opposing party. The other random half was told the survey was about the internet. For the people who were made to think about their political identity (i.e., who were asked political questions), when they later responded to questions about personality traits, they looked "psychologically" more like their "partisan team" than did respondents who were told the survey was about the internet.

In the language of social identity theory, a couple of different things might be happening here. On the one hand, maybe priming partisan identity caused people to want to "perform" as good members of their partisan teams—and answering questions about personality traits gave them that opportunity. But it might also be that highlighting partisan identity motivated people to embody the traits that made them feel like a part of their team. Bakker, Lelkes, and Malka conclude their study by outlining the democratically problematic consequences of both: "From a normative standpoint, this adds a concerning wrinkle to the standard story on political polarization. Specifically, political polarization may be exacerbated by people on different sides of the ideological spectrum adopting—or perceiving themselves as possessing—different personality traits. Rather than merely reflecting non-political psychological differences, opposite political loyalties might motivate people to enhance such differences."[37]

The Epistemology of Populism

Not every study shows a link between American partisanship and ways of comprehending the world. Kevin Arceneaux and Ryan J. vander Wielen explored whether a preference for intuition over evidence was associated with American partisanship in 2015 and found *no* differences by party.[38] Note, however, that their study was conducted just months before Donald Trump announced his bid for the Republican presidential nomination, in which he referred to people emigrating from Mexico as "bringing drugs . . . bringing crime . . . and [being] rapists." If, as the findings of Bakker, Lelkes, and Malka suggest, political context causes partisans to increasingly embody (or at least *report* embodying) the epistemic traits of their team, then maybe the lack of findings in 2015 makes sense. It is certainly possible that years of political identity reinforcement under a Trump presidency might make these correlations stronger.

In research that Erin Maloney, Amy Bleakley, Jessica B. Langbaum, and I conducted immediately after the 2020 presidential election, we explored how the ways that people report comprehending the world–through feelings and intuition or through evidence and data–are associated with political preferences and with belief in misinformation.[39] The study, published in the *Journal of Social and Political Psychology*, was conducted in the context of the larger COVID-related project discussed in the last chapter. Because that work required two separate samples–one for Americans ages 18–49 and one for Americans ages 50 and over–these data are presented within each of those age groups. The national survey we conducted in November–December 2020 asked participants how much value they placed in intuition and emotions as pathways to truth, and how much they valued evidence and data.[40] We found that those who reported "trusting their gut to tell them what's true and what's not" and "trusting their initial feelings about the facts" were more favorable toward President Trump. Meanwhile, those respondents who reported trusting "facts, not their instincts," and who agreed that "evidence is more important than whether something feels true" were less favorable toward Trump and more likely to be liberal and Democratic.[41] Trump support was a stronger correlate of "ways of coming to truth" than was party or ideology.

To illustrate these relationships here, I've categorized participants as low or high in valuing intuition and emotion and low or high in valuing evidence and data (split at the means). These two categorical variables were then *crossed* to identify individuals with a combination of high intuition and low evidence ("intuition-based thinkers") and a combination of low intuition and high evidence ("evidence-based thinkers"). The figure on page 117 illustrates the average favorability toward President Trump within each of these two groups, broken down by party affiliation. Among Republicans, Independents, and

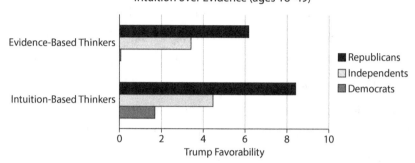

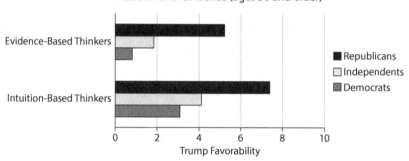

Trump Favorability by Party and Type of Thinking

Democrats alike, intuition-based thinkers rated Trump more favorably than did their evidence-based thinking counterparts, across both age groups.

Next, we wanted to understand how these patterns were associated with belief in misinformation about COVID and the 2020 election. We found that belief in both sets of misinformation was higher among Republicans, conservatives, and Trump supporters. But most importantly, like our colleagues R. Kelly Garrett and Brian Weeks, we found that belief in misinformation was highest among those who valued intuition and emotions and rejected evidence and data. The figure on page 119 shows the number of pieces of COVID misinformation that individuals somewhat to strongly agreed with out of three statements, including: "The coronavirus is a hoax," "The coronavirus vaccine will be used to implant people with microchips," and "The flu is more lethal than coronavirus." It also shows how many pieces of election misinformation that individuals somewhat to strongly agreed with. These three statements were as follows: "The fact that Trump lost means that the election was rigged," "There was widespread voter fraud in the 2020 Presidential election," and "We can never be sure that Biden's win was legitimate." As illustrated in the figures, more value placed in intuition and emotions was associated with higher rates of misperceptions of both COVID and the election, in both age groups. This relationship was most pronounced among Republicans, such that the highest rates of misperceptions were found among those Republicans who reported placing high value in intuition and emotion. Importantly, these relationships were still significant even when we held constant various sociodemographic characteristics.[42] As J. Eric Oliver and Thomas Wood write, "Intuitionism not only amplifies America's ideological divisions, it exerts its own power on public opinion."[43]

You may notice that several of the misinformation beliefs explored in our study were rooted in a classic conspiracy theory narrative. Statements like "The coronavirus is a hoax," "The coronavirus vaccine will be used to implant people with microchips," and "The fact that Trump lost means that the election was rigged" are all tales of bad, powerful people operating in the shadows to harm the public and hide the truth. Conspiracy theories such as these are a staple of populist political rhetoric and populist beliefs.[44] They were also a part of President Trump's political biography as he leveraged speculation about President Obama's birthplace to garner political and media attention back in 2011. Oliver and Wood explain that "conspiracy theories are so common in populist movements that many scholars view these as one of the primary forms of populist

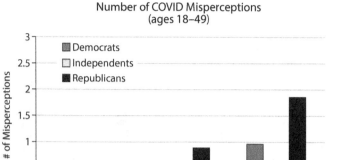

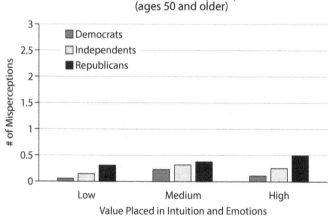

Misperceptions by Party and Level of Intuition-Based Thinking   (*continued*)

discourse, how ordinary people understand power structures."[45] In their re-search, they also find that "magical thinkers" (their intuitionists) score higher on political and cultural populism.

Intuitionism and the rejection of evidence and expertise are especially com-patible with conservative populism. As discussed in chapter 3, populism is an ideology that is thin on substance or policy positions. Instead, it is the rhetoric

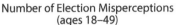

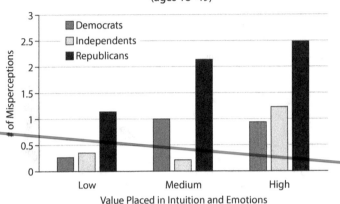

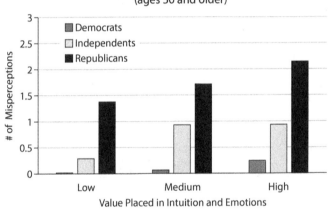

(*continued*)   Misperceptions by Party and Level of Intuition-Based Thinking

of populism, with its adulation of "the pure people" and their moral distance from the "corrupt elites," that defines it.[46] In solidarity with the crowd, populists appeal to "common sense" and gut instinct.[47] They reject experts and intellectualism, instead prioritizing group affiliation and symbolism. As rhetorician Jennifer Mercieca writes, President Trump is a "rhetorical genius" when it comes to populist appeals.[48] His engagement with the world—and his communication style—is guided by instinct and intuition. In 2018, he told the *Washington Post*, "My gut tells me more sometimes than anybody else's brain can ever tell me."[49] That same year, Trump's adviser, Peter Navarro, discussed his role as Trump rolled out new tariffs on steel and aluminum imports: "This is the president's vision," Navarro said. "My function, really, as an economist is to try to provide the underlying analytics that confirm his intuition. And his intuition is always right in these matters."[50] Phil Bump of the *Washington Post* highlighted how this intuition-driven approach makes it challenging to get to truth and to engage in democratic governance: "If there are no agreed upon facts, all that's left is opinion. But even when there are facts that could inform decision-making, willfully ignoring them in favor of trusting the president's gut makes changing Trump's view nearly impossible. How do you reason with someone's instincts?"[51]

Don't Be Fooled

Prioritizing intuition and emotions while *rejecting* evidence and data can increase our susceptibility to misinformation and conspiracy theories.[52] This combination is also associated with more polarized views on political issues and more animosity toward members of the opposing political party.[53] Given these trends, it's tempting to want to conclude that intuition-based thinking is always bad, that evidence-based thought is always good, and that we should, as Arceneaux and vander Wielen write, "tame our intuition." But while emotional, intuitive approaches to understanding the world can lead us to inaccurate conclusions, they are not inherently bad. Psychologists Jonathan Evans and Keith Stanovich explain that the notion that "intuitive, heuristic processes are responsible for all bad thinking and that reflective, analytic processes necessarily lead to 'correct' responses" is the most "persistent fallacy" in thinking about how people come to understand their worlds.[54] Psychologist Seymour Epstein acknowledged that careful, reflective thinking is cognitively taxing and a huge pain (my words) as well as "a very inefficient system for responding to everyday events."[55] This is especially true given that intuition and emotions seem to work pretty well most of the time. Psychologist Martie Haselton's concept of adaptive rationality emphasizes just this: that humans have adapted to make rational decisions from "irrational" (read: intuitive and emotion-based) processes. We instinctively know that a big animal baring its teeth is something to avoid, and that when crowds of people are moving rapidly in one direction, we probably should go with them. These shortcuts guide us in the direction of solid decisions most of the time.[56]

Epistemology, Identity, and Humility

While "dual systems" approaches to the study of human cognition have been popular for decades, the reality of what is going on in the brain is likely far more complex.[57] According to newer dynamic models of cognition, all of us use a combination of intuition and emotions, on the one hand, and evidence and reason, on the other, to various degrees in different contexts.[58] All told, it seems that characterizing intuitive emotional approaches as separate from or worse than evidence-based or rational approaches is an oversimplification. Worse, to do so might exacerbate the social and political divisions we've discussed thus far.

If partisan identity can trigger people's conscious embrace of—or performance of—distinct epistemic traits, perhaps politicizing ways of coming to truth is a bad idea.[59] Explicitly linking reason and evidence-based approaches to liberal politics could very well encourage a deliberate rejection of seemingly evidence-based approaches (like science, for example) among those on the political right. It could also, hypothetically, lead to a citizen at a town hall meeting opposing science-based public health measures on the grounds that she has "a bachelor's degree in logic, a master's in motherhood, and is board certified in being a freedom loving American."

While Jonathan Evans and Keith Stanovich challenge the notion that evidence-based approaches are normatively good and intuitive approaches are normatively bad, they acknowledge that the more efficient, heuristic approaches can be strategically manipulated to cause harmful, dysfunctional outcomes.[60] When the cues we receive from our information environment are authentic (like an actual tiger baring its teeth), our heuristic responses (scared = run!) will generally lead to functional outcomes. They refer to this as a "benign" information environment, where the cues are authentic and so the responses are generally appropriate. But sometimes we find ourselves in an environment in which cues are manipulated and used strategically to exploit our efficient heuristic processes. They refer to this as a "hostile" information environment. And in a hostile information environment, our heuristic responses may lead us astray.

Given the role of political identity salience in activating accompanying epistemic traits, conservative populists can make strategic use of partisan identity to activate intuition and emotions to efficiently spread self-serving disinformation and conspiracy theories among their supporters.[61] If "people like me" think through intuition and emotion, then I will tend to prioritize my preexisting values and beliefs over disconfirming observations and evidence. But if "people like me" think through evidence and data, I will prioritize new observations and evidence over my preexisting beliefs. In other words, the direction and strength of the arrows linking theories, values, and beliefs with observations will depend on the ways of coming to truth that I feel are valued by my team.

And yet, unless you are personally conducting controlled trials on the efficacy of vaccines or conducting audits of election outcomes, the observations you're making are not direct observations of data and evidence but rather observations of what credible sources and experts say *they* have observed. So, really, these "evidence-based thinkers" are not being directly guided by evidence but rather are guided by their *trust in experts who are being guided by evidence.* This would imply that trusting sources who are guided by evidence and data might be less of a cognitive process related to the evaluation of evidence and more of an identity-driven shortcut related to trust.[62] "People like me trust scientists." This is a heuristic cue. It is a form of System 1 processing—an efficient decision-making process *just like the one that social conservatives use.*

In fact, identifying as the kind of person who relies on evidence and data may become part of one's social identity on the political left, regardless of how liberals really form judgments. I think about this whenever I see those signs posted in people's front yards that say, "In our home, we believe that Black Lives Matter, love is love, and . . . science is real." Science is real. If I put this in my yard, would it serve as a description of how I arrive at truth? Through evidence, data, verification, falsification, and not removing myself from doubt? Or would it signal what team I'm on?

This question was especially salient in the later months of the COVID pandemic as the scientific findings and recommendations regarding the efficacy of face masks evolved. During the initial deadly COVID wave in the spring of 2020, face masks were shown to be a highly effective way of preventing the spread of the virus. In April 2020, the Centers for Disease Control and Prevention released new guidelines recommending the use of a cloth face covering to help stop the spread of COVID, especially since new research indicated transmission was possible even from asymptomatic carriers and that a face covering significantly limited the amount of virus that people could expel into the air.[63]

But wearing face masks became politicized. Politicians and media person-alities on the political right framed face mask mandates as a threat to individual liberty.[64] Research I conducted with my colleagues at the University of Delaware in the fall of 2020 showed that Trump supporters who were especially psychologically reactant (who reported experiencing high levels of anger when their freedom of choice was restricted) were among the least likely to engage in masking behaviors outside the home.[65] For those on the political left, engaging in masking behaviors starting in the spring of 2020 was an evidence-based behavior guided by trusted experts.[66] But over time, the mask became embedded with elements of a liberal social identity. Masking became a symbol of protecting people in your community and reflected a sense of collective responsibility. It was also more likely among liberals who were conflict averse—meaning they likely believed in the efficacy of masks but also didn't want to get in arguments with people for not wearing one.[67]

As the months went by, we learned more about COVID's transmissibility outdoors and the role of masks in slowing its spread. Evidence indicated that outdoor transmission was highly unlikely, especially if people were more than three feet apart.[68] In an article in *The Atlantic* titled "The Liberals Who Can't Quit Lockdown," Emma Green explores the challenge for some on the left as COVID restrictions loosened in the spring of 2021: "For this subset, diligence against COVID-19 remains an expression of political identity—even when that means overestimating the disease's risks or setting limits far more strict than what public-health guidelines permit. . . . For many progressives, extreme vigilance was in part about opposing Donald Trump."[69]

As someone who lives in a predominantly liberal community and whose friends and family are mostly liberal, I admit I felt a social pressure to continue masking outdoors long after restrictions were lifted, as a way of signaling my good standing as a part of my team. I found myself being skeptical of information that suggested masks were unnecessary when outside. What may have started out as an "evidence-based behavior" had become a part of my social identity, and once it did it was very hard to go back, despite the changing evidence. My community saw masks to be a sign of goodwill, and we put faith in them as a way of controlling the spread of a deadly virus. For my team, "belief in science" meant "belief in the efficacy of masks," and I found it difficult to stop wearing them while I was walking the dog or at an outdoor barbecue. It had become hard for me to allow challenging or disconfirming evidence to update my beliefs about masks. The irony here, of course, is that the spirit of scientific inquiry *requires* that we seek out disconfirming evidence and that we update our theories, knowledge, and beliefs in light of it. But for me, what had started out as a science-based practice had—at least in some contexts—become an identity-based performance.

The Power of Admitting We Might Be Wrong

At the heart of the epistemology of wrongness is an unwillingness to allow new information to update our beliefs. But is there anything that can increase our willingness to engage with and be moved by new information and evidence? One of my favorite concepts in this area is that of intellectual humility (IH). IH is an individual-level characteristic that captures how much we "recognize that a particular personal belief may be fallible, accompanied by an appropriate attentiveness to limitations in the evidentiary basis of that belief and to one's own limitations in obtaining and evaluating relevant information."[70] IH is about how much we embrace—and adjust to—the fact that we might be wrong. Psychology professor Mark Leary developed the following six items to capture IH: (1) "I question my own opinions, positions, and viewpoints because they could be wrong"; (2) "I reconsider my opinions when presented with new evidence"; (3) "I recognize the value in opinions that are different from my own"; (4) "I accept that my beliefs and attitudes may be wrong"; (5) "In the face of conflicting evidence, I am open to changing my opinions"; and (6) "I like finding out new information that differs from what I already think is true."[71]

Like the AOT scale, IH captures how much people value the role of new information and evidence in updating their existing beliefs,[72] but while the AOT scale frames these as prescriptive principles that people ought to live by, IH frames these as descriptive aspects of the self. So rather than AOT's "People should do and think these things," IH captures how much "I do and think these things."

Notice that IH does not make a firm distinction between ways of knowing, either through intuition or through evidence. Rather, it captures how much people recognize that their beliefs may be inaccurate—regardless of how those beliefs were arrived at—and how much they are open to challenging and updating their views. One of the many benefits of IH is a reduction in susceptibility to misinformation. People who score higher on IH are more likely to scrutinize health information and less likely to belief misinformation about COVID-19.[73] They hold fewer antivaccination attitudes, have higher intentions of receiving the COVID vaccine,[74] and are less prone to believe in conspiracy theories more broadly.[75] Psychologist Adam Grant writes, "Arrogance leaves us blind to our weaknesses. Humility is a reflective lens: it helps us see them clearly. Confident humility is a corrective lens: it enables us to overcome those weaknesses."[76] It seems that being open to the possibility that we could be wrong might very well increase our chances of being right.

Part II: The Process

The first half of this book has unpacked how human beings are wrong about lots of things all the time. Our innate needs to understand our worlds (comprehension), to have agency in our lives (control), and to form a sense of belonging (community) shape what we see and the conclusions we draw. We've seen how social identity is a powerful force that influences what the three Cs end up looking like. And we've seen how, in today's America, lots of us—even those of us who don't think of ourselves as especially *political*—have "good partisan prototype fit." Because of overlapping sociodemographic, political, and cultural identity categories, tapping into and activating our political mega-identities can be done all kinds of ways—through politics, yes, but also through references to religion, race, ethnicity, culture, lifestyle, and even ways of coming to truth, all of which tend to cluster us under a blue tent or a red tent. We have explored how this process of social sorting has harmful implications for democracy and even how it shapes how we make sense of our worlds.

What we have yet to discuss is how these same dynamics are a goldmine for anyone looking to engage and rile up lots of people all at once. The second half of this book thus dissects the process through which our mediated political world enhances American wrongness. Political elites, news organizations, partisan media, and social media platforms make use of our political mega-identities to mobilize supporters, attract audiences, and engage users. And every time they do, those identities become a more potent, purer version of what they were before. They become *distilled*, like an expensive whiskey. And as they do, they increase our capacity for wrongness.

So, let's head to part 2: the story of political identity distillation through our mediated political world, how it fuels a cycle of asymmetrical American wrongness, and what can be done to disrupt it.

Part II

The Process

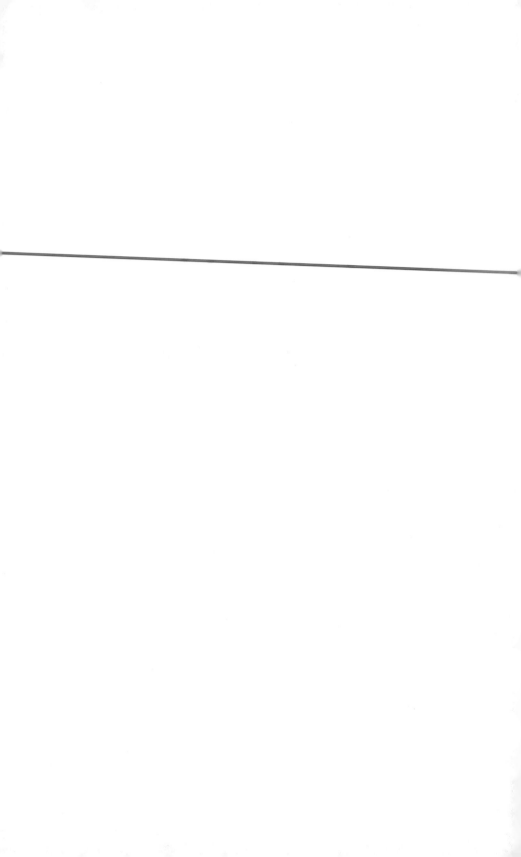

Chapter 6

Exemplify Us

Identity Reinforcement through Political News

THE MARCH 2022 SUPREME COURT nomination hearing for Judge Ketanji Brown Jackson marked the nomination of the first Black woman to serve on the country's highest court. A graduate of Harvard Law, Judge Jackson came to the nomination as a "conventional and mainstream" highly credentialed judge,[1] with a measured judicial philosophy that seemed—on its face—unlikely to ruffle the feathers of Republican lawmakers. Given that Supreme Court nominees have historically been confirmed with "a substantial majority of votes for confirmation,"[2] one might expect the hearings for Judge Jackson to be rather perfunctory and uncontroversial. But while confirmation hearings had historically occurred with overwhelming bipartisan support (except in rare instances like President Reagan's nomination of Justice Robert Bork or President H. W. Bush's nomination of Clarence Thomas), over the past two decades, these proceedings have been increasingly tinged with partisan conflict. In 2016, President Obama's nomination of Judge Merrick Garland was stalled by Republican senators, who refused to hold a hearing or a vote on Garland's nomination. Soon thereafter, President Trump's nominees, Justices Neil Gorsuch and Brett

Kavanaugh, were confirmed with just a minimum number of Democratic votes—and Justice Amy Coney Barrett with no Democratic votes at all.

As the nomination hearings for Justice Jackson unfolded, it was evident that she, too, would be subject to the kind of browbeating that had come to define contemporary Supreme Court nomination hearings.[3] Republican senator Josh Hawley of Missouri challenged the judge's sentencing record on cases of child sex abuse materials, suggesting that she had been too soft on child pornography criminals, and voicing his fears of his own children being exploited. Republican senator Lindsey Graham of South Carolina questioned the judge's defense of detainees held as enemy combatants in Guantanamo Bay, Cuba, after the 9/11 attacks. Frustrated by the committee chair's defense of Judge Jackson, Senator Graham raised his voice, expressing anger at the idea of these prisoners' early release. "As long as they're dangerous, I hope they all die in jail if they're going to go back and kill Americans," he said, before turning off his microphone and storming out of the hearing.[4]

Republican senator Ted Cruz of Texas questioned the judge on the meaning of critical race theory, a frequent topic of conversation among conservative media hosts like Sean Hannity and Tucker Carlson. An academic theory introduced by Harvard legal scholars in the 1970s, critical race theory (CRT) explores how institutions and systems perpetuate racial inequality. And while CRT is not technically taught in elementary or secondary schools, in 2020 and 2021, conservative critics began describing antiracist and social justice curricula in public schools as "CRT."[5]

Senator Cruz's CRT-related questioning included the dramatic use of props, like an antiracist children's book from the library of the private school where Judge Jackson served on the board. Gesturing to oversized illustrations from the book propped up on an easel behind him, the senator asked Judge Jackson, "Do you agree with this book that is being taught to kids that babies are racist?" The senator then used his time to read various passages from several of the school's books, including the provocative quote, "Can we send white people back to Europe?"[6]

In reference to Senator Cruz's aggressive questioning of Judge Jackson, Michael Barbaro, host of the *New York Times*'s *Daily* podcast, asked Supreme Court correspondent Adam Liptak, "What exactly is Cruz up to here?" Liptak suggested that the Republican senators were engaged in a strategic performance, that they "need[ed] a reason to vote against the first Black woman to serve on the Supreme Court," and that these questions were an "effort to find something that will sell to at least [their] constituents that she likes terrorists, that she's soft on people involved in child sexual abuse, that she endorses racist baby books in private schools. Whatever force these critiques have, their real purpose seems to be to provide a rationale for a vote against Judge Jackson."[7]

Connecting these dots would allow Republican lawmakers to convince more moderate conservatives that their rationale for opposing the nomination was sound, while also tapping into wedge issues that would mobilize their conservative base. In the ideologically polarized and socially sorted reality of contemporary elections, the latter of these is especially important. Every public-facing moment is an opportunity to avoid "getting primaried"–that is, losing their party's nomination to a more ideologically extreme challenger. And the threat of "getting primaried" is real. Between 2010 and 2014, one-third of Republican senators seeking reelection found their vote totals under 60 percent owing to challenges from the Right, and three of them lost their seats.[8] The threat posed by conservative Tea Party Republicans to establishment members of the GOP during that time transformed the party. This ideological shift was fueled by a well-oiled machine of conservative interest groups–organizations such as the Club for Growth, FreedomWorks, and Heritage Action stepped in to financially support and promote ideologically conservative candidates, including Senator Ted Cruz and Senator Rand Paul of Kentucky.[9] In that sense, the behavior of elites in Congress—including their performances during Judge Jackson's nomination hearings—is a defensive strategy.

Partisan Prototype Performances

For a racially, religiously, geographically, and culturally homogeneous Republican Party, avoiding "getting primaried" is about successfully performing the role of a prototypical party member. Remember the prototypical Philadelphia Eagles fan adorned with face paint and throwing snowballs at Santa? Not the average member of the party but the *best* member of the party. The behavior of Republican senators during the hearings illustrates their performance of "identity ownership," a term coined by political communication scholars Daniel Kreiss, Regina Lawrence, and Shannon McGregor. The performance of identity ownership involves political elites' strategic "attempts to create the perception and remind voters that they, and their parties, best represent particular social groups."[10] For decades, political scientists studied the related concept of issue ownership to describe how each political party was considered especially capable of addressing certain issues. As a result, party leaders would work to center elections on the issues their party "owned."[11] It is only appropriate that in a socially sorted and identity-driven political context, politicians are working *less* to own policies or issues and *more* to own their side's political mega-identities, proving they are "appropriate, credible 'prototypes' of particular groups—and manifesting a good 'fit' with a group's characteristics, values, and norms."[12]

For Republican senators in 2022, aggressively questioning Judge Jackson on the teaching of CRT in schools or on child pornography sentencings was an effort to do just this: prove to voters that they are a strong fit with the Republican Party's values and norms centering on race, religion, crime, and the vulnerability of (white) children. Notice that all these values and norms are group based, emphasizing values of one social category in opposition to other categories, including white versus nonwhite, evangelical versus secular, and less educated versus college educated.

Notice also that strategic use of identity-centered approaches does not require that lawmakers share (either deliberately or inadvertently) false information. Yet, through their performance of identity ownership, they set the wheels in motion to facilitate identity-based misperceptions on the part of their supporters. Political leaders "connect the dots" across social and cultural issues, creating associations and developing schemas from which partisans can draw conclusions (maybe true ones, maybe false ones). Following Judge Jackson's nomination hearings, experts warned that although the questions did not technically contain false information, the framing of Senator Hawley's questions tapped into a long-standing web of right-wing conspiracy theories alleging that Democratic elites have some involvement in child trafficking or pedophilia.[13] The QAnon conspiracy theories in particular—which have spread around the world since 2016—are based on false claims about a network of satanic child sexual predators operating in the highest ranks of government and media. Just through mere power of association, Hawley's questions could tap into the same mental schema, thus enabling the reinforcement of cognitive connections between the judge and these insidious conspiracy theories.

Hawley's questioning might have facilitated connections with the known QAnon catchphrase "Save the children" frame as well—one that connects conservative opposition to both the mandatory use of face masks and the teaching of CRT in schools. As the *Washington Post*'s Phil Bump writes, "It's not necessarily that Hawley is specifically trying to appeal to QAnon supporters. . . . But QAnon's focus and Hawley's politics share a common point of origin: elevating and amplifying the fears of parents. And in both cases, that amplification overlaps with hyper partisan attacks on the political left."[14] In this way, both Hawley's questions about child-pornography sentencing decisions and Senator Cruz's questions about the contents of antiracist children's books likely reinforced the same mental schema and, in so doing, placed it at the center of what it means to be a prototypical Republican.

A Symbiotic Relationship

But is that it? Were these senators just performing their identity ownership to the most extreme partisan voters, in the hopes they don't lose their seats in the primaries? Probably, yes. But remember that our understanding of politics is mediated. We're not in the room at the hearing. We rely on mediated constructions of events to have a sense of what happened—or as Walter Lippmann wrote in 1922, "The only feeling that anyone can have about an event he does not experience is the feeling aroused by his mental image of the event." In other words, what we respond to are not actual events we have witnessed directly, but to "pictures in our heads" of those events.[15] So, yes, these displays of identity are about shaping the pictures in voters' heads, but lawmakers know that these pictures get there by way of media, and they know that the press cannot resist dramatic, aggressive performances of partisan identity. Senators' dramatic identity-based performances serve two goals simultaneously: they prove their culture war credentials to their base, and they appeal to journalistic routines (habits of reporters and news producers) that earn them press coverage. Even Democratic Judiciary Committee chair Dick Durbin, when asked about his "very testy exchange" with Senator Lindsey Graham, replied with a laugh, "Lindsey knows how to get on CNN."[16]

This exploitability of the mainstream press, like politicians engaging in dramatic displays of identity ownership knowing they'll be rewarded with media attention, is attributable to long-standing journalistic routines—habits of the press that inform how they select, produce, and frame news stories. Political communication scholar W. Lance Bennett describes the outcomes of these press routines as "content biases" in the news.[17] For example, news media tend to focus on drama over harmony, individual personalities over institutions and systems, and fragmented events over abstract policies and concepts.[18] These biases are generally done in anticipation of what it is that media organizations think that we, the audience, want. We want drama. We want people. We want stories. Or so media executives tell themselves. The negative effects of these press biases are wide ranging, from fueling political cynicism to encouraging audiences to blame individuals for their roles in their own misfortunes instead of considering system-level solutions.[19]

These content biases in favor of conflict, personality, and isolated events are so well established and predictable that political actors and interest groups have used them to their own advantage for decades, making "getting spun the norm rather than the exception."[20] Historically, these dynamics have been captured by the phrase "the professionalization of politics,"[21] which includes how political handlers stage photo-ops to associate persuasive visuals with policy rollouts. Or how communication teams produce "pseudo-events" to create good "optics" to garner media attention.[22] Professional communications teams work to create experiences, events, scandals, and moments to be captured and distributed by media organizations. These dynamics are also captured by the concept of the "mediatization of politics," wherein the behaviors of both media producers and political leaders are governed more by the logics of media than by the logics of politics.[23]

The predictability of the press's content biases is why the press and politicians are in a long-term "you scratch my back and I'll scratch yours" relationship. Politicians need the press to help create "pictures in voters' heads," and the press needs politicians to give it the raw ingredients for the political spectacle of the day.[24] And because they need each other, each of these entities feeds into and rewards the needs and biases of the other. As our political context has (d) evolved through polarization and sorting, the nature of the mediatization of politics has (d)evolved, too.[25]

The professionalization of America's political campaigns throughout the 1980s and '90s was a strategic response to advances in the production standards of television news. As political news became highly produced and edited, politicians found fewer of their own words being included in the news, and more editorializing from reporters against a backdrop of aesthetically pleasing visuals.[26] Michael Deaver, President Reagan's media adviser, who orchestrated countless positive press cycles for the president, explained that he and his team understood that the business of television news in the 1980s was not journalism but entertainment. Embracing the needs of the press meant producing good "wallpaper" (pretty pictures) to accompany their stories, like arranging for President Reagan to be filmed riding a horse, eating jellybeans, or drinking beer with working-class voters in Boston—the latter occurring on the same day he cut the corporate income tax rate.[27]

But recall that in 1986, the United States was not ideologically polarized at the level of elites or the public. Legislation was frequently passed with bipartisan support. Affective polarization was significantly lower than what we find among partisans today.[28] The parties were less separated along the lines of race, religion, and culture than they are today. They were not as socially sorted—both the Democratic and the Republican Parties included mixes of racial, religious, geographic, and educational categories. And although trust in government wasn't as high as it had been back in the 1960s, in 1986 trust was hovering around 40 percent—a stark difference from the mere 20 percent of Americans currently reporting they can trust the government to do what is right most of the time.[29] For politicians like Reagan, creating "pictures in voters' minds" against this backdrop—of relative elite bipartisanship, moderately ideological voters, amicable relations between regular Democrats and Republicans, and some trust in government—meant curating positive pictures of strength (Reagan riding a horse), grandfatherly kindness (Reagan eating jellybeans at work), and approachability (Reagan drinking with the guys). Such moments appealed to the press's bias in favor of personalized, fragmented news while appealing to the political spirit of the moment.

But for politicians to make it into the news today—in an era of elite polarization, sorted and ideological voters, popular disdain for members of the other party, and woefully low trust in government—they must appeal to a different iteration of these same biases. In today's context, personalization is firmly *conflict* centered, as illustrated by the popularity of negative emotional displays and up-close camera angles in political programming.[30] In-your-face programming, in which partisan actors yell at, insult, and interrupt each other, is good for the audience metrics of media and bad for the citizen metrics of democracy. These uncivil exchanges increase viewer attention and arousal—two positive metrics that please media producers and advertisers while increasing viewers' hostility toward the opposing side and making them evaluate the other side's arguments more negatively.[31]

For Senators Cruz and Graham, tapping into today's press biases to maximize coverage while also creating positive pictures in the minds of today's sorted, polarized, untrusting Republican voters means emotionally, aggressively challenging the opposition while proving their prototypical group fit. Intense emotional displays about child pornography, terrorists, and racist baby books appeal to the press's bias in favor of personalized, fragmented, and dramatized news while also allowing these elected officials to prove that they "own" their party's identity. Bennett was right when he said that "members of Congress have learned how to play the media game."[32]

In the days after the nomination hearings, I watched as the outrage cycle came full circle. In my Twitter feed, I saw a post from Senator Graham saying, "The Game Has Changed" along with a one-minute video arguing that Democrats had been ruthless and relentless in their questioning of Trump's Supreme Court nominees but had given a free pass to "activist" Judge Jackson. The video ended with the proud proclamation: "Senator Graham Voted Against Judge Ketanji Brown Jackson for the U.S. Supreme Court," with a call to donate to his reelection campaign (see below).

The emotional intensity of the current polarized and social-identity-laden political world means that political conflict and aggressive exchanges about divisive social and cultural issues will be most likely to make the news. They appeal to media's biases in favor of conflict, personalities, and fragmented events. And they help lawmakers perform the partisan prototype, all while emotionally engaging their most attentive partisans. Put simply: if you berate a Supreme Court nominee about pedophiles, racist baby books, and terrorists, that clip will

Senator Lindsey Graham Online Ad from April 2022

Ted Cruz Appears to Search for His Own Name on Twitter during the
Judge Jackson Hearings on March 23, 2022.
Photo by Kent Nishimura / Los Angeles Times via Getty Images

probably end up on television. You'll probably go viral on social media too. Perhaps that is precisely what Senator Cruz was contemplating in the photo that *Los
Angeles Times* photographer Kent Nishimura snapped of the senator appearing to
search for his own name on Twitter on the afternoon of the hearings (see above).

Conflict Frames and the Primacy of Social Identity

At the center of today's symbiotic relationship between politicians and the press
is a press routine that is so common in political news that it's difficult to imagine political coverage without it: conflict framing. In conflict framing, news stories are told in terms of competing factions, either groups or individuals, and
it is especially prevalent in news coverage of politics. Because of its inherent

appeal to the press biases of personalization, drama, and fragmentation, and because conflict frames allow journalists to maintain an "objective" stance in their treatment of a topic while framing Democrats and Republicans in a war against one another, the conflict frame dominates political news.[33] In the context of campaign coverage, conflict framing often focuses on elements of the "horse race," such as who is ahead and who is behind, and on strategies used by the various sides that are pitted against each other in a "battle" for victory.[34] There is an economic basis behind the press' fascination with election strategy and the horse race, though. First, elections are indeed contests that do involve campaign strategy. To pretend otherwise would be disingenuous. And second, audiences—especially politically engaged audiences—seek out election stories focused on the horserace and campaign strategy.[35] So, these stories are lucrative. The trouble, I submit, is not the mere existence of such stories, but rather, a press that only reports on politics through the lens of partisan conflict to the exclusion of substantive reporting on issues, policy, and democratic processes.

In their 1996 book *Spiral of Cynicism*, Joseph Cappella and Kathleen Hall Jamieson demonstrate how exposure to these kinds of conflict narratives caused people to become more cynical about politics. While cynicism is bad for democratic health, today, as affective polarization and social sorting have come to dominate America's political landscape, it seems the implications of conflict frames might be even more dire. In today's environment, in addition to fostering cynicism about politics, political conflict frames in the news contribute to our political mega-identities and to hostility toward the other side. In a set of experiments, political psychologists Jiyoung Han and Christopher Federico examined the effects of exposure to two different conflict frames: news stories framed in terms of conflict between genders, and news stories framed in terms of conflict between the political parties. Their goal was to understand not just the effects of these frames on polarization but the specific psychological mechanism through which these effects occurred.[36]

Respondents read an article about Facebook's and Apple's new policies to cover female employees' costs for freezing their eggs. But respondents read the piece framed in one of two ways: either in terms of partisan conflict, with the headline "Egg-Freezing Rekindles Partisan Debates on Workplace Inequality," or in terms of gender conflict, with the headline "Egg-Freezing Rekindles Debates on Gender Inequality in the Workplace." Results showed that exposure to both the political conflict frame and the gender conflict frame increased participants' "self-stereotyping." After reading the article, participants' attitudes toward the egg-freezing issue matched their perception of their in-group's view on that issue (based on either gender or party depending on their experimental condition). It was this process that best accounted for their polarized attitudes on the topic. In other words, participants who read the political conflict frame were more likely to anchor their attitude toward egg-freezing policies to what they thought was the attitude of their party. And those in the gender conflict frame condition were more likely to anchor their attitude to what they thought was the attitude of their gender. This is how the attitudes of the different groups (Democrats versus Republicans and men versus women) moved even further apart on the egg-freezing issue.

In short, partisan conflict frames activate our partisan identities. We read a story where our team is in a fight with another team, and we immediately respond as a member of our team. Whether that team is defined in terms of gender or political party, once activated, we respond as a good team member would respond. This means that the very way that news stories are most frequently told and the way that political events and issues are most frequently presented (as partisan conflicts) are constantly driving us apart: activating our partisan identities and influencing us to match our attitudes to those of our party.

The phenomenon of the "partisan pundit" is another useful television (especially cable) news routine that embraces the conflict frame while offering emotionally evocative performances of partisan identity. Pundits are talking heads who appear on the news not to "report" news but to talk *about* the news.[37] Cable news programs frequently assemble panels of pundits (for example, journalists, experts, and partisan commentators) who argue about the topic, tie that topic to broad themes in the culture war, and typically do so with the "in your face" interpersonal conflict style that increases viewer engagement while also increasing viewers' hostility toward the other side.[38] Among CNN's past pundit panel topics are questions of whether President Trump is a racist,[39] the role of racism in immigration policy,[40] and the security of American elections.[41] In fact, put this book down for just a second and google "'panel erupts' and 'CNN.'" It appears that "erupting panels" has been an entire subgenre at the cable network, especially in 2017 and 2018. Among the results are "Panel erupts over conversation of race," "Panel erupts over death threats to press," and "Panel erupts over Ivanka Trump rabbi meeting."

Through interruption and insult, huffs, puffs, and eye rolls, the conflict inherent in partisan pundit panels can activate and reinforce viewers' partisan identities yet again.[42] And while viewers' partisan identities become more salient and refined in ways that will inevitably shape how they view the world, these panels also provide partisan operatives the opportunity to *directly* misinform audiences. At the nonpartisan fact-checking organization Politifact, researchers fact-check statements made by pundits and on-air guests at the major cable networks. A 2015 report showed that of the pundit claims they checked, almost 60 percent on Fox News were rated as mostly false or false. This was true of 44 percent of pundit claims at MSNBC and 20 percent of pundit claims on CNN.[43]

Recall the concept of intellectual humility from the last chapter? Intellectual humility is the extent to which people are open to the possibility that they might be wrong. Well, partisan pundit panels are characterized by performances of intellectual arrogance or "I am not listening because I just want to show I'm right." Intellectual arrogance plays well on television, whereas intellectual humility does not. In fact, we rarely see intellectual humility modeled in our mediated political world. When we do, it's from the occasional appearance of scientists—people trained to never prove things or remove themselves from doubt. They don't speak in absolutes or forevers. They speak with caveats and conditions and often answer with "Time will tell" and "For now this seems to be the case." But in our mediated information-scape, their humility makes them come across as unsure, ambivalent, weak, or waffling.[44] As the late Neil Postman wrote in 1985, "When a television show is in process, it is very nearly impermissible to say, 'Let me think about that' or 'I don't know.'"[45]

Hostile Identity Performance Is Rewarded by the Press: A Case Study

To better understand how aggressive performances of identity ownership are rewarded with press coverage, I examined media coverage of Senators Cruz and Graham during the week of the nomination hearings. To perform a comparison, I needed to explore media coverage of a senator who had also used the hearings to do more talking than listening but whose comments were less in keeping with the conflict-centered content biases of the press. Reader, I offer you New Jersey Democratic senator Cory Booker.

During the nomination hearings for Judge Jackson, Senator Booker used his time to praise the judge and tell her how much her nomination meant to him. He emphatically told her that he would not let anyone in the Senate "steal his joy." His voice trembled as he said, "I want to tell you when I look at you, this is why I get emotional. . . . You're so much more than your race and gender. You're a Christian, you're a mom. You're an intellect, you love books, but for me, I'm sorry, it's hard for me to look at you and not see my mom, not see my cousins."[46] While Booker's performance was emotional and tapped into aspects of identity, it was not aggressive or oppositional. There was no fight to show. Would the New Jersey senator receive the same news coverage extended to Senators Cruz or Graham?

Using the Lexis-Nexis news database, I searched various news outlets for stories mentioning the Supreme Court as well as each of the three senators' names during the week of the hearings.[47] The results are consistent with a national press obsessed with conflict driven by partisan identity. When examining the proportion of "Supreme Court" news stories from each outlet that mentioned each senator's name, Senator Booker received far less media coverage for his joyful, tearful "pep talk" than did Senators Cruz or Graham for their aggressive culture war questioning (see figure below).

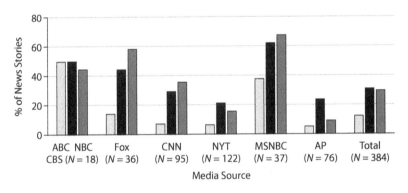

Media Mentions of Cruz, Graham, and Booker. Aggressive performances of identity ownership and identity threat are rewarded with press coverage.

On the broadcast news networks, all three senators were mentioned in about half of the Supreme Court stories. But on cable news, Senators Cruz and Graham enjoyed more than twice the coverage of Senator Booker: Senator Graham was mentioned in over half of the Supreme Court stories on the conservative Fox News and 68 percent of the stories on the more liberal MSNBC, and Senator Cruz was mentioned in 44 percent and 62 percent, respectively, of the Supreme Court stories. In the *New York Times* and the Associated Press (AP), the overall proportion of Supreme Court coverage mentioning each of the senators was lower than on television or cable, but Senator Cruz still benefited from over three times the coverage of Senator Booker, with mentions in just under a quarter of their stories. Also note that liberal-leaning MSNBC amplified Cruz's and Graham's identity performances as well. As explained by Jeff Berry and Sarah Sobieraj in their book *The Outrage Industry*, partisan programs like those on MSNBC and Fox News are chiefly in the business of producing "outrage programming" that focuses on the identification of partisan threats.[48] Partisan opinion shows cover stories and issues that they believe will outrage their partisan audiences. If you're a producer at liberal-leaning MSNBC looking to steep your audience in outrage, covering the identity performances of conservative senators Cruz and Graham at Judge Jackson's nomination hearings is as good a plan as any. The logic of media has become the logic of politics. In this polarized and socially sorted political context, the press's biases in favor of conflict and personalities reward negative emotional outbursts and the weaponization of political mega-identities with press coverage.

Following the New Rules of the Game

Although both Democrats and Republicans have become more ideologically and socially sorted, as illustrated in chapter 3, these trends have been significantly more pronounced on the right than on the left.[49] With a commitment to ideological purity over the building of coalitions, Republican lawmakers are under much pressure to perform their identity as devout ideological conservatives. In doing so, they reconstruct the role of a Republican lawmaker. Take author J. D. Vance. A Kentucky native, Vance came to fame after the 2016 publication of his memoir, *Hillbilly Elegy*. The book tells the story of his poor, white, working-class upbringing in America's Rust Belt in the 1980s and reveals how, despite his traumatic family history of abuse and alcoholism, he was able to achieve the new American Dream through his hard work.[50] Following the publication of his book, Vance was a media darling. The press, eager to understand how they had so underestimated the popularity of culturally conservative Donald Trump, turned to Vance—and midwestern diner patrons[51]—to understand the inner machinations of the white working-class voter. Vance was a relatable source for members of America's legacy press. He attended Ohio State and Yale Law School and, in 2016, declared himself a proud "never Trumper," even calling then candidate Trump "reprehensible." In one of his since-deleted tweets from a month before Trump's presidential victory, Vance wrote, "Trump makes people I care about afraid. Immigrants, Muslims, etc. Because of this I find him reprehensible. God wants better of us."[52]

But Vance soon developed political aspirations and announced his candidacy for a coveted US Senate seat in Ohio in July 2021. After this announcement, his public commentary completely changed. By that summer, he had deleted his anti-Trump tweets and was appearing on Fox News to disavow his prior criticisms of the conservative populist president.[53] This disavowal was rewarded with financial support and endorsements from conservative billionaire Peter Thiel, conservative Republican senator Josh Hawley, and controversial right-wing congresswoman from Georgia, Marjorie Taylor Greene.[54]

In an asymmetrically polarized and socially sorted political world, there may not be a place for a moderate, anti-Trump, Ivy League–educated Republican candidate J. D. Vance. But there *may* be a place for a culturally conservative populist pro-Trump J. D. Vance—one who signals his commitment to Republican values by supporting the idea of cutting funding for universities that teach critical race theory, and who says things like "The professors are the enemy"[55] and "The childless left [has no] physical commitment to the future of this country."[56]

After the January 6 insurrection at the US Capitol, those few Republicans who dared criticize the party's embrace of the Far Right (or vote with Democrats) were insulted or rebuked by other party members. Republican Party rising star (and daughter of the former vice president) Liz Cheney of Wyoming was removed as Republican conference chair after voting to impeach President Trump and criticizing his role in the events of January 6. Utah senator and 2012 Republican presidential candidate Mitt Romney was the only senator to vote to impeach his own party's president in Trump's first impeachment trial and did so a second time after the attack on the Capitol. Romney also voted in favor of Judge Jackson's appointment to the Supreme Court. After Far Right members of Congress Marjorie Taylor Greene and Paul Gosar appeared at a pro-Putin rally and addressed white nationalists, Senator Romney remarked on their appearance with a quote from the film *Butch Cassidy and the Sundance Kid*: "Morons. I've got morons on my team." He described as "almost-treasonous" the Far Right members of his party speaking out in support of the Russian president during Russia's horrific assault on Ukraine. He also acknowledged the mediated political incentives driving these Far Right identity performances, saying, "Of course they do it because they think it's shock value and it's going to get them more eyeballs and maybe get a little more money for them or their network. It's disgusting."[57]

While traditional conservative Republicans like Cheney and Romney tried to push back against the fringe elements of their party, the mediated political logics continued to incentivize and reward extremist displays of Republican identity. Following Senator Romney's vote in favor of Justice Jackson's appointment to the court, Marjorie Taylor Greene tweeted that Romney and the two other Republicans who voted yea were "pro-pedophile," a reference to the questioning by Senators Hawley and Cruz regarding sentencing for child pornography charges, and a barely veiled (but convenient) reference to the QAnon conspiracy theory centering on false claims of satanic pedophilia rituals by political elites. Greene's "pro-pedophile" tweet was covered by all the major news sources, including CNN, MSNBC, the *Washington Post*, and the *New Yorker*. The aggressive performance of the Republican mega-identity got the last word.

Who Gets Covered?

In the 1990s, W. Lance Bennett, the scholar who gave us the concept of content biases, became interested in (and concerned by) what appeared to be invisible constraints placed on the range of perspectives that journalists included in mainstream national news coverage. Bennett coined the term "indexing" to refer to the press practice of "indexing" acceptable points of view (perspectives that would be included in news coverage) to the range of positions expressed by congressional lawmakers.[58] The result was the compression of representations of public opinion "to fit into the range of debate between decisive institutional power blocs."[59] To the extent that voices of the public fit within that range of elite opinions, those viewpoints might be included in the news. But voices of the public that were further left or right of the "institutional power blocs"–defined by the positions expressed by congresspeople–would be excluded from news coverage or framed as deviant or dangerous. But today, as the ideological extremity of members of Congress increases, and as elites make explicit appeals to their parties' sorted and polarized social identities, the range of policy positions promoted by lawmakers is expanding. So, how does that affect the range of opinions that is deemed acceptable enough to be treated as "legitimate" by the press?

Well, it turns out that the ideological extremity of lawmakers is *rewarded* with press attention. Political scientists Mike Wagner and Mike Gruszczynski examined the amount of press coverage received by members of Congress serving between 1992 and 2013 to assess how lawmakers' ideological extremity (based on the ideological leaning of their floor votes) related to the amount of press coverage they received.[60] The strongest predictor of the amount of press coverage given to any individual member of Congress—especially coverage of members of the House of Representatives—was their ideological extremity. Ideologically extreme members of the House received three times the amount of newspaper coverage that more centrist lawmakers received, and twice the amount of broadcast television news coverage. Wagner and Gruszczynski conclude that "in an era of increased partisan polarization at the elite level, extreme politicians are good fits for modern journalistic norms of judging newsworthiness."[61] When broken down by party affiliation, their results show that "ideologically extreme Republicans tended to net more news coverage than ideologically extreme Democrats."[62] This difference was so stark that when looking only at Democratic lawmakers, there was almost no correlation between ideological extremity and press coverage. But among Republicans, political extremism yielded a sharp increase in press coverage. Once again, these mediated political incentives are profoundly asymmetrical. They are *lopsided.*

From a journalistic standpoint, the problem is that the professional norm of objectivity discourages journalists from taking a side in the reporting of political and social issues and events. The practice of press objectivity naturally encourages reporters' reliance on official sources and the indexing of political perspectives according to the institutional power blocs within houses of

Congress. If members of one party have embraced positions and rhetoric that flirt with white nationalism, promote falsehoods about the legitimacy of the presidential election outcome, and otherwise challenge democratic norms and institutions, then embracing objectivity would mean leaving those claims unchallenged to avoid allegations of press bias.

In his 2014 *Atlantic* article headlined "Yes, Polarization Is Asymmetric— and Conservatives Are Worse," journalism scholar Norm Ornstein of the American Enterprise Institute warns of the dangers of false equivalence, also known as "bothsidesism": "Saying both sides are equally responsible, insisting on equivalence as the mantra of mainstream journalism, leaves the average voter at sea, unable to identify and vote against those perpetrating the problem."[63] Ornstein was writing two years before the election of Donald Trump and six years before the challenges Trump would pose to America's democratic institutions through false claims of voter fraud and election insecurity. So, when faced with the January 6 insurrection, what was a journalist to do? In this context, bothsidesism ran the risk of placing lies on equal footing with the truth. In the weeks following the 2020 election, journalism scholar Jay Rosen identified a new, insidious version of journalistic bothsidesism that became commonplace in national news: "dueling realities stories." These were stories that covered Democrats and Republicans operating with two understandings of reality but that failed to acknowledge that one of these realities—one of these sets of "facts"—was false. One was *empirically inaccurate,* contradicted by evidence and expert consensus. This is how bothsidesism in the press fuels asymmetric wrongness.

Rewarding the Performance of Populism

With a nearly nonexistent public media infrastructure in the United States, we rely on a media system that is concerned first and foremost not with the public good but with maximizing profits and minimizing production costs.[64] Such a system will reward charismatic authoritarian populists over what rhetorician Jennifer Mercieca calls "normie" democratic politicians: those who embrace the norms of democratic discourse and respect the legitimacy of democratic institutions. The content biases of personalization, dramatization, and fragmentation all stem from a deregulated media industry that is incentivized to generate profit through sensationalized, audience-centered, cost-effective production routines. The focus on individuals over issues, conflict over harmony, and isolated events over static systems is a way to maximize eyeballs while decreasing production costs. Populist leaders, with their emotional, common-sense appeals and their charismatic criticisms of abstract institutions, are a great fit for contemporary media norms.[65] Populism expert Cas Mudde emphasized these dynamics when he wrote about the audience-oriented pressures that encourage media producers to "focus on more extreme and scandalous aspects of politics." He concludes that "all this provides a 'perfect stage' for populist figures who find 'not just a receptive audience, but also a highly receptive medium.'"[66]

Candidate and then president Donald Trump was unpredictable, prone to improvisation and insult, and played into the audience's cynicism and distrust of government and media. Trump understood that in an era of ratings-chasing journalism, even antagonistic relationships between politicians and the press are symbiotic. Candidate bashes press, press covers those insults with outrage and incredulity. Repeat. Journalism scholars Matt Carlson, Sue Robinson, and Seth Lewis propose that Trump used news media's audience-driven content biases to get airtime, thereby increasing the viability of his candidacy while also transforming journalism in the process:

Trump took advantage of journalistic conventions to increase his presence in the news; He used press bashing as a type of political performance commensurate with his populist rhetoric; He demonstrated the expansiveness of the contemporary media culture through his use of social media, political rallies, and right wing media to reach the public; He boldly invented or misrepresented facts in ways that strained reporting norms; And, in doing all of this, he challenged the institutional character of journalism.[67]

Political communication professor Dave Karpf put it simply: "Trump was demonstrably good television and reliable click bait."[68] Karpf points to the commentary of CBS chairman Les Moonves, who stated that Trump's candidacy "may not be good for America, but it's damn good for CBS."[69]

In the wake of Trump's presidency, we have seen more Republican elected officials playing by Trump's rules—both in their rhetorical style and in their attacks on governmental institutions and the press. We saw Florida Republican governor Ron DeSantis criticizing medical experts and the Centers for Disease Control and Prevention, issuing an executive order prohibiting schools from requiring face masks during COVID-19 and tweeting, "If the corporate press nationally isn't attacking me, then I'm probably not doing my job."[70] We saw Congresswoman Marjorie Taylor Greene blaming mainstream media for her attraction to conspiracy theories like QAnon and then declaring that COVID was not real and vaccines did not work—all while receiving press coverage that continued to raise her profile and amplify her claims.[71] As Jay Rosen put it, "It is very obvious . . . that being 'hated by the media,' as she would put it, is the basis to Greene's appeal. Therefore, critical coverage is not actually accomplishing what we think of it as doing: accountability. It's actually building her résumé."[72]

These populist political figures capitalize on the routines of journalism to build their reputations while eroding faith in the journalistic institutions themselves. Both DeSantis and Greene have been rewarded for their aggressive attacks on the press with, you guessed it, more press. In fact, Governor DeSantis had become such a sought-after Fox News guest that, following the 2020 election, he was invited to appear on Fox News just about every day during a three-month period.[73]

Nationalization of Wrong

As I write about Governor Ron DeSantis and Congresswoman Marjorie Taylor Greene, I find it fascinating that these names—of the governor of Florida and a member of the House of Representatives from Georgia's Fourteenth Congressional District—have become household names. In a normal political moment, the average American would not, and need not, know these names. And yet, regardless of whether you live in Tallahassee, Columbus, Denver, or Boston, you have likely heard of both Ron DeSantis and Marjorie Taylor Greene. This is because in addition to being mega-identity-centered, American politics are highly nationalized. Americans' political attention and interest tend to be driven by considerations of the national political scene over and above those of local or state politics. On the one hand, this includes the fact that voters are increasingly likely to vote for the same party for state and local elections as they do for the presidency.[74] On the other hand, as political scientist Daniel Hopkins explains, nationalization also includes "when voters are engaged with and knowledgeable about national politics to the exclusion of state or local politics."[75] Nationalization is about what aspects of American political life citizens attend to, think about, and allow to shape their partisan identities. Put simply: big-ticket, national culture war issues take prominence over local- and state-level issues.

In accounts of *why* Americans pay more attention to national politics than they do to state and local politics, scholars point to the same phenomena that have been the focus of the book so far: the ideological polarization of the two parties, affective polarization among the public, geographic and social sorting, and the primacy of partisan identity as a cue guiding citizens' vote choice.[76] Together, these factors create a political climate in which public officials running for local- and state-level offices see a strategic advantage to playing politics "nationally." Because, as Hopkins writes, "national politics is rife with people and issues that are evocative to voters."[77] Instead of campaigning down in the weeds of state and local issues, candidates can perform their identity as a party prototype on the national stage.

For political media producers with hours of airtime to fill, millions of eyeballs to attract, and millions of dollars to save, nationalization is a lucrative cost-cutting mechanism. Rather than reporting on complicated policy proposals that may have different implications across different communities, nationalized politics rewards the coverage of high-profile culture war issues that can be covered from 30,000 feet. Through "erupting" partisan pundit panels and conflict-framed stories of Right versus Left, televised political news can talk about national culture war topics without having to invest much in local or investigative reporting.

On the audience side, the growth in media choice through cable and internet allows politically interested citizens to immerse themselves in America's *national* political scene (by watching CNN, MSNBC, and FOX) while the politically disinterested tune out from political information altogether.[78] Because there is so much emotionally evocative, conflict-ridden national political news to take in, politically passionate Americans tend to engage with their state and local news less and less.[79] And since national politics tends to be more partisan than local politics, as we turn our attention away from the local and toward the national, we activate our partisan identities even more.[80] It is this interplay between the economics of news and the salience of political identities that explains Americans' "declining engagement with state and local politics."[81]

Local Goes National

But what about local news? Can't Americans disrupt their political mega-identities by anchoring themselves in their actual communities and by paying attention to local and state politics through local news? Yes! Not only are the audiences for local journalism in decline, but since 2004, the industry itself has been demolished. Today, financial organizations like hedge funds, private equity firms, and investment groups—organizations with little interest in journalism or the public good—have discovered the value of buying up local newspapers, gutting them, and in many instances, eliminating them altogether.[82] At the University of North Carolina's Hussman School, researchers have found that once these financial organizations acquire a local paper, their standard operating procedure is "aggressive cost-cutting, the adoption of advertiser-friendly policies, the sale or shuttering of under-performing newspapers, and financial restructuring, including bankruptcy."[83] As of 2018, thousands of American counties were served by only one local newspaper, and 200 counties had no local newspaper at all. During the coronavirus pandemic, this trend worsened, with over 100 local newsrooms closing in 2020 and 2021.[84] For Americans across the country, the choice isn't whether to consume local news or national news, but to consume national news or *no news at all.*

While the death of local news means local officials can get away with more shenanigans without the watchful eye of journalists, it also contributes to Americans' disdain for the opposing political party. Political communication scholars Joshua Darr, Matthew Hitt, and Johanna Dunaway have explored how consumption of national news "in the absence of a local newspaper" exacerbates political polarization.[85] In counties where local newspapers had closed, citizens were significantly less likely to engage in split-ticket voting (voting for candidates for multiple parties) than citizens in counties with local newspapers. Darr, Hitt, and Dunaway argue that the death of local newspapers causes a shift in citizens' attention to national politics, which is inherently more polarized than state and local politics, and is focused on the most contentious and most uncivil behaviors of political elites. According to *The Atlantic*'s Elaine Godfrey, as local newspapers disappear, "all news becomes national news": "Instead of reading about local policy decisions, people read about the blacklisting of Dr. Seuss books. Instead of learning about their own local candidates, they consume angry takes about Marjorie Taylor Greene."[86] Godfrey highlights the crucial substantive content of local newspaper stories as "the connective tissue of a community; they introduce people to their neighbors, and they encourage readers to listen to and empathize with one another. . . . As local news crumbles, so does our tether to one another."[87]

After the publication of Darr, Hitt, and Dunaway's 2018 study, the executive editor of the *Desert Sun*, the daily paper of Palm Springs, California, had an idea. Editor Julie Makinen decided to try to reduce her community's political polarization by "refocusing the paper's opinion page on local authors and issues" and avoiding commentary or cartoons related to national politics.[88] This provided researchers with an amazing opportunity to run an experiment in real time that would examine how citizens' political attitudes and beliefs changed in communities with and without a local paper that focused on local issues. Results showed that following the shift to local news, readers of the local paper in Palm Springs (where Makinen had localized her newspaper) experienced less social and political polarization compared with the control community in nearby Ventura (whose local paper's opinion page continued to include national issues).[89]

While these findings are heartening, there is still intense pressure on local news outlets to cover the conflict-ridden mega-identity-focused national political spectacle.[90] Indeed, as local newspapers have shuttered, local television news programming and online local news sites that emphasize national politics have flourished.[91] As of October 2022, conservative Sinclair Broadcast Group owned approximately 200 local television stations across the United States, reaching about 40 percent of US households.[92] As Sinclair acquired these local TV networks, the company infused local news content with conservative-leaning frames and topics while also moving *away* from the local and toward more national political stories.[93] When local stations are acquired by Sinclair, not only does news content become more ideologically conservative, but the amount of national political news increases substantially and the amount of local news drops.[94]

What about online local news, you ask? Unfortunately, despite the potential for the internet to expand local news through websites and blogs, by 2011, media scholar Matthew Hindman had found "almost no evidence" that such digital local news expansion had come to pass.[95] Jump forward in time another decade, and the online local news situation had become even worse. Instead of local news sites simply not existing at all, thousands of fraudulent and partisan sources had popped up masquerading as local sites.[96] Journalism scholars and practitioners have come to refer to these sources as "pink slime," in reference to the low-grade beef discards that are used to make fast-food burgers.[97] Chief among the pink slime sites was Journatic, a centralized "journalism" company founded by former journalist and conservative entrepreneur Brian Timpone in 2006. Timpone hired writers and researchers, many based in the Philippines, to write "local stories" using the tools of the internet. Stories were then sold to local papers around the country.[98]

The Journatic business model—a centralized company hiring workers from afar to create cheap content for local news—proved both profitable and exploitable. By 2021, its exploitability was exemplified by Metric Media, a network of media companies that boasted over 1,000 "local"—yet ideologically conservative—news websites across the country. While Journatic had created generic news stories for local papers looking to save money on staffing, Metric Media offered cheap local news with a conservative frame. Research by the Tow Center for Digital Journalism at Columbia University revealed that Metric Media's partisan content was funded by conservative organizations connected to the Tea Party movement.[99] And one of the key people at the helm of Metric Media? The same guy who started Journatic in 2006: Brian Timpone.

In recent years, liberal pink slime sites have emerged as well, but in far fewer numbers than the conservative pink slime infrastructure. In 2019, progressive Super PAC Priorities USA had invested in four "local news" sites to mimic the Timpone model on the left but at a smaller scale: publish liberal-leaning stories on local news sites in swing states to defeat President Trump in the 2020 election.[100] The progressive organizers admitted this plan was made possible through the death of local newspapers—especially in such states as Michigan, Pennsylvania, Florida, and Wisconsin, where many local newspapers had been dissolved.[101]

Fortunately, most people are not immediately receptive to information from unknown sources, which is a good thing.[102] But, *given* exposure to information from unknown—even deceptive—sites, readers' attitudes and beliefs *do* change in the direction of the perspective advanced in those stories.[103] Researchers warn that low trust in traditional media might work together with social media recommendations to increase people's willingness to read information from less credible sites like pink slime sites. Given the extensive work by psychologist Lisa Fazio and her team demonstrating that repeat exposure to false information increases beliefs in false claims *regardless* of perceptions of source credibility, none of these findings is particularly reassuring.[104]

While not all pink slime stories contain explicitly false information, they tie local stories to national partisan identity in ways that may increase misperceptions through the lens of political identity. An analysis by progressive journalist Judd Legum showed that the conservative "local news" sites funded by Brian Timpone were instrumental in tying the 2020 Virginia governor's race to the divisive issue of "teaching critical race theory in schools."[105] (See next page.) Through its 28 "separate" "local" "news" sites across the state and hundreds around the country, Timpone's network published "tens of thousands of stories about Critical Race Theory," many of which falsely suggested that CRT was being taught in Virginia public schools. Immediately following Republican Glenn Youngkin's gubernatorial win, one of his chief fund-raising operatives, Gerrit Lansing, posted a celebratory tweet with a link to a story from Timpone-owned *West Nova News*. The headline read, "Loudoun County Public Schools Spent $422K on Controversial Critical Race Theory Curriculum in Past Two Years." Above it, Lansing wrote, "The story that started it all."[106]

At the time of the writing of this book, a visit to the *West Nova News* website under a section labeled "Loudoun County Public Schools" brings up the headlines in the following list. Please note, this is not a *selection* of headlines. These were the top six stories on the site on April 7, 2022:

- "'To Kill a Mockingbird' remains on Loudoun County schools' curriculum"
- "LCPS' equity team draws mixed reaction, school spokesman says district values 'all the input we receive'"
- "Loudoun County schools signs new contract with social justice consultants"

POLITICS

New website to publish which residents of Isle of Wight and Southampton Counties voted, did not vote in gubernatorial election

POLITICS

New website to publish which residents of Shenandoah Valley voted, did not vote in gubernatorial election

POLITICS

New website to publish which Augusta and Bath County residents voted, did not vote in gubernatorial election

POLITICS

New website to publish which Lancaster and Northumberland County residents voted, did not vote in gubernatorial election

POLITICS

New website to publish which Arlington residents voted, did not vote in gubernatorial election

POLITICS

New website to publish which Central Virginians voted, did not vote in gubernatorial election

Examples of Metric Media's Automated "News" Sites for Different Towns. These Metric Media sites for towns across Virginia generate "local" news that all looks the same, and all sites feature thematically similar content that resonates with national culture war issues.

Judd Legum, *Popular Information*, November 8, 2021.

- "PACT founder calls conciliation terms between Loudoun County schools, local NAACP 'reprehensible'"
- "Loudoun County school official: Measures 'should reduce suspension rates,' 'ultimately close disparities'"
- "Loudoun resident: School plan the wrong approach on racial issues"

The nationalization of political parties, activist groups, and candidates makes it more likely that national political battles—like those regarding racial policy and the teaching of race-related aspects of American history—will play out at the local level. In *Laboratories against Democracy*, political scientist Jacob Grumbach highlights the dangers of nationalization in the US political context: democratic backsliding at the state level, especially in states with Republican-controlled legislatures. He concludes that "the Republican Party has eroded democracy in states under its control," largely through the actions of nationally coordinated Republican groups, including a coalition between "the very wealthy on the one hand, and those motivated by white identity politics and cultural resentment on the other."[107] Crucially, these coordinated efforts to nationalize local and state politics do so by activating our political mega-identities through references to culture war issues.

So, what about those six *West Nova News* headlines I found on April 7— all on the topic of CRT and diversity in public schools? Those stories invite white conservative Republican audiences to activate their aligned white conservative Republican identities in their engagement with their local communities. And as these "local" news stories prime those identities and identify threats, they also connect local stories directly to the national political scene, where Republican leaders like Ted Cruz make CRT a centerpiece. Since these "local" news sites are funded through investments by national conservative advocacy groups and super PACs (e.g., DonorsTrust and Liberty Principles), it is efficient to connect local stories to national themes like "white identity politics and cultural resentment." So, while Senator Cruz signals partisan prototypicality with his questions during Supreme Court nomination hearings, these deceptive news sites bring the issue home. For residents of Loudoun County reading these stories, this is now about *our* community—*our* children in *our* schools. Importantly, even if these nationally focused, partisan pink slime stories do not contain explicitly inaccurate information, the political-identity-driven narratives masquerading as "news" reinforce the conditions under which a "misinformation society" thrives.[108]

The Perfect Progressive Partisan Prototype

Because the dynamics explored throughout this book are identity driven, and given that the Republican Party has experienced more racial, religious, geographic, and cultural homogenization than the Democratic Party, it follows that identity-related consequences are likely asymmetrical. However, the nationalization of politics has not been limited to exemplars from the Republican Party. Liberal partisan prototypes have emerged from within the Democratic Party in recent years to receive significant attention on the national stage. Most iconic, perhaps, were the female members of Congress elected in 2018, referred to by commentators on both the left and the right as "the Squad." All under the age of 50 at the time of their election, Alexandria Ocasio-Cortez ("AOC") of New York, Ilhan Omar of Minnesota, Ayanna Pressley of Massachusetts, and Rashida Tlaib of Michigan boasted ideological liberalism on both fiscal and social issues. And while ideologically conservative Republican national stars like Missouri senator Josh Hawley and Texas senator Ted Cruz are devout Christians, the Squad's Congresswomen Omar and Tlaib are two of only four Muslims to have ever served in the US House of Representatives.

The Squad is distinct not just for its youth, gender, and religious affiliations but also for its racial and ethnic diversity—situating these four congresswomen at the center of the national political spectacle's identity-driven narratives. Representative Omar is Somali American, Representative Tlaib's parents emigrated from Palestine, Representative Pressley is African American, and AOC's parents are Puerto Rican. The distinctiveness of the four female representatives wasn't lost on them, either. In fact, they coined the term "the Squad" at a 2019 photoshoot.[109]

Just weeks after the four freshman lawmakers were sworn in, President Trump placed them firmly in the camp of the racial, ethnic, and political outgroup, tweeting "Why don't they go back and help fix the totally broken and crime infested places from which they came."[110] The progressive social and fiscal positions of these congresswomen made it easy for reporters to feature them in conflict-framed stories purporting to be issue centered but that facilitated personalized, identity-centered stories. The conservative *New York Post* ran a story with the headline "AOC, Far-Left Pols Urge Biden to Bypass Congress on Energy, Immigration and More."[111] In that piece, the reporter Mark Moore linked Representative Ocasio-Cortez to the other members of the Squad, describing their positions on immigration and crime as "radical," and implicitly signaling the issue of race to readers: "Progressive House Democrats like Rep. Alexandria Ocasio-Cortez and other members of the 'Squad' are urging President Biden to sidestep Congress and use the power of his pen to authorize dozens of radical policies on issues like immigration, criminal justice, climate change and student loan debt."

Representative Ocasio-Cortez, in particular, has become a favorite target of conservative politicians and commentators. Media Matters for America, a liberal media watchdog, found that over the course of 42 days in 2019, the conservative cable networks Fox and Fox Business mentioned the freshman congresswoman 3,181 times.[112] Scholars have theorized that Ocasio-Cortez embodies the spirit of intersectionalism—occupying minority categories across gender, age, class, and ethnicity. Writes Eleanora Esposito,

> Ocasio-Cortez never made a mystery of the fact that she was born to a Puerto Rican family in the Bronx and took jobs as a bartender and waitress to help her family fight foreclosure of their home. All these inseparable aspects of her lived-experience and identity contribute to her depiction as an outsider in the largely white, male, upper-middle class game of politics, and provide multiple cues for aggression and delegitimization.[113]

When we combine AOC's overlapping social and cultural identities with her progressive ideology and the reality of political mega-identities, we have a recipe for a perfect progressive partisan prototype on the national stage—one that can be used to mobilize and inspire in-group members (liberal Democrats) or to anger and threaten out-group members (conservative Republicans). This is exactly what local and state political campaigns did in 2020. AOC was mentioned in ads for both Democratic and Republican candidates to mobilize voters—through excitement in the former, and through anger in the latter.

Warning Republican voters about AOC was especially popular among more conservative candidates in more conservative districts.[114] Consider the campaign ads of Georgia's far right candidate Marjorie Taylor Greene that warned, "AOC wants to plunge us into Communism,"[115] and Colorado's far right candidate Lauren Boebert, who stated, "I am ready to be the one that steps up for conservative values and takes on AOC."[116] In one of her final campaign ads against incumbent Republican representative Scott Tipton, Boebert juxtaposed the congressman with pictures of the Squad (see opposite).[117]

Campaign Ad for Lauren Boebert, Republican Candidate for Congress in Colorado's Third District. Boebert's ad against incumbent Republican congressman Scott Tipton in 2020 uses members of the Squad to trigger identity threat.

Both Marjorie Taylor Greene and Lauren Boebert went on to win their elections and were sworn in as freshman members of the US House of Representatives in January 2021. In a socially sorted, polarized political context, in which the Republican Party is racially and culturally homogeneous and the Democratic Party is racially and culturally diverse, identity-based campaigns conducted by Republicans in opposition to the perfect progressive partisan prototype apparently work quite well.

In *Why We're Polarized*, Ezra Klein argues that "to appeal to a more polarized public, political institutions and political actors behave in more polarized ways. As political institutions and actors become more polarized, they further polarize the public. This sets off a feedback cycle."[118] One central piece of the story of how and why so many of us are so "wrong" stems from

these transformations of our democratic and media institutions and the consequences of their perpetual reinforcement of political identity. The logic of
media has dominated our political institutions for decades. But today's political leaders are incentivized to play into press biases while *also* performing the
kind of partisan prototypicality that is rewarded by a polarized and sorted
American public. In the words of Senator Lindsey Graham, this is one of the
ways that political elites can attempt to "stay relevant."[119]

Chapter 7

Separate Us

Identity Distillation through Partisan Media

FOR 24 YEARS I'VE STUDIED how media exposure influences individuals' attitudes, knowledge, and behaviors. After almost a quarter century of running experiments and conducting surveys, I've concluded that early media scholars like Paul Lazarsfeld and Joseph Klapper were right: mass media are better at reinforcing existing attitudes than they are at changing them. However, unlike those scholars, I don't see reinforcement as an indication that media's effects on people are "limited." On the contrary, I see reinforcement as the most significant influence of all, especially right now.

Recall that we believe things that satisfy our needs for comprehension, control, and community. Also recall that how those needs become articulated (what we use to satisfy those needs) depends on the identity-driven theories, beliefs, and values that we start with. If I primarily value freedom and individual liberties, for example, then my need to feel in control and like I am part of a community will be satisfied by vastly different attitudes, beliefs, and behaviors than if I primarily value equality and diversity. And since the specific manifestation of those needs depends on values rooted in my social identity, they also depend on what social identity is most salient to me at that moment. Thus, exposure to media content that reinforces what I value, what I believe, and what team I'm on can be hugely influential—*even if it isn't changing my mind.*

In the 1970s, media scholar Todd Gitlin proposed that media's capacity to reinforce our existing beliefs is consequential in itself. We know through decades of social science research that reinforcing an existing attitude increases its influence on subsequent behavior.[1] If you remind me how much I love chocolate ice cream, I'm going to eat more chocolate ice cream. But, Gitlin went further, suggesting that reinforcement of existing attitudes "can be understood as the crucial solidifying of attitude into ideology," a "relatively enduring . . . configuration which determines how people may perceive and respond to new situations."[2] Not only will activating and reinforcing my attitude toward chocolate ice cream increase my likelihood of eating it, but chronic reinforcement over time might create a broader cognitive framework that will guide how I engage with chocolate-ice-cream-adjacent stimuli—you know, things like chocolate cake or cookies or perhaps even Fudgsicles.[3]

Reinforcement in a Low-Choice Media Environment

When Gitlin was writing in the 1970s (and when Lazarsfeld and Klapper were writing in the decades before that), mass media—broadcast television and radio and physical newspapers—were highly centralized with few options. There were three major broadcast networks in the United States. No cable television. No internet. And little specialization—that is, very few niche outlets designed specifically for different types of people.

Magazines were an exception—a rare medium with titles geared toward distinct audiences with specific interests. Through the success of early "ladies" magazines in the nineteenth century, magazine publishers knew the viability of specialization as a business model. So, when television exploded in popularity in the late 1940s and national advertisers abandoned the pages of general-interest magazines like the *Saturday Evening Post* for television, the magazine industry pivoted. It saved itself by creating titles for smaller, unique audiences, featuring content that made an attractive home where smaller specialized products and services could be efficiently advertised. Titles such as *Seventeen*, *Jet*, *Good Housekeeping*, *Yachting*, and *Gourmet Magazine* successfully catered to specific kinds of readers and featured specific kinds of ads that could, in the words of communication professor Theodore Peterson in 1956, "capitalize on the tastes and interests of a large share of [their] audience. Indeed, those tastes and interests helped to establish a magazine's raison d'être."[4]

Why this detour into the history of *Ladies Home Journal*, you ask? This pivoting of the magazine industry in the 1950s is analogous to what the television industry did in the 1980s after the emergence of cable and, later, the internet. This is the story of media fragmentation. And the story of media fragmentation is the biography of the contemporary media environment. With the introduction of cable and the internet, the number of outlets increased. As the number of outlets increased, the economic model that previously sustained the media industry fell apart. As outlets proliferated, the number of people watching any one thing shrank. Suddenly, the industry that had been built on the sale of advertiser access to giant diverse mass audiences (e.g., audiences of ABC, CBS, and NBC in the 1960s) had to pivot. The solution was the deliberate creation of content that would separate distinct kinds of audiences—or more accurately, distinct kinds of consumers. Television executives used sociodemographic, psychological, and personality data, as well as information about viewers' hobbies, interests, and purchases, to create outlets and programming to appeal to different types of people. In *Breaking Up America*, Joseph Turow describes how media executives in this new, fragmented environment appealed to advertisers by touting the "efficient separation" of their distinct audiences with whom they had developed "special relationships" through their specialized content.[5] It is in this environment that we find the birth of MSNBC in 1996, in the very same month that Comedy Central introduced its news satire show *The Daily Show*, both just three months before the birth of their eventual foil, Fox News Channel.

Back in the 1940s–1970s, it was understandable that American media scholars would downplay the consequences of "reinforcement" as a media effect. With only a handful of networks, media producers sought to appeal to as wide a swath of the American public as possible, typically by offering viewers what NBC vice president Paul Klein called "least objectionable programming."[6] It was in this climate that media sociologists Paul Lazarsfeld and Robert Merton suggested that the potential for American mass media to be used as conduits for propaganda was limited. Since it was in the interest of private corporate owners of American media to maintain the status quo, and since business was about giving people what they already wanted, Lazarsfeld and Merton argued that media would "operate toward the maintenance of the going social and cultural structure rather than toward its change."[7]

But this was also a time of relatively high trust in media and in government, with little elite polarization. Before the partisan racial realignment in the 1960s and '70s, the two political parties were not particularly distinct ideologically, racially, or religiously. In this political context, "giving Americans what they wanted" through a handful of top-down media sources meant providing them a lot of homogeneous, status-quo-affirming (read: unobjectionable) programming. It made sense for media effects researchers at that time to say, "Don't worry, folks. Media only reinforce people's preexisting beliefs."

By the 1970s (even in the still-low-choice media environment), media scholars began theorizing about the ways media reinforcement might be of consequence. "Uses and gratifications" research explored how people used media content rather than what media content did to people. This approach suggested that people used media to serve specific needs and fulfill desires, whether to monitor what was happening in the world, to feel social connection, to escape from everyday life, or to reaffirm one's own values,[8] all of which were motivated by a goal of reinforcing interests, beliefs, and identity.

In the late 1970s, George Gerbner and his colleagues at the University of Pennsylvania's Annenberg School developed a provocative and sweeping theoretical framework to describe the cumulative effects of media reinforcement. They suggested that television had become America's cultural storyteller and was shaping our collective *perception of reality*—how we perceived the real world. Through the introduction of cultivation theory, these scholars proposed that television content was largely homogeneous, with meta-narratives like interpersonal violence and traditional gender roles dominating programming across network and across timeslots. Their survey research confirmed that people who consumed heavy amounts of television were more likely to view the world in keeping with these dominant themes in TV content; viewers with heavy TV exposure overestimated their likelihood of being the victim of a crime and were more likely to hold gender stereotypical views than those with less TV exposure.[9]

The cultivation researchers also found that people from different sociodemographic categories, whose real, lived experiences were quite different, looked more alike in their perceptions of reality when their television viewing was especially heavy. In the *absence* of television viewing, people of different races and income groups reported varied levels of fear of crime. As one might expect, those from demographic categories most likely to experience crime in real life (racial minorities and those from lower-income categories) were far more likely to report that fear of crime was a "very serious personal problem." But at high levels of television exposure, these differences eroded, especially among high-income and white respondents, who reported significantly higher levels of fear of crime, consistent with the prevalence of violence on television. The authors described this as a "mainstreaming effect" of media exposure, writing, "The 'mainstream' can be thought of as a relative commonality of outlooks that television tends to cultivate. By 'mainstreaming' we mean the sharing of that commonality among heavy viewers in those demographic groups whose light users hold divergent views."[10]

Reinforcement in a High-Choice Media Environment: A Different Beast

As cable fragmented the television landscape in the 1980s and 1990s, cultivation research moved in a new direction. With more thematically diverse viewing options, it became harder to argue that all media content had the same effect on heavy television viewers.[11] Instead, researchers began thinking about how exposure to *specific* media genres or programs was shaping viewers' perceptions of reality. This approach centered on how mediated depictions of the world (of events, relationships, and power dynamics) shaped the cognitive representations (mental models) viewers came to hold in their minds.[12] Watching shows that depicted traditional romantic relationships, for example, informed our brain's schematic representations of what "romantic relationships look like."[13] We would then draw on those "mental models" to make sense of the *real world*.[14] In other words, exposure to specific media content served as an "observation of the world" that we then used to inform our knowledge, theories, and beliefs about what reality was like.

On average, media provide just *some* of the many observations that we use to understand our worlds. This helps explain why the strongest media "effects" tend to emerge in the context of issues and topics with which we have the least real-world experience.[15] Researchers have found that the effects of watching stereotypical depictions of minority groups on television are strongest among those with little interaction with members of those groups in real life.[16] Similarly, the effects of media exposure on perceptions of police are greatest for those with the fewest real-world interactions with police.[17] If media provide some fraction of the observations that we use to inform our understanding of the world, then media's influence will be strongest in the context of phenomena we have the least opportunity to directly "observe" on our own.

Putting this all together, from the 1960s to the 1980s, centralized low-choice media technologies were operating against the backdrop of low elite polarization, high(ish) trust in institutions, and sociodemographically mixed (not very sorted) political parties. In their quest to offend as few people as possible, media producers created broadly appealing, status-quo-affirming television content that was associated with viewers looking more and more similar in their worldviews the more they watched.

But what happens in a decentralized, high-choice, fragmented media environment in which media producers deliberately create content to separate—and create relationships with—different kinds of people? And what happens when this strategic audience segmentation occurs in a climate of increasing political polarization, institutional distrust, and the social sorting of the political parties? Well, the fact that MSNBC, Fox News Channel, and the political news satire program *The Daily Show* were all launched in 1996 is no accident. Recall that the 1994 Republican revolution marked a seismic shift in American politics. It coincided with a sharp increase in ideological polarization of elites, increased affective polarization among the public, and the increased social sorting of the two parties. All these trends were making American media consumers harder to please, especially in terms of their perception of bias in political programming. It was in the 1980s that scholars identified a "hostile media effect," a perceptual error in which partisan viewers perceive objective political programming to be biased against their side.[18]

As cable outlets proliferated, one of the domains that media producers could use to efficiently separate and develop special relationships with distinct audiences was politics. And it worked. Research by Kevin Coe and his colleagues conducted in 2004–2005 found liberals were more likely than conservatives to watch the liberal satire show *The Daily Show*, and conservatives were more likely than liberals to watch the conservative Fox News Channel. Partisans perceived less bias in programming that agreed with their politics: Fox was perceived as less biased among conservatives than among liberals, and *The Daily Show* was perceived as less biased among liberals than conservatives. Like-minded partisan content was also perceived as more interesting and informative.[19]

This fragmentation of the media landscape not only allowed politically interested partisans to seek out content they found interesting and informative but also allowed a whole lot of people to tune out from politics altogether. Political scientist Markus Prior has demonstrated that the fracturing of our media landscape through cable and internet allowed politically disinterested Americans to avoid consuming any political news.[20] Instead, these less interested folks fled explicitly political content for entertainment and sports, leaving "news" and "public affairs" to the most partisan among us.

As these politically interested partisans engaged in selective exposure—tuning into the content consistent with their worldview—that worldview was thus reinforced.[21] But unlike media reinforcement in the 1970s and '80s, where broadly appealing "least objectionable programming" reinforced the things Americans had in common, "reinforcement" in today's fragmented media landscape reinforces the things that divide us. In a quest to satisfy a politically divided, untrusting population, producers are producing one side's "most objectionable programming" as an efficient way to appeal to the other side.

For years, political communication researchers worried that because audiences could opt out of media programming that disagreed with their political views, we would all end up in echo chambers, avoiding anything that disagreed with us and moving further in the direction of our preexisting views. It turns out that most people don't do this. Even though we tend to seek out information that agrees with our politics,[22] most of us consume at least some political media content that contradicts our views.[23] Unfortunately, the problem isn't what "most people do." The problem is what the highly engaged, highly interested, strong partisans do.[24] Scholars have found that it is here—among the most politically interested and engaged partisans—where people enter a partisan echo chamber, watching and reading media that support their beliefs and avoiding content they disagree with.[25] And unfortunately, it's among these engaged partisans where we're likely to find the kind of heightened emotional responses—especially anger—that contribute to even more like-minded exposure later on.[26]

Does it matter that politically interested partisans avoid media that disagree with them? The problem is what "attitude reinforcement" looks like among people who already hold strong attitudes. Political scientist Matthew Levendusky has studied what happens to individuals' political attitudes and beliefs after watching partisan cable media (like Fox and MSNBC). His book *How Partisan Media Polarize America* makes a compelling case that politically biased media lead us to privilege what we already believe over what is empirically true.[27] Levendusky explains how exposure to attitude-reinforcing content makes us think of ourselves more in terms of our political "team," worsening these (non)sense-making tendencies: "Priming this sort of salient identity

increases viewers' directional goals—it heightens their desire to reach a conclusion in line with their partisanship, thereby strengthening their biases
toward attitudinally congenial information."[28] These effects are greatest (read:
worst) at the margins, where highly engaged partisans experience identity-
reinforcing effects that move them further in the direction they were already
heading. Among those who are highly attentive to politics, being able to select
like-minded news media is associated with greater partisan-ideological alignment, such that highly politically engaged Democrats are more liberal as their
media options increase, and highly engaged Republicans are more conservative.[29] Levendusky writes, "These programs contribute to polarization not by
shifting the center of the ideological distribution, but rather by lengthening
the tails (i.e., moving the polarized even further away from the center)."[30]

Reinforcing Political Identity
and Identity Threats

Since political mega-identities have come to capture ideological, racial, religious, and cultural identities, tapping into cultural politics has proved to be an
especially effective (highly profitable) mechanism to separate different kinds
of audiences and different kinds of consumers. And because of the growing
alignment of various dimensions of identity, political identity signals not just
what belief systems we hold but how we engage with the world, what kind of
lifestyle we have, and even what aesthetics media producers should use to make
that content as appealing as possible.[31]

By studying viewers and tracking their movement across various platforms,
media executives use partisan social identities to guide what they cover and how
they cover it. Advances in data analytics allow them to capture patterns in viewer
engagement in real time—both with the programming itself and on social media.[32] Media scholar Dave Karpf proposes that this focus on analytics is what

allowed populist candidate Donald Trump to become a media juggernaut. Karpf writes, "The increasing reliance on newsroom analytics created a positive feedback loop, in which journalists and their editors became so attuned to Trump's clickworthy campaign that they continually devoted outsized attention to his candidacy, which in turn sustained and supported his polling numbers, which thus gave news media even more reason to provide overwhelming coverage of his campaign."[33]

In an investigative report detailing the operations and success of conservative outrage program *Tucker Carlson Tonight* on Fox News Channel, the *New York Times*'s Nick Confessore described how media analytics pushed Carlson's programming further into the realm of culturally conservative identity politics.[34] As one Fox employee told Confessore, audience analytics motivated Fox executives to call for more of "the grievance, the stuff that would get people boiled up. . . . 'They're coming for you, the Blacks are coming for you, the Mexicans are coming for you.' 'They're all obsessed with the minute-by-minutes,' said a former Fox employee. 'Every second that goes on that network now gets scrutinized.'"

All told, the consequences of media reinforcement depend on how much media producers know about us in the first place. Data analytics make the study of audiences possible at a granular level, integrating individual sociodemographic and consumer behaviors with our real-time engagement with television and social media content. But—and this is essential—these methods do not result in the production of media content that reflects and reinforces who we *are.* Rather, they result in the production of media content that reinforces the most emotionally engaged, attentive versions of ourselves, since that is what is most financially viable for the media industry. If there is anything that ignites the attention and emotional response of viewers—especially threat-monitoring culturally conservative viewers—it's threats to their team. Viewed this way,

Carlson's meta-narrative of "they're coming for you" was a safe bet in terms of viewer engagement, retention, and profitability.

The notion that reinforcement itself is a powerful media effect is at the heart of media scholar Mike Slater's Reinforcing Spirals Model.[35] Rather than a simplistic account of media's direct influence, the model acknowledges that people are goal directed in their use of media. Our social identities shape how we interpret messages while also guiding our selection of media in the first place. We anticipate what messages and programs will complement our social identities, then we seek them out. It's the "people like me watch shows like this" calculus. As we view this content through our social identity lens, our identities are further reinforced. The next time we seek out media content, the identity that guides us in that selection has become even more crystallized and salient than before—hence Slater's description of the process as an ongoing "spiral." Over time, as we consume more media to support our group identity, the process repeats itself and we become more entrenched in our role as a member of our team.

Slater's model also highlights the role of "identity threat" in these dynamics, where threats to our social identities increase our likelihood of seeking out identity-reaffirming media content. If I encounter media content that makes me feel like someone is coming for my team, I'm going to want to seek out content that makes me feel good about my team and keeps tabs on rival teams. Slater explains that a sense of identity threat can happen "during political campaigns or . . . when rival ideologies are becoming salient, or at times of economic or social strain," at which point, "selective use of attitude- and identity-consistent content should increase."[36] Identity threat is increased when people encounter opposing views that challenge fundamental beliefs or values associated with their social group. In fact, after strong partisans experience a threat to their partisan identities through interactions with people of competing political views, they seek out more like-minded political content.[37] Under conditions of identity threat, they turn to their team's partisan programming to reinforce their role as a member of their team. Identity threat can also be increased when public debate is "framed as a threat to core values and beliefs."[38] In American politics today, elites strategically tie public policy debate to the values and beliefs that are at the heart of political mega-identities. On the right, those values are freedom, tradition, and the protection of innocent children. On the left, they are equality, diversity, and caring for the less fortunate.[39] Even at the local level, where community debates are being nationalized, we see policy discussions framed in these very terms, like those conservative "local news stories" that tied school curriculum discussions to critical race theory.

Since threats to our identity increase our desire for identity-reaffirming media exposure, partisan media producers have perfected a genre predicated on identity threat. In chapter 6, I showed how both Fox and MSNBC made extensive use of Senator Cruz's and Senator Graham's outbursts during Judge Jackson's nomination hearings (MSNBC even more so than Fox). By highlighting out-group protypes, MSNBC emotionally engages its audience while reinforcing the concept of identity threat from the right.

Meanwhile, conservative outrage hosts directly threaten a white conservative social identity with content that says "they're coming for you." A 2021 analysis by political scientists Jeff Berry, James Glaser, and Debbie Schildkraut shows that Fox viewers are 94 percent white and just 1 percent Black, compared with MSNBC's audience, who are 67 percent white, 24 percent Black, and 9 percent other.[40] In a country that is 76 percent white, these numbers matter.[41] They also help us understand why in just five months, from February to June 2021, the term "critical race theory" was mentioned 1,860 times on Fox News shows.[42] Political communication scholar Kathleen Hall Jamieson explains Fox's obsession with the alleged teaching of critical race theory in schools in terms of the threat-monitoring propensity among Fox's conservative viewers: "If you are on high alert to threats to your identity, then if it's happening in any place, it's worrisome to you."[43] In the end, these content choices are about reinforcement: reinforcing the fears, outrage, and identities of their threat-monitoring viewers. And as Jamieson says, "It works. It holds audiences. The goal is sustaining viewership."

Asymmetrical Identity Distillation

The anticipation of political mega-identities by political elites, media producers, and social media algorithms encourages the creation and spread of identity threats and thus identity-reinforcing content. This content provides observations that we then use to make sense of the world; and since it was created to tap into our partisan identity, it reinforces it every time we watch.

When master distillers make whiskey, they first mix grains like corn and wheat, boil the mixture, and then add alcohol to begin a process of fermentation. The resulting "wash" is then put through a process of distillation—it is brought to a boil to evaporate the alcohol. The evaporated alcohol is captured, condensed, and turned into a raw form of whiskey. But good whiskey puts that already-distilled liquid through the distillation process again, removing even more impurities through evaporation and collecting the alcohol product. Double- and triple-distilled whiskey gets purer and purer, increasing the proof every time. This process is akin to what our political media ecosystem does to our social identities—refining and purifying our idea of who we are and how people like us think, feel, and act, then drawing on those purified identities to repeat the process again and again.

While both liberals and conservatives have their identities distilled through partisan-reinforcing media content,[44] the nature of the conservative media ecosystem and the alignment of Republican sociodemographic and cultural categories streamline these dynamics.[45] Meanwhile, the psychological profile of social conservatives, capitalizing on heuristics like emotions and intuition, increases the potential for conservative media to reinforce beliefs and distill mega-identities on the right.[46] In a study of how the Reinforcing Spirals Model operates differently for conservatives and liberals, Jay Hmielowski and his team found that "reinforcing effects were more likely to occur for conservative media outlets compared to liberal media outlets."[47] The extent to which underlying beliefs predicted subsequent media behaviors—tuning into like-minded content—was greater for conservatives than for liberals. Not only are conservatives more likely to seek out like-minded content when their political identity is made salient; they are also more responsive to the statements of political elites than liberals are.[48] So once again, the process is lopsided, creating an identity distillation apparatus that is more efficient on the right than on the left.

From a media programming standpoint, one of the problems is that as political mega-identities become distilled and salient, these audience members become increasingly hard to please.[49] According to the literature on the hostile media effect, as partisans become more entrenched in their identity, they come to see anything other than like-minded media content as increasingly hostile to their side.[50] The machinery of partisan outrage constantly reminds viewers that their team—and their entire way of life—is under threat. As highly interested and engaged partisans consume like-minded content, their views become more extreme.[51] Over time, strong partisan viewers' needs for comprehension, control, and community will come to take a very narrow and extreme identity-centered form. They will increasingly perceive objective counterattitudinal content as hostile to their side and will perceive it as especially hostile if it comes from a source that is supposed to be "on their side."[52] When someone who is on my team threatens my team's core values and beliefs, they are threatening my sense of self.

"Fox Knew"

A vivid illustration of how this process plays out in the conservative media eco-system can be found in the days after the 2020 presidential election. It took four days for news organizations to officially declare Joe Biden the winner of the 2020 election. But, on Election Day itself, ahead of other news organizations, the Fox News decision desk called the state of Arizona for Joe Biden. Four days later, on November 7, Fox News's Bret Baier announced, "The Fox News decision desk can now project that former vice president Joe Biden will win PA and Nevada putting him over the 270 electoral votes he needs to become the 46th president of the United States." Cohost Martha MacCallum then stated that President Trump "would be denied a second term" and urged viewers to "keep in mind the Trump campaign is in the midst of waging legal challenges in several states, but the path is clear for the new President Elect."[53]

For Fox viewers and Trump loyalists who had spent the better part of a year hearing tales of likely voter fraud from Fox opinion show hosts and from Trump himself, Fox's early call on Arizona and its announcement of Biden's electoral victory constituted the ultimate identity threat.[54] As Fox News's Chris Stirewalt put it on National Public Radio, "Part of the problem, of course, was that there were opinion hosts on Fox who, for months and months and months, had been repeating the baseless claim that Trump was going to win the election for sure or that we were going to do it again or don't listen to the polls."[55]

Ratings data confirm that in the weeks after Fox News made the call in favor of Biden, fringe conservative media outlets, like Newsmax TV, benefited. The Trump-loyal, Big Lie–embracing Newsmax TV channel enjoyed an increase in viewership to the tune of 500 percent.[56] As CNN's Brian Stelter writes, Trump's electoral loss "changed the cable TV calculus. Viewers who were frustrated when Fox admitted the truth of Trump's loss sought other options. Trump encouraged them to try Newsmax."[57] And so they did—so much so that on December 7, 2020, Newsmax surpassed Fox's ratings during a primetime slot among the key 25- to 54-year-old demographic. In interviews with former Fox viewers who had left the network to watch Newsmax after the election debacle, *Washington Post* reporter Jeremy Barr heard tales of grief.[58] Some reported feeling like moving on from Fox was akin to "losing a friend" or a "part of the family." Yet others felt satisfied by the "appreciation" they felt from Newsmax, as though Fox had been taking them for granted.

In early 2021, contending with the competition posed by more conservative media outlets, Fox News faced the incompatible challenges of offering attractive conservative opinion programming while also supporting a news operation that was charged with reporting the truth. The Fox outrage opinion hosts offered identity-rooted content to satisfy viewers' needs for comprehension (Biden did not really win), control (Trump is the rightful winner), and community (We are in this together, and the Democrats, RINOs [Republicans in name only], and mainstream media are against us). Meanwhile, the Fox News desk was still trying to report on what was empirically, observably, true. But as weeks went by, Fox News's editorial direction leaned in favor of the identity-driven outrage programming and away from empirical truth. Or, as the *New York Times*'s Michael Grynbaum put it, Fox's content moved "Trumpward."[59]

This Trumpward shift at Fox included media hosts modeling a way of knowing rooted in intuition and gut instinct over evidence. Tucker Carlson, for example, amplified a discredited conspiracy theory about giant suitcases of fraudulent ballots, saying, "We're going to show you a video you may have already seen today. It seems real. It's pretty unbelievable," followed up by "We spent all day trying to find out exactly the context here. . . . We know that fraud took place. We know ballots just kind of showed up in various places."[60] Fox News personalities Sean Hannity and Brit Hume also floated false claims that "leftists" and "bad actors" including "Antifa" were probably responsible for the violence at the Capitol on January 6, which they were not.[61] Their coverage thus became guided by what reinforced their shared political mega-identity—by what "felt right"—rather than what was empirically true.

For some at the network, the Trumpward shift in programming went too far, especially after the insurrection at the US Capitol.[62] In December 2021, longtime Fox News anchor Chris Wallace announced his departure from the network as he headed to rival CNN. After 18 years at Fox, Wallace lamented the recent shift in the truth value of Fox programming, stating, "I'm fine with opinion: conservative opinion, liberal opinion . . . But when people start to question the truth—Who won the 2020 election? Was Jan. 6 an insurrection?—I found that unsustainable."[63] Wallace's comments highlight what happens when political programming chases ratings by moving away from evidence and truth, in the direction of identity-based content. When identity dominates, truth no longer matters.

Several lawsuits filed against conservative outlets and personalities following the 2020 election highlight the epistemic divide discussed in chapter 5, between truth arrived at through intuition and emotion, on the one hand, and truth arrived at through evidence and data, on the other. In the context of law, truth is based on considerations like how evidence is used, what evidence is admissible in court, and what is meant by a "preponderance of evidence."[64] Note that it is *not* about intuition, hunches, or what we (or our viewers) "want to believe to be true." So, when facing legal challenges, conservative sources that reinforce identity threats by knowingly spreading false claims rooted in intuition or hearsay face an uphill battle.

After the election, Trump surrogates appeared on conservative media networks and repeatedly peddled conspiracy theories about voting technologies rigging the election in favor of Joe Biden.[65] Fox hosts like Tucker Carlson and

Sean Hannity platformed election deniers and amplified these false claims on their shows. In response, election technology companies Smartmatic and Dominion Voting Systems filed billion-dollar defamation lawsuits against conservative media personalities and outlets. Smartmatic alleged that conservative outlets OAN, Newsmax, Fox News, and Fox Business Network "knowingly and intentionally disseminated a continuous stream of falsehoods that harmed Smartmatic and negatively impacted the company's business."[66]

In a separate $1.3 billion defamation lawsuit, Dominion Voting Systems sued Sidney Powell, an attorney who propagated vote-rigging conspiracy theories on Fox and elsewhere. In her defense in that case, Powell proposed that "no reasonable person would conclude that the statements [she had made about Dominion] were truly statements of fact."[67] Recall political scientist Michael Bang Petersen's proposition that elite-spread disinformation is more about mobilizing than informing.[68] Perhaps he was onto something.

In 2021, Fox News was hit with a $1.6 billion defamation lawsuit by Dominion alleging that while the network was providing a platform to Powell and other election misinformation peddlers (including Trump's personal attorney Rudy Giuliani), decision makers at Fox knew the claims were false. Dominion's lawsuit sought to show that Fox executives displayed actual malice by knowingly and willfully airing false claims of voter fraud and rigged voting machines.[69] Depositions and private communications between Fox News hosts and producers revealed that many Fox personalities viewed the claims by Powell, Giuliani, and others to be absurd, but they aired them anyway. Carlson texted a producer that "Sidney Powell is lying." Laura Ingraham described Powell in a text as ". . . a bit nuts." And in a deposition, Sean Hannity stated, "That whole narrative that Sidney was pushing. I did not believe that for a second."[70] As Dominion states in their January 2023 brief, "Fox knew. From the top down, Fox knew the Dominion stuff was total B.S."[71]

The documents made available through the Dominion lawsuit illustrate the very phenomena I described earlier: identity distillation, the hostile media effect, and a partisan audience steeped in identity-threatening content. Following Fox's call of Arizona for Biden, Tucker Carlson texted a producer, "We're playing with fire, for real . . . an alternative like Newsmax could be devastating to us."[72] After the election, Fox higher-ups and show hosts met to assess the damage from their Arizona call (which was accurate) and their election call (also accurate). Chief executive Susanne Scott stated that if they had not made the call for Arizona, "our ratings would have been bigger."[73] Scott maligned Bill Sammon, the head of Fox's Decision Desk, saying that he should have been more concerned with protecting "the [Fox] brand."[74] Meanwhile, news anchors like Martha McCallum explained that "in a Trump environment," making election calls based off the vote count alone might be inadequate. *The New York Times'* Peter Baker explains that both McCallum and news host Bret Baier suggested "that viewer reaction should be considered" when making election calls.

To protect ratings and market standing after the election, Fox gave viewers what they wanted rather than what was true. As producer Abby Grossberg texted host Maria Bartiromo, "To be honest, our audience doesn't want to hear about a peaceful transition." Bartiromo responded, "Yes. Agree."[75] Fox gave audiences a way to understand how Trump could have lost—through vote rigging and cheating by Democrats (thus fulfilling viewers' need for comprehension). Fox showed viewers what entities to hold accountable, including local election officials, Democratic lawmakers, mainstream media, Smartmatic, and Dominion (thus fulfilling their need for control). And Fox provided a friendly environment where this narrative was communicated across programs by their favorite hosts (thus fulfilling their need for community). I should note that in April 2023, Fox settled the lawsuit with Dominion for $787.5 million. The litigation leading up to this landmark settlement and information revealed in discovery spurred several events at Fox News, including a lawsuit filed by producer Abby Goldberg against Tucker Carlson for creating a hostile work environment, and perhaps most stunningly, Fox's abrupt "parting of ways" with Tucker Carlson on April 24, 2023.

Given the feedback loop that drives the identity-distillation apparatus, Fox News' *response* to the Dominion allegations was especially revelatory. In a counterclaim filed against the voting software company, Fox lawyers wrote, "Dominion brought this lawsuit to punish [Fox] for reporting on one of the biggest stories of the day—allegations by the sitting president of the United States and his surrogates that the 2020 election was affected by fraud. . . . The very fact of those allegations was newsworthy."[76] In other words, the false claims about the election were news because newsworthy people were making them.[77] But this ignores the fact that newsworthy people were incentivized to make these claims because months of identity-threatening content guaranteed that these claims would be effective. It was a lucrative—and insidious—symbiotic relationship. In *The Propagandist's Playbook*, sociologist Francesca Tripodi highlights the symbiosis between conservative lawmakers and the right-wing media ecosystem. She explains how conservative propaganda machinery reinforces the white conservative Christian cultural identity along with the existential threats against it (from the Left, minorities, immigrants, and media). Conservative media hosts repeat a chronic refrain that the mainstream media cannot be trusted, which "deepens [conservatives'] resolve to seek out so-called alternative facts, and 'do their own research'"[78] This research, spurred by identity threat, is conducted not with a goal of getting closer to truth but with a goal of satisfying their needs for comprehension, control, and community in keeping with their conservative mega-identity. And in the context of the 2020 election, this pattern reinforced the Big Lie.

As is true of most of the underlying dynamics explored throughout this book, these processes also operate on the left, but not as effectively. The apparatus is not as well oiled, and the liberal identity categories are not aligned to run efficiently, but it does run. Consider, for example, how MSNBC opinion show host Rachel Maddow covered the Steele Dossier, an unverified file of documents by former British intelligence officer Christopher Steele alleged to contain evidence of Trump colluding with Russia, and salacious details of sex acts performed with sex workers in Moscow. But an FBI investigation raised "significant questions about the reliability of the Steele reporting," including questions about who funded the work and what other ties Steele might have had.[79] While Maddow conceded that the dossier was unverified and that the claims of Trump colluding with Russia were not corroborated, on her show the dossier remained at the center of speculation for weeks.[80] On March 8, 2017, she said, "But even if [the claim of Trump/Russia collusion] is as yet in itself uncorroborated and undocumented. . . . All the supporting details are checking out, even the really outrageous ones. A lot of them are starting to bear out under scrutiny. It seems like a new one each passing day."[81] This looks a whole lot like reporting on what seems to be true based on salient partisan identity threat, rather than reporting on what is true based on evidence.

Writing about how partisan cable news distills the political identities of our most interested and engaged partisans is admittedly depressing. And because these highly engaged partisans are also highly influential, the effects on their beliefs tend to affect the people around them through interpersonal conversation.[82] Your uncle Jim watches Fox News and is increasingly convinced of the dangers of demographic "replacement." He tells his friends and family about these theories, and they start to share his concerns. This two-step flow effect, where media influence the beliefs of the highly attentive, who then shape the beliefs of the people they talk to, means that the impact of partisan media on the public is more widespread than it might appear based on audience size alone.[83]

The influence of partisan cable television—especially conservative media—on the distillation of identity and belief in misinformation was especially palpable during the COVID-19 pandemic. Misinformation about mask wearing was more prevalent on Fox News than on any other mainstream, print, or cable news outlet.[84] Viewers of Fox News were more likely to believe misinformation and conspiracy theories about COVID than viewers of broadcast media.[85] People prone to conspiratorial thinking were more likely to seek out conservative media sources (read: Fox News) in the first place, then grew to hold even greater misperceptions about COVID over time.[86] Conservative media users were not only more likely to believe COVID misinformation and conspiracy theories but also more likely to believe that "public health experts over-estimated the severity of the pandemic."[87] Perhaps unsurprisingly, then, viewers of Fox News were among the least compliant with social distancing orders,[88] held significantly more negative attitudes toward the COVID vaccine,[89] and were significantly less likely to receive the COVID vaccine.[90]

In my conversation with misinformation experts David Rand and Gordon Pennycook[91] I asked them, "In your ideal world, if the vectors of influence could operate at any level with infinite funds, where would you stage an intervention [to reduce belief in misinformation]?" Pennycook responded without hesitation: "I would delete Fox News." Rand agreed, "I would say de-platforming bad elites." Pennycook continued: "The [United] States has an insane media ecosystem. It is not the same in other countries. Even Canada. We don't have Fox News. . . . That is the issue."

These are two scholars who study the psychological and sociological factors that contribute to misinformation beliefs. They explore how interventions staged on social media slow the spread of misinformation and which kinds of people are more likely to believe misinformation. And when asked what lever they would pull to stop the spread of misinformation and conspiracy theories, they would delete Fox News and deplatform bad elites. Given the primacy of "free speech" doctrine in the United States and our history of a hands-off libertarian approach to media policy, such a lever doesn't exist. But it is essential to acknowledge that experts recognize that the synergy between America's demographically sorted political landscape and the identity-threat-propelled engine of conservative media has created something uniquely bad for democratic—and physical—health in the United States.

Until you look at the profile of the American news audience in comparison with other nations, you might think this is just the way it is everywhere. But it's not. The United States is unique in the magnitude of its news audiences' ideological polarization—especially, you guessed it, on the right. For years, scholars at the Reuters Institute at the University of Oxford have studied the profile and behaviors of news audiences around the globe.[92] Their work shows that even though liberals and conservatives in many countries are gravitating to distinct ideological news sources, the US situation is striking. In most other countries, the largest audiences (indicated by the size of the circles in the figure opposite) are ideologically moderate, leaning slightly left. There are partisan audiences that lean left and right, like the UK's *Guardian* (left) and the *Daily Mail* (right), but these audiences are smaller in size than more mainstream news audiences. In the United States, politically middle-of-the-road audiences are small. Instead, we see sizable liberal audiences gravitating toward the *New York Times* and CNN. And on the right, we find one hugely popular media source being consumed by an audience that is distinctly far right: Fox News. Unlike right-wing news audiences in most other countries, the right-wing audience of Fox is sizable, attracting as many, if not more, audience members as any other major news outlet explored (see figure).

The size of the conservative news audience in the United States makes sense given what we know about conservatives' trust in mainstream news

CROSS-PLATFORM NEWS AUDIENCE POLARISATION – SELECTED COUNTRIES

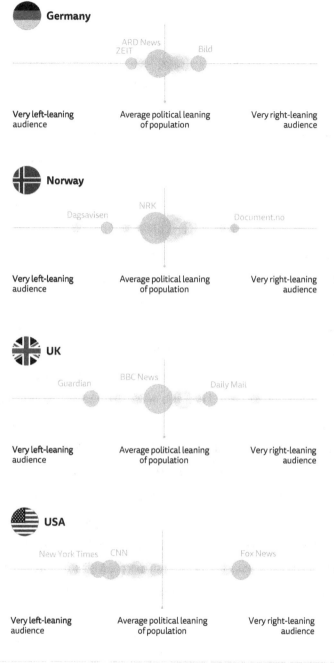

Germany

ARD News
ZEIT
Bild

Very left-leaning audience
Average political leaning of population
Very right-leaning audience

Norway

Dagsavisen
NRK
Document.no

Very left-leaning audience
Average political leaning of population
Very right-leaning audience

UK

Guardian
BBC News
Daily Mail

Very left-leaning audience
Average political leaning of population
Very right-leaning audience

USA

New York Times
CNN
Fox News

Very left-leaning audience
Average political leaning of population
Very right-leaning audience

Q1F. Some people talk about 'left', 'right', and 'centre' to describe parties and politicians. With this in mind, where would you place yourself on the following scale? Q5A/B. Which of the following brands have you used to access news offline/online in the last week? *Base: Germany = 2002, Norway = 2010, UK = 2410, USA = 2036.*

Polarization of News Audiences in Different Countries. America's news audiences are more ideologically polarized than those in many other democratic countries.

From: Newman, N., Fletcher, R., Robinson, C. T., Eddy, K., & Nielsen, R. K. (2022). Reuters Institute Digital News Report 2022. Reuters Institute for the Study of Journalism. https://reutersinstitute.politics.ox.ac.uk/digital-news-report/2022.

sources. A 2020 Pew report found that of 30 news sources that Americans were asked about, conservatives distrusted 20 of them. Less than a third of Republicans reported trusting CNN, the *New York Times*, the *Washington Post*, *Time Magazine*, or any of the major television network news organizations. But 65 percent of those same Republicans reported trusting Fox News.[93]

In a high-choice media environment in which republicanism signals not just ideological conservatism but also whiteness, Evangelicalism, rural geography, and cultural values, centering editorial decisions on a Republican mega identity is good business. And it works best when it reinforces most: focusing on the fundamental values and beliefs shared by those overlapping categories and reinforcing the audience's perception that their identity is under threat. While reinforcement in the mid-twentieth century was a homogenizing influence that muted differences between different kinds of Americans, reinforcement today is a mechanism for sectarianism and, in some instances, extremism. Rather than coming to a shared understanding of the world through increased media exposure, we come away from partisan media with perceptions of reality that (1) interpret events in a way that fits with the ideological and cultural values of our team (comprehension), (2) empower us to think and act in service of our partisan identity (control), and (3) reinforce our connection to our team (community). In the next chapter we turn our attention to digital technologies' contribution to American "wrongness," where many of these same concepts are at play: media fragmentation, partisan identity threats, data analytics, and the power of media reinforcement. But the nature and economics of our largest social media platforms—decentralized, interactive, networked, user driven—compound these dynamics, distilling partisan identity and driving wrongness even more.

Chapter 8

Curate Us

Identity Distillation through Social Media

IN AN *ATLANTIC* ARTICLE FROM APRIL 2022 titled "Why the Past 10 Years of American Life Have Been Uniquely Stupid," social psychologist Jonathan Haidt suggests the answer is simple: it is the fault of social media.[1] Haidt argues that the rise of social media is largely responsible for America's devolving sense of community, our cultural fragmentation, our eroding trust in institutions and each other, our balkanization along political lines, the spread of misinformation and conspiracy theories, and the rising mental health challenges experienced among our young people.

And although Haidt concedes that Americans were divided before the introduction of social media, he suggests the ascendance of social media was the equivalent of the biblical tale of the fall of the Tower of Babel: social media made us unable to communicate with each other and unable to have a shared reality necessary to work together to solve societal problems. He attributes the destructive power of social media to what he refers to as metaphorical "dart guns" (tweets and Facebook posts) that "give more power to trolls and provocateurs while silencing good citizens" and "give more power and voice to the political extremes while reducing the power and voice of the moderate majority."

On these last two specific points, I believe Haidt is correct. Social media empower the margins and are especially good at encouraging the polarization of extremes, as we will see. But what Haidt downplays are the synergistic influences—political, journalistic, economic, and cultural forces—that are driving identity-based sectarianism. These forces are capitalizing on social media machinery just as social media are capitalizing on them. After its publication, Haidt's *Atlantic* article caused a kerfuffle in scholarly circles and (somewhat ironically) on social media, where scholars took issue with the breadth of the brush that Haidt used to paint his bleak picture. My critique is somewhat different. I am less concerned that Haidt may have overstated the harm posed by social media, and more concerned about the powerful people, entities, and influences that Haidt let off the hook—namely, those covered in the previous chapters.

Let's face it: social media *are* wildly different from earlier media technologies. They are decentralized, networked, and interactive in ways that can both benefit and devastate democratic health and the "reality-based community" at large. They are well suited to persuasion and mobilization, which means they are also well suited to propaganda and exploitation. But whether social media facilitate one set of consequences over another depends largely on the actions of political elites, journalists, partisan media, and the actions of users—us.

Like television and news media content, social media newsfeeds and time-lines provide some of the "observations of the world" that inform our understanding of what is true. But these observations—especially on large platforms like Facebook, Instagram, and Twitter—have been curated in anticipation of our most passionate emotional responses. And these emotional responses are most efficiently activated by identity threat. Social identity has become the backbone of social media logic—media logic being the processes that shape not only how media organizations and platforms function but also the kinds of content that we receive (and create) through them.[2] The observations of the world that we receive through our newsfeeds are shaped by who we're connected to and by algorithms that prioritize what we have emotionally responded to in the past (through likes, reactions, or shares) and what other people "like us" have liked or responded to in the past. I say "like us" because these determinations are made by linking us to others with shared sociodemographics, interests, and network characteristics. They might not actually be like us at all. So, these three things—who we are connected to, how we respond to emotional content on the platform, and what most people "like us" watch, like, and share—are all influenced by how we categorize ourselves (that is, what team we're on). This is why I say social identity is the backbone of social media logic. And in the United States right now, political mega-identities are the most all-encompassing, efficient, and threat-inducing social identities of all.

The Internet: Doing Exactly What It Was Designed to Do

When I teach my students about the potential influence of digital technologies and social media, I first remind them of the features, capacities, and limitations of analog mass media—the media I grew up with in the early 1980s: printed newspapers, broadcast television, and radio. Most of my undergraduates do not remember life without internet access in the home. Their media experience has always been a digital one, a networked one, an interactive one. So before discussing the unique features of digital technologies, I first explain how traditional mass media before the 1990s were a one-to-many proposition. One powerful message producer (publisher or network owner) would disseminate a message to a giant diverse audience of many people largely disconnected from one another and with little ability to talk back directly to message producers. It was the one-way, top-down nature of mass media that caused media sociologists such concern about the potential for powerful media effects on audiences dating back to the 1930s and '40s.

To understand how social media platforms work, it helps to remember that the internet was designed in part to solve the problem of the inherent vulnerability of a centralized information infrastructure. When the Soviet Union placed nuclear-capable missiles on the coast of Cuba within range of the United States in 1962, it revealed core vulnerabilities in the US military's information systems. Their systems were hierarchical and centralized. Command centers were home to data and strategy, on which military officials relied. If one information hub were destroyed, or if the physical information infrastructure were damaged, the military's capacity to respond would be compromised.[3] The 1969 creation of the first decentralized information network was the US government's solution to the vulnerability of information centralization. Through the technology of "packet switching," information could be sent through an interconnected system, made redundant across the network, and decoded at various destinations.[4] In other words, people could receive the same information anywhere on the network, even if one of the hubs were destroyed. No one person or entity controlled the network.

In traditional top-down analog mass media systems, media organizations controlled what messages entered the flow of information. These gatekeepers— people like editors, producers, even reporters—chose what stories to cover. Network executives, network censors, and advertisers also exerted control over what messages were produced and distributed and what they looked like. But the internet was designed to be decentralized and horizontal, with little room for a centralized gatekeeper who could control (or limit) the flow of information. It was also designed to facilitate many-to-many communication—interconnected message recipients become message creators and distributors.

Gatekeepers are like the bouncers at the entrance to a nightclub. Depending on your choice of attire, who you know, how much money you have, or even your gender, the bouncer (my students like to give him a name, like Biff) might allow you to enter the club, or not. Before the era of the internet and social media, Biff had total control over who got into the club or information space. In this analogy, Biff is the powerful newspaper editor, television producer, or record label executive who determines what gets "in" to the flow of information—the stories on TV, on the radio, or in the pages of the newspaper. If Biff didn't let you into the club, you weren't getting in.

But digital technologies and social media are the equivalent of a dozen new—unguarded—doors around the back of the nightclub. Note that Biff the bouncer is still there at the front door. Newspaper editors, TV producers, and record label executives do still exist, after all. But now, if Biff doesn't let you in the main door, you can just go around back and enter the club through another door. You could write a blog post, upload your video to YouTube, share your song online, or perform your stand-up comedy bit on social media.

From the early days of the internet, scholars and journalists wrote with overwhelming optimism about the likely impact of this shift, which took control away from elites and formal organizations (away from Biff) and sent it downstream to citizens, consumers, and audiences. This was especially true with the birth of Web 2.0 in the mid-2000s, characterized by user-centered platforms that better capitalized on the networked and interactive nature of digital technologies. These included the social media platform Myspace launched in 2003, Facebook in 2004, YouTube in 2005, and Twitter in 2006—all platforms designed to promote horizontal, interpersonal communication between users and to empower individual users to create content and distribute it through the network. Scholars (including me) were especially optimistic about the likely impact of this transformation on democratic health.[5]

As formal gatekeepers lost their monopolistic control over what got into the flow of information, regular people became the new center, with more opportunities to have their voices heard, raise issues and stories that were important to them, and share their own perspectives in a way that the traditional gatekeepers hadn't allowed. The networked nature of the internet also helped groups of individuals mobilize toward collective action. In the spring of 2011, the world watched as citizens throughout the Middle East made use of social media platforms to challenge authoritarian leaders. Across the region, citizens demanding economic and political reform capitalized on the decentralized control of the internet to communicate, criticize their existing political regimes, and organize protests. In Tunisia and Egypt, activists used Twitter and Facebook to help mobilize democratic revolutions.

Historically marginalized groups capitalized on these same features of digital technologies and social media to create counternarratives, organize, and mobilize toward representation and justice—as we saw with movements such as Black Lives Matter and #MeToo.[6] With fewer gatekeepers and a networked communication infrastructure, social media platforms offer power and voice to those whose stories are often excluded from mainstream media content. As social movement scholar Sarah Jackson writes of Twitter, "It expanded the set of voices all of us have to hear."[7] Scholars have documented how the use of social media hashtags "allows users who are territorially displaced to feel like they are united across both space and time,"[8] and how the interests and perspectives of Black users can enter the national conversation through #BlackTwitter.[9] Anthropologists Yarimar Bonilla and Jonathan Rosa document how minority communities use hashtags like #HandsUpDontShoot to "construct counter-narratives" and "reimagine group identity" surrounding police violence.[10] The decentralized control of digital technologies allows less powerful communities to influence the decisions of traditional media gatekeepers, thus amplifying their perspectives through mainstream media. Through a computational analysis of over 40 million tweets, for example, digital politics scholar Deen Freelon and his team showed how the social movement Black Lives Matter was able to attract mainstream press coverage through their engagement on Twitter.[11] In sum, while social media do not create social or political movements, they certainly facilitate the kind of decentralized, horizontal, networked communication that empowers marginalized voices, amplifies counternarratives, and helps people organize and mobilize.[12]

But this same combination of a lack of information gatekeepers and hyper-networked communication also places a powerful new tool in the hands of propagandists.[13] If Biff the bouncer allows only his friends or people who slip him some cash to enter the club, then the existence of a dozen other unguarded doors around back is a win for good folks who are now able to get inside. But if Biff had stopped a guy from entering the club because that guy regularly threatens violence, and then that guy comes in through an unguarded back door, that is probably bad for everyone.

The Exploitability of Social Media by Disinformation Peddlers

If you were on social media during the 2016 US presidential election campaign between Hillary Clinton and Donald Trump, you may have seen posts or memes arguing that American police departments consisted primarily of KKK members or that Black Lives Matter protesters were responsible for the deaths of police officers. Maybe you saw or shared a meme featuring a photo of a woman holding a gun that reads: "Why do I have a gun? Because it's easier for my family to get me out of jail than out of a cemetery." Crucially, none of these was authentic content created by American citizens. They were all Russian disinformation created by internet trolls; the Kremlin paid people to spend hours online using false social media accounts to post memes and videos, and to comment on and share information that would divide Americans and weaken American democracy.[14]

In her book *Cyberwar: How Russian Hackers and Trolls Helped Elect a President*, political communication expert Kathleen Hall Jamieson illustrates how Russia took advantage of the decentralized and networked nature of social media to spread divisive, hateful, and false information among the American public, to weaken American democracy. Russia is a repeat offender in this space.[15] In the summer of 2021, Facebook removed hundreds of Russian-linked accounts that were part of a COVID-19 vaccine disinformation network.[16] Various investigations have found that the Russian and Chinese governments were drivers of COVID-related conspiracy theories and disinformation through their state-run news media organizations, which then spread through social media.[17] They also used fringe websites to spread conspiracy theories through social media platforms with stories doubting the vaccines' safety and falsely alleging the Biden administration was launching a "forced" vaccination campaign.[18] In the summer of 2022, US security experts warned of Russia's inevitable plans to use disinformation to suppress American voter turnout in the 2022 midterm elections, exacerbate cultural divisions, and sow public doubt about the fairness of the elections.[19]

In the spring of 2020, communication scholar Shannon McGregor and I published an essay in the *Washington Post* reflecting on how social media are particularly well suited to exploitation by malicious actors.[20] We framed the piece using the same criteria outlined in the influential 1948 essay by social psychologists Paul Lazarsfeld and Robert Merton discussed in chapter 7. Their essay was intended to quell societal fears about the potential for media to have direct, powerful effects on individuals and society.[21] They argued that three criteria would have to be met for propaganda to be successful. And because these three criteria were nearly impossible to satisfy in the United States (in 1948), such powerful media effects were unlikely. But 2020 was a long way—and many technological advances away—from 1948. McGregor and I explained how today's social media are tailor-made to satisfy the very criteria that Lazarsfeld and Merton argued had safeguarded us back then. Those three criteria were as follows:

Monopolization—Mediated propaganda can only thrive in the absence of counterpropaganda.

Canalization—Mediated propaganda can only succeed if it capitalizes on preexisting attitudes and beliefs.

Supplementation—Mediated propaganda can only work if the message is supplemented by interpersonal communication with trusted people.

So, how are the three unmet criteria that safeguarded us in 1948 being facilitated by social media today?

Monopolization (the absence of counterpropaganda): Because mediated communications in 1948 were disseminated to large, unfragmented masses, big, diverse media audiences were bound to hear the "other side" (or at least "an other side") of a story or issue. But today users can curate their social media experiences to receive content that is favorable to their worldview or bolster their social identity. And while social media users still tend to encounter information that opposes their views,[22] in carefully curated spaces, users can be exposed to belief-disconfirming content while still having their beliefs reinforced in the process (more on that later).[23]

Canalization (capitalizing on preexisting attitudes and beliefs): Without intimate knowledge of audience members' preexisting beliefs, designing propaganda that takes advantage of those beliefs is impossible. And without a personalized medium to reach individual people, distributing propaganda that taps into individual beliefs is also impossible. But the interactive nature of digital technologies gives platforms access to endless data that capture individual user preferences, attitudes, and behaviors. Today propagandists *do* know individuals' attitudes and values, and they use this information to develop attitude-consistent messaging and to target small (tiny) groups of users who will be most receptive to those messages.

Supplementation (supplementing mediated propaganda with interpersonal messaging): In the mid-1900s, audiences of newspapers, radio, and television were largely anonymous to one another, with little ability to connect or collaborate. Media content was not experienced within interpersonal communication networks. Researchers soon learned that the influence of media messages on audiences was filtered through friends, family, and community members, dubbed "opinion-leaders."[24] But today, media messages are embedded within and experienced through interpersonal networks. We encounter media messages that have been liked and shared by friends and family. We engage with others in replies and react to media content—together. Platforms that offer a hybrid of interpersonal communication and media messaging are excellent places for media-fueled interpersonal conversation, meaning supplementation is baked into social media logics.

Identity-Driven Disinformation

Together these features make social media an efficient apparatus for disinformation peddlers to push out false narratives—especially those that center on social identity. As Jamieson documents in *Cyberwar*, Russian disinformation efforts in 2016 were designed to highlight cleavages along racial, religious, and cultural lines, most directly by trying to mobilize white evangelicals and veterans while demobilizing Blacks and progressives.[25] And they are still at it. A Facebook report published in 2021 revealed that in the months leading up to the 2020 election, the Kremlin-affiliated online troll farms were still reaching identity-based target audiences with "Facebook Pages" geared toward Christians, Black Americans, and Native Americans.[26] As many as 140 million Americans per month received identity-centered messaging from these inauthentic pages.

Communication scholars Madhavi Reddi, Rachel Kuo, and Daniel Kreiss coined the term "identity propaganda" to refer to disinformation efforts that leverage social identity in service of power or profit.[27] They show how propagandists weaponize social identity through rhetorical strategies including "othering," "essentializing," and "authenticating." Identity propaganda persuades and mobilizes by exploiting primal constructions of identity—especially those tied to race, gender, and culture. It often includes false and misleading information in the process. But even in the absence of explicitly false information, identity propaganda facilitates false narratives by subtly affecting how we seek to satisfy our needs for comprehension, control, and community.

In a study of Russian-generated disinformation during the 2016 election, Deen Freelon and his colleagues found that the fake Russian social media accounts with the highest user engagement were those that presented themselves as Black.[28] The authors conclude, "Race is a critical variable in the analysis of disinformation uptake and should be a key focus area in future research on the topic."[29] Russian disinformation is not just about spreading false information, explains propaganda expert Nina Jankowicz. It's also about eliciting emotional responses and building online communities centered on shared social identities.[30]

It's crucial to recognize that false information spread by bad actors isn't the only way that social media platforms encourage identity-driven wrongness. The platforms facilitate wrongness indirectly, by encouraging us to always think of ourselves in terms of our social identity. This dynamic, as we already know, encourages us to understand the world in keeping with who we are and who we want to be like, rather than in terms of what is empirically true. As media sociologist Zeynep Tufekci writes, "Belonging is stronger than facts."[31]

The Identity Distillation Machine

What makes social media so well suited to the activation of social identity isn't just their defining features—decentralization, networked communication, interactivity—but the economic model that capitalizes on them. Just as the content and function of cable news are influenced by the economics of advertising, so, too, are the content and function of social media. Back in 2015, Facebook's advertising sales generated $17 billion in revenue.[32] This represents advertising sold across all Facebook's holdings, including Facebook, Instagram, Facebook Messenger, and WhatsApp. Since then, the company's ad revenue has increased exponentially, to $114.9 billion in 2021 alone (see figure opposite).[33] In October 2021, Facebook changed its parent company name to Meta; that year, ad sales were responsible for 99.4 percent of Meta revenue. Whatever the company's name, it's clear from its financial reports that the social media behemoth is best described as an advertising company.

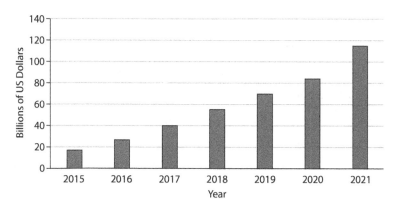

Meta/Facebook Annual Advertising Revenue in Billions of US Dollars

In contrast to the ads on cable television, advertising on social media is based on the sale of huge numbers of highly customized, microtargeted ads delivered to tiny specific audiences. Thus, data analytics are king. But when we use social media, we don't generate data just from being *on* Facebook or YouTube. We generate data when we *do things* on Facebook and YouTube—when we click on something, like something, react to something, share something, comment on something. These behaviors are how we leave evidence of who we are, what we like, and what we might do or buy in the future. These activities leave bread crumbs that data analysts can follow and extrapolate from. Recommendation algorithms prioritize content that will get us to leave those bread crumbs, content that makes us *do something*.

And content that makes us do something is content that makes us feel something.

And content that makes us feel something is content that taps into our social identity.

In the fall of 2021, former Meta employee Frances Haugen made headlines for leaking secret internal Facebook documents and testifying before the

US Congress about Facebook's recommendation algorithms and their potential harm to users and society.[34] Through Haugen, we learned about the logic governing Facebook's newsfeed and tensions between Facebook researchers and executives about the ethics of their programming decisions.[35] Haugen's testimony and the leaked documents highlighted how Facebook's programming decisions prioritized user engagement (stickiness) and upweighted content that was emotionally evocative. We learned that Meta (Facebook) researchers had found that Instagram users experienced "stress and anxiety" related to the number of likes their pictures received, but when likes were hidden, engagement decreased, so the company brought the feature back. We learned that in August 2019 researchers were concerned that Facebook's "core product mechanics"—namely, "virality, recommendations, and optimizing for engagement"—contributed to misinformation and hateful speech. We learned that employees had written with concern in 2020 about how Facebook's recommendation system can "very quickly lead users down the path to conspiracy theories and groups." We learned that Facebook researchers found high rates of misinformation shared through "reshares," where users share a post that was shared with them by someone else.[36]

In 2016, Facebook increased users' options beyond the mere "like" and "share" buttons with the introduction of new emoji buttons that allowed users to emotionally react to posts with the "love," "ha-ha," "wow," "sad," and "angry" emojis. In the internal documents shared by Haugen, known as the Facebook Papers, we learned that these features not only were a mechanism to optimize user engagement but also were relied on to inform newsfeed recommendations. From 2017 through 2019, Facebook's algorithm gave emotional reactions (like "love" or "anger") five times the weight of a traditional "like" in determining what posts to prioritize in individuals' newsfeeds.[37]

Each individual piece of content (i.e., each post) is scored by Facebook on thousands of criteria, or "signals" specific to each user. These scores determine where each piece of content should appear in a specific user's feed. And although Facebook sought to "demote" potentially problematic posts by cutting scores, savvy users knew how to exploit the algorithm. As reported by the *Washington Post*'s Jeremy Merrill and Will Oremus, the angry emoji button, in particular, was known to be problematic among Facebook's data scientists. They saw that hateful, harmful, and misleading content was disproportionately likely to elicit the angry emoji, even though, on average, it was the least used of all the reaction buttons. Researchers had concluded that the angry button rewarded emotionally evocative content and was "being weaponized" by political elites who used it to rile up supporters and get algorithmic priority in the process.[38]

Features that increased user engagement and encouraged virality, then, were the ticket to Facebook's capacity as a microtargeting advertising juggernaut. Facebook facilitated user interactivity not to empower people but to extract meaningful data from them. These data became valuable bread crumbs. From the introduction of the "like" button in 2008, the company realized its unique capacity to sell ads on the basis of an unheard level of user specificity. In Sheera Frenkel and Cecilia Kang's book, *An Ugly Truth*, they explain how "[the like button] represented an entirely new capability and scale of collecting insights into users' preferences"[39]—insights that could be used to inform the creation and dissemination of identity-reinforcing and identity-threatening content.[40]

Social Identity: The Backbone of Social Media Logics

Countless scholars working in this space have all argued that social media logics capitalize on social identity. MIT's Sinan Aral explores how the "hyper-socialized" world of social media encourages us to rely on social cues about how we should think, feel, and consume.[41] Sociologist Christopher Bail emphasizes how social media allow us to efficiently monitor our social environments and "give us much more flexibility to present carefully curated versions of ourselves."[42] Drawing on sociologist Erving Goffman's concept of the "presentation of self,"[43] Bail proposes that we are deliberate and careful in our online presentation of self. "Social media is . . . like a prism that refracts our identities—leaving us with a distorted understanding of each other and ourselves."[44] He shows how social identity, social comparison, and status-seeking all contribute to the harmful effects of social media, including political polarization, radicalization, and the appeal of misinformation. He even illustrates how anonymizing our social media platforms might disrupt these harmful dynamics. If our social media contributions were not tethered to our social identities, perhaps we'd feel less compelled to defend in-groups, threaten out-groups, or contribute to hateful and polarizing discourse.

In Siva Vaidhyanathan's *Antisocial Media: How Facebook Disconnects Us and Undermines Democracy*, the media scholar characterizes user behavior on social media as "a public performance of our cultural affiliations."[45] Vaidhyanathan sees social media expression more as a performance of who we are and who we want to be like and less as proclamations of information or truth. "We share content regardless of its truth value or its educational value because of what it says about each of us. 'I am the sort of person who would promote this expression' underlies every publication act on Facebook."[46] Research by Gordon Pennycook and his colleagues illustrates how the fast, automated nature of social media use exacerbates this trend. Pennycook concludes, "People may share news that they do not necessarily have a firm belief in. As a consequence, people's beliefs may not be as partisan as their social media feeds seem to indicate."[47] Well, that's good. I guess.

Which brings us to one of the most compelling books I've read about these dynamics. It comes from political scientist Jaime Settle. In *Frenemies: How Social Media Polarizes America*, Settle explains why the reality we experience through social media is so *un*real. She illustrates how social media encourage psychological aspects of political polarization through three processes that all center on social identity: "identity formation and reinforcement, biased information processing, and social inference and judgment."[48] Her END Framework (for expression, news, and discussion) outlines how social media expression, news consumption and sharing, and interpersonal discussion are "seamlessly interwoven into a wider variety of socially informative content."[49] Her model is based on the same political concepts we have covered here, like the social sorting of the parties, the alignment of partisan sociodemographic categories, and the disproportionate likelihood of strong partisans to be the most engaged in political discussion and news consumption. Settle shows how social media provide endless skewed "signals" that leave us with stereotyped perceptions of our friends' and families' political beliefs and values. These signals lead us to make inaccurate inferences about what regular members of the other party are like, so we overestimate ideological differences and are left with more hostility toward members of the other party. Writes Settle, "Using Facebook strengthens people's recognition of political identity. The users generating END content are the most partisan and likely have polarized attitudes at the outset; their motivation to express their identities while informing and persuading other people in their networks only serves to reinforce these already strong identities."[50] In fact, according to a 2021 report by the Pew Research Center, 25 percent of all Twitter users are responsible for posting 97 percent of all Twitter content.[51] That is one hyperpolitical, ideological, identity-conscious bunch. And research spearheaded by my graduate students Brooke Molokach and Erin Oittinen suggests these folks may also lack intellectual humility. Remember that trait, "intellectual humility" that captures whether we acknowledge the limits of what we know and are open to updating our views? Molokach and Oittinen found that in 2021, among Americans 50 and over, people who reported posting and sharing information on social media the most also reported the *least* intellectual humility.[52] Given that they also found the highest rates of COVID misinformation beliefs among the *least* intellectually humble, it stands to reason that we should be concerned about just what kind of content expressive social media users are contributing to our information environment.

It's Not the Echo Chambers—It's Our Identities

Scholars have long feared that social media would encourage us to bathe in like-minded content while avoiding content (and people) that disconfirmed (or contradicted) our views—a phenomenon referred to as "filter bubbles" or an "echo chamber." But study after study has suggested that, by and large, most people are exposed to belief-disconfirming content online.[53] Today, most scholars in this research space push back against the narrative of filter bubbles on social media.[54] R. Kelly Garrett describes the echo chamber conversation as a "distraction," warning that "effectively responding to disinformation campaigns requires that we find ways to undermine beliefs that persevere *despite* encounters with counter-evidence."[55] Media scholar Axel Bruns says that a focus on echo chambers is causing us to misunderstand the roots of our current political crises, which are more about affective political polarization and social sorting than about social media "silos."[56] Most revelatory here is the fact that the people who are most ideological, most divided, and most likely to dislike the other side are *more*, not *less*, likely to be exposed to belief-disconfirming content. Writes Bruns, "It turns out that those whom we most expect to be caught in filter bubbles—hyperpartisans on the political fringes—are also most actively engaged with the mainstream media, even if they read them from a critical, oppositional perspective."[57]

Philosopher C. Thi Nguyen argues that the term "echo chamber" conflates two different things: (1) a lack of exposure to belief-contradicting viewpoints and (2) exposure to belief-contradicting viewpoints in a way that signals distrust by discrediting or delegitimizing them.[58] It's one thing for my liberal aunt Sally to see a story critical of gender-affirming care for transgender youth (exposure to belief-contradicting content). It's another for that story to be shared by her friend Rita along with the comment: "These Republicans are barbaric. This is an outrage!" (thus discrediting those beliefs). In the context of social media, it is not mere exposure to belief-disconfirming information that matters, but the discussion *around* belief-disconfirming information that matters. Media sociologist Zeynep Tufekci highlights how it is our social identities and the embeddedness of communication within networked communities that complicate the echo chamber concept:

> The problem is that when we encounter opposing views in the age and context of social media, it's not like reading them in a newspaper while sitting alone. It's like hearing them from the opposing team while sitting with our fellow fans in a football stadium. Online, we're connected with our communities, and we seek approval from our like-minded peers. We bond with our team by yelling at the fans of the other one.[59]

Although Aunt Sally initially read the belief-disconfirming story about transgender youth while she was sitting at her kitchen table, now she sees it online, shared by her friend Rita along with the comment about barbaric Republicans.

Now Sally's entire experience of reading that article about that belief-challenging topic is framed in terms of the identity-activating comment from Rita.

The Problem on the Margins

For more than a decade, social media researchers have been trying to learn how these dynamics affect users. How do these features influence user attitudes, beliefs, and behaviors? How do advertisers use individual data to microtarget their appeals, and what do these customized appeals look like? Social media companies, especially Meta, make this kind of research very difficult to do—or at least to do well.[60] But despite the difficulty in getting adequate access to user data or to internal decisions relating to algorithms and recommender programming, scholars have found creative ways to study social media processes and effects. We've conducted surveys that ask folks about their beliefs, knowledge, and behaviors, as well as their social media use. Some scholars go to social media users directly to ask for access to their newsfeeds and social media behaviors while also studying their attitudes and behaviors offline. Academics have also used novel experimental methods to re-create the conditions of the social media experience to see how these dynamics play out. Some platforms collaborate with academics. For example, prior to a policy change announced by Elon Musk–led Twitter in February 2023, for years the platform had granted researchers and developers free access to the "firehose" of tweets and supporting APIs (application programming interfaces) that allowed researchers to study how information diffuses across the network.[61] And yes, Facebook has facilitated academic studies related to certain aspects of misinformation and belief correction.

Yet another obstacle to our accurate understanding of the influence of social media stems from the fact that many of the most problematic dynamics are occurring on the margins, among a small number of people. And since the most dangerous behaviors and outcomes are most prevalent among this small percentage of users, they are difficult to find with traditional sampling techniques, techniques that capture a cross-section of *typical* users.

But if it's a small percentage experiencing problematic outcomes, does this matter? Yes, it matters. It matters because the total number of social media users is *so massive*, a tiny percentage of users on the margins can still wreak havoc. In 2021, Pew reported that almost 70 percent of Americans reported using Facebook.[62] With the US population at 331.9 million, a harmful trend among just one-half of 1 percent of Facebook users would still be experienced by about 1,161,650 people. Brandon Silverman, cofounder of the research analytical tool CrowdTangle, writes, "Instead of using measurements that try and capture some sort of mythological average experience across the entire user base of these platforms, I think we need to focus more on the potential harms within particularly vulnerable communities where there are outsized implications."[63] Stanford's Matthew Gentzkow echoed these sentiments, observing that most researchers have been focused on "how social media affects the average person." But he suggests we ought to be most concerned about the margins, where "a small number of people with very extreme views are able to find each other and connect and act."[64]

By and large, research on the effects of social media on information polarization, affective polarization, or belief in misinformation and conspiracy theories all points to the problems on the margins. The people who encounter the most false information on social media are those who spend a *lot* of time online.[65] The people most likely to come away from social media believing in conspiracy theories are those who already have a strong propensity toward belief in conspiracy theories.[66] And the people most likely to consume fringe political content on social media are highly engaged and highly politically partisan.[67] These engaged partisans are the same people creating most of the user-generated political content on social media.[68] Social media effects on political knowledge and attitudes are strongest in the context of these extreme partisans as well.[69]

Today, scholars around the world are studying online radicalization and the dangers that may exist on the margins. Some research shows that recommendation systems occasionally result in users escalating from moderate to fringe political and cultural content. This appears to be happening in small numbers, as in less than 0.001 percent,[70] but again, even tiny percentages of individuals being pushed to more extreme content online can still be consequential when the user base of these platforms is so large.

Perhaps the more challenging problem is the *problem of demand*—that is, people seeking out extremist content. In a study of exposure to fringe and extremist content on YouTube, for example, Annie Chen and her team found that the small number of users who see fringe and extremist content on You-Tube have largely self-selected into those channels. These are people who "previously expressed high levels of hostile sexism and racial resentment."[71] There has been an increase in the production of right-wing online cultural content (so-called intellectual dark web, alt-lite, or alt-right content) on YouTube over the past several years. YouTube's recommendation systems *are* capable of exposing people to more extreme content the more they consume the "lighter" right-wing fare.[72] However, to receive an offer of deluxe extremist content, users would need to choose to view hate-adjacent content in the first place. Is this better or worse than social media algorithms radicalizing "normies" and luring them into the margins? The *New Yorker*'s Gideon Lewis-Kraus suggests that "algorithmic radicalization is presumably a simpler problem to solve than the fact that there are people who deliberately seek out vile content."[73]

While consumers of extremist online content score high in hostile sexism and racial resentment, the ones most likely to *generate* hostile online content are those who are status-driven risk takers.[74] Meanwhile, those folks who are least concerned with status are unlikely to talk about politics online. Which leaves the online world dominated by a *lovely* lot of folks, it would seem. These findings are consistent with work by Emily Sydnor that shows that people who are "conflict approaching" (individuals who find arguments interesting and entertaining and who are not made uncomfortable by disagreement) are more likely to consume political media and experience positive emotions in response to political conflict.[75] A project led by my doctoral student Huma Rasheed points to a similar pattern when predicting who expresses their political views on social media.[76] People who are "conflict approaching" are significantly more likely to post, comment on, or share things about politics online, whereas those who are conflict averse do not. So, not only is social media dominated by the most ideological and partisan voices among us, but it's also dominated by people who like to fight and who are status seeking. What kind of content might these highly partisan, conflict-approaching, status-seeking people create when on social media? Well, provocative, identity-protective, and identity-threatening content, of course. Or, as a team of psychologists and political scientists from Yale and NYU call it, "moralized emotional content."[77]

"This Is an Outrage!" The Moralized Emotional Content Problem

"Moralized content" is content that argues something is "good" or "bad" for society and articulates what *should* be happening in a perfect, just, proper world.[78] As psychologists William Brady, M. J. Crockett, and Jay Van Bavel explain, moralized content is typically expressed through emotional language— as in the case of your aunt Sally's friend Rita sharing the news story about transgender youth being denied gender-affirming care, prefaced by, "These Republicans are barbaric. This is an outrage!" Content that highlights events, people, or objects as good or bad for society and does so using emotional language is especially likely to spread through online networks.[79] It is shared a lot. It's "contagious." And it's good at going viral, Brady explains, because it taps into our social identities. When we experience threat from an out-group (as Rita did when she read this "value-violating" news story), our sense of what is right or wrong is violated and we respond emotionally. We respond with outrage and contempt (as Rita did) or with gratitude for our in-group, elevating who "we" are and what "we" stand for. Remember, we are social animals: we survive in groups, we monitor for threats to our group, and we are readily mobilized to protect our group. Given all that, this moralizing emotional content rooted in identity threat grabs our attention in a way other content does not. Take, for example, this moralized emotional tweet from conservative activist and writer Christopher Rufo from July 2022 that was rewarded with over 34,000 likes and 7,000 retweets: "No child has an innate sense of being 'genderqueer,' 'pansexual,' 'two-spirit,' or 'gender-fluid.' Adults impose these ideological constructs on children and facilitate their adoption as sexual identities. It's manipulative, destructive, and wrong."[80] By stating that "adults impose these ideological constructs on children," framing the concept of gender identities in terms of "sexual identities," and using the words "manipulative, destructive, and wrong," Rufo succeeds in identifying a threat, tapping into conservative morals, and emphasizing his points with the emotional language of outrage.

Moralized emotional content happens to be one of the most common vehicles for *misinformation* as well.[81] This is because the sharing of misinformation online is rarely about the truth value of the content. It's about contempt for the out-group.[82] Its truth value is beside the point.[83] This also helps explain why authoritarian populists make expert use of social media, often spreading misinformation in the process. Railing against what's wrong, what needs to be different, and how mad we should be while pitting the pure people against elites is the bread and butter of populist rhetoric.[84] It also offers the viral combination of being identity based, emotional, divisive, and moralized. And so social media logics reward identity-driven misinformation and populist messaging.[85]

The Problem of Asymmetry (yes, again)

Like most things in this book, the prevalence and impact of moralized emotional social media content in the US are lopsided.[86] Conservative leaders and causes benefit more from it than do liberal leaders and causes. In a study of the diffusion of Donald Trump's and Hillary Clinton's social media posts in the 2016 campaign, William Brady and his colleagues found that Trump benefited significantly more than Clinton did from using moralized emotional language in his posts—meaning, his moralized emotional posts were more likely to be shared than hers were. Looking at how moralized emotional language affected the diffusion of social media posts by Senate candidates in the 2016 election, Brady and his team again found a "conservative advantage in moral contagion."[87] And when his team extended the analysis to *all* congressional candidates in the 2016 election, the ideological asymmetry was even more pronounced. Conservatives benefited more than liberals did from including moralized emotional language in their social media posts.

Political and data scientist Joshua Tucker has found political asymmetry in Americans' exposure to inauthentic "social bots" online during the 2016 presidential election. He found that while most Americans never came across one of these bots, Republican men came across them a lot.[88] Politics professor Andy Guess and his colleagues found that conservatives were more likely to share false information online than were liberals.[89] In the context of the 2016 campaign, Guess found that Facebook was a "key vector" sending people to websites containing false information—sites that were overwhelmingly conservative and pro-Trump. Although *most* people were not consuming false information online, the data showed how the consumption of false information was highly concentrated among the most conservative Americans, concluding, "6 in 10 visits to fake news websites came from the 10% of people with the most conservative online information."[90] In 2022, researchers found evidence that a 2018 tweak to the Facebook algorithm, in favor of posts from closely connected friends and family (called "meaningful social interactions"), "likely increased the visibility and spread of information from local conservative political groups."[91] Researchers have also documented an asymmetry in how well people identify and respond to false information they encounter online, with conservatives more likely to believe false information than liberals.[92]

With this asymmetry in misinformation engagement comes asymmetry in the misinformation *supply*, with false content online favoring conservative views and causes over liberal ones.[93] A sweeping examination of images shared on Facebook in fall 2020 conducted by Yunkang Yang, Trevor Davis, and Matthew Hindman found conservative-leaning images contained more than five times the amount of false information that liberal-leaning ones contained.[94] While part of this asymmetry may stem from the sociodemographic homogeneity of American conservatives that lends itself to identity-driven wrongness, it is also facilitated through the well-organized right-wing media machinery. As Deen Freelon and his colleagues explain, the conservative media ecosystem "is a densely interlinked region of the media network that stands far apart from other media in terms of digital, professional, and ideological connections."[95] Ring-wing disinformation is distributed more broadly on social media than left-wing media content.[96] Even though the Center Left has greater overall representation on Twitter, Freelon and his colleagues found a vastly broader reach of disinformation from right-wing media sources on the platform.[97]

The Trouble with Policing Misinformation
on the Side of Supply

In 2018, Meta founder and CEO Mark Zuckerberg explained that there's no way to know whether an individual is intentionally trying to deceive people by sharing information they know to be false (disinformation) or is sharing something they believe is true but just *happens to be* false (misinformation).[98] Through a partnership with independent fact-checking organizations that launched in 2016,[99] the company promised to tackle misinformation by flagging it, reducing its distribution, and demonetizing it.[100] Yet, misinformation continued to spread on the platform, even when it had been debunked by fact-checking organizations.[101]

The tandem misinformation crises related to the COVID-19 pandemic and the 2020 US election put new pressure on Facebook to tackle the problem of misinformation on the platform. In December 2020, Facebook decided that regardless of intent, users were not allowed to be "wrong" about COVID.[102] The site's updated policy mandated removal of certain inaccurate COVID-related claims.[103] In early September 2020, Facebook also announced a revised policy on US election-related misinformation, banning false claims relating to voting (like fake poll locations and voting rules), imposing warning labels on false claims (including claims that sought to delegitimize the election), and changing its algorithms to promote stories from credible news organizations and reduce distribution of questionable sources.[104] Although Facebook eliminated the "Stop the Steal" Facebook group in November 2020 (the group pushing the Big Lie and whose page was the site for the organization of the January 6 DC rally), the platform continued to allow posts that questioned the legitimacy of the election outcome through the insurrection.[105] The early months of 2021 marked the first work of the Facebook

Oversight Board, a quasi-independent body of experts and scholars who would be called on to review particularly contentious content decisions and issue binding verdicts. Most notably, these reviews included that of Facebook's decision to suspend President Trump's Facebook account following the violent insurrection on the US Capitol—a decision that the Oversight Board upheld, noting that Facebook would need to clarify how it would handle future cases dealing with disproportionately influential public officials.[106]

If the problem is the supply (sources and content) of misinformation online, then an obvious solution would be to suspend those accounts and remove those posts. But who decides what is true? The platforms? Meta? And if we define misinformation in terms of "evidence and expert consensus" as many scholars do, which evidence and which experts?[107] Journalists? Government? Academics? At present, the governments that have laws against misinformation include China and Belarus, where information critical of the regime is often declared to be "misinformation." The potential exploitation of misinformation laws by bad acting public officials has led most scholars in this space to consider speech freedoms paramount to the protection of democratic health.[108] Even though misinformation poses a problem for democratic health, democracy experts overwhelmingly oppose the idea of governments getting in the business of regulating misinformation content.

So, should *users* decide what is true? Twitter has experimented with a user-based effort known as the Birdwatch Community, which uses crowdsourcing to find and flag misleading content. Such efforts reduce belief in and sharing of misinformation,[109] as do "accuracy prompts"[110] and other friction-based interventions designed to slow users down and encourage them to think critically before clicking.[111] These efforts are effective and even scalable, which is promising. But if interventions slow us down and reduce our emotional responses, wouldn't that also reduce the number of bread crumbs we leave? If

I pause and think critically, that means I am less likely to like, share, and comment on a post. With fewer bread crumbs, the platform has fewer data points to inform my ad targeting. And with 99.4 percent of Meta's almost $115 billion in profits in 2021 coming from ads, why would the company ever want to support such interventions unless required to do so?

I've thought a lot about Lazarsfeld and Merton's larger point about the limits of media effects back in 1948. They argued that powerful media organizations had a vested interest in maintaining the status quo—the existing political, social, and economic order. And I've asked myself, is the same true today? More specifically, do social media platforms benefit from a stable American democracy? I think that while social media platforms might benefit from the economic stability and prospects for innovation afforded by American democracy, they might benefit even more—in the short term—from identity-based political sectarianism.

Social media's targeting criteria, metrics, rankings, and recommendation algorithms are shaped by users' emotional responses, which are the easiest responses to capture, quantify, and leverage through identity appeals and identity threats. Political sectarianism primes the pump for this kind of engagement and makes it easier to extract the fuel that powers their machinery. So, just as I'm skeptical that Meta would support efforts that slow users down, I'm also skeptical that Meta (or any advertiser-supported social media platform) would voluntarily support efforts that would disrupt political mega-identities.

Identity-fueled wrongness is a synergistic process, one that involves not only our own social psychology but also the behaviors of political elites, institutions, journalists, and technology executives. So, in considering why American life has become, in the words of Jon Haidt, "uniquely stupid," my sense is we need to move upstream and think about how powerful entities interact with our innate social and psychological needs—and with each other. Americans did not fall from the sky, land on YouTube, and search for "critical race theory." We didn't show up on Facebook and join a group that believes big government is tracking us through microchips. These behaviors are tied to our need to comprehend our world, to control those things that feel chaotic or threatening, and to be a part of a community—needs that take shape in keeping with our political mega-identities, which have become easy to ignite and exploit. Yes, the content of social media may accelerate these processes on the margins, but much of the groundwork for identity-driven wrongness originates upstream. In the final chapter we'll head upstream to consider some of the ways we might disrupt these dynamics. We'll explore various changes that might disrupt our political mega-identities, reduce our identity-driven attraction to misinformation, and maybe even improve American democratic health in the process.

Chapter 9

Disrupt Us

Solutions to Identity-Driven Wrongness

BEING WRONG ISN'T ABOUT BELIEVING factually inaccurate pieces of information. It's not even about believing lies people tell us. It's about our psychological and social needs: our need to understand our world (comprehension), have agency within it (control), and feel socially connected to people on our team (community). And when endless dimensions of identity all fit together in a little partisan package, this multidimensional political mega-identity influences all three needs. We look to comprehend our world in ways that advantage our team, we seek to control our world in ways that benefit our team, and we think and behave in ways that better connect us to our team. When false beliefs satisfy these needs, we will embrace them—even demand them. This explains the stickiness of false claims of a rigged election. It also accounts for many Americans' misperceptions of the origins and severity of COVID-19. Yes, fact-checking this information as it appears is crucial. But the well of identity-driven misinformation never runs dry. There are infinite falsehoods we (and others) can formulate to satisfy these needs, and this is why we must disrupt the system that distills political mega-identity in the first place.

It's easy to feel overwhelmed at the scope of identity-driven wrongness and how it is embedded within America's political, journalistic, and media institutions. It can feel like there's no way out. But when there are synergistic factors that work together to make a system go, it means that altering even one of these factors could make the system stop, or at least slow down. When it comes to identity-driven wrongness, there are many levels we could explore to disrupt this apparatus. Chief among them are structural changes that would, in the words of Eli Finkel and his colleagues, "create incentives for politicians and other elites to reduce their sectarianizing behaviors."[1] These include curbing partisan gerrymandering and altering campaign finance law to stop rewarding voices on the extremes. The behaviors of elected officials and political candidates play an outsized role in activating identity threat and in defining the "normal" behaviors and expressions of members of our team. Changing the electoral and financial incentives that govern their political and media behaviors could bring the identity distillation machinery to a halt. Unfortunately, as long as political elites benefit disproportionately from political sectarianism and the identity-driven needs it fosters, there is little incentive for them to change on their own or to push for structural changes that would disrupt these processes. Similarly, in the land of partisan media like Fox News, the industry of identity threat remains highly lucrative. Absent a moral obligation to the health and longevity of American democracy, executives at these outlets have little reason to change how they do business; they are likely to continue until their identity-threatening content stops padding their pockets.

In this chapter, which looks at solutions to identity-driven wrongness, I focus on the aspects of identity distillation that I think *are* disruptable: in journalism, in social media, and among individuals. Because these entities operate synergistically, changes at these levels might also alter the calculus of partisan elites in the realms of both politics and media. To that end, I recommend the following:

In journalism: engaging in democracy-centered reporting, not rewarding or incentivizing partisan performances of identity, abandoning conflict framing in the coverage of politics, and expanding community-centered local news and funding for public media

In social media: transparency requirements regarding algorithmic content rankings and ad targeting, making data available to social science researchers to understand these trends and develop research-based recommendations for the platforms and lawmakers

Among regular people: cultivating intellectual humility, disrupting our performances of political identity, making a seat at the table for those unlike us, and increasing our demand for democracy-centered political information

Underlying this work and the solutions I outline below are several non-negotiables.[2] First, America is a multiracial, multiethnic, multifaith society that requires a pluralist vision of democracy to survive and thrive. Unequal power, voice, or democratic representation by race, ethnicity, religion, or sexual identity or orientation is incompatible with a pluralistic liberal democracy. Second, freedom of expression is paramount to democratic health. To the extent that solutions to the problem of identity-driven wrongness violate any of these nonnegotiables, they are not solutions at all.

Solutions in Journalism

In 2020, I was one of over 60 political communication scholars from around the country to help develop guidelines for journalists to center democracy in their coverage of politics and elections. That group, the Election Coverage and Democracy Network, came up with specific actions and practices that journalists and news producers could do (or avoid doing) to protect American democracy when reporting on elections.[3] The recommendations that I offer here are rooted in that same literature but extend beyond election coverage to political news more broadly.

Democracy-centered reporting is a kind of journalism that puts voters and democratic institutions (rather than partisan elites or political operatives) at the center of political stories. In election reporting, this means centering stories on issues, voters, and election workers rather than on the contest between the candidates. In the context of political news more broadly, it means centering stories on issues, policies, institutions, processes, and citizens. Abandoning partisan conflict framing in our coverage of politics is an efficient way to recenter journalism on democratic processes rather than on political mega-identities.

Consider headlines like "The Biden-Trump Rematch, in Many Ways, Has Already Begun"[4] in the *Washington Post*, or Politico's "Biden and Trump Step into a Pennsylvania Proxy War,"[5] or NBC News's "The 2022 Midterms Are Just Another Battle between America's Entrenched Divides."[6] Stories framed as battles between the Left and the Right reinforce the notion that our political divide is insurmountable while reinforcing the audience's partisan identity salience.[7] They also contribute to the practice of "bothsidesism" as they imply that both parties are equally engaged in conflict and thus equally responsible for the mess of political life. Instead, framing political stories in terms of issues and policy would encourage readers and viewers to think about concrete solutions to social, economic, or environmental problems, rather than just where the good members of their team stand on those issues. And framing political stories in terms of the functioning of democratic institutions and processes, instead of Right versus Left, would encourage readers and viewers to think more in terms of one's allegiance to American democracy than to one's political party.

At present, partisan performances of identity (like Senator Ted Cruz holding up the *Antiracist Baby book* in Judge Jackson's nomination hearing) are rewarded and incentivized by the press. Political leaders engage in these displays not only because they mobilize voters but also—as explored in chapter 6—because they get covered in the news. But imagine news producers and editors deliberately exercising restraint in the face of these elite identity displays. Instead of replaying them, including direct quotes, or centering their stories around them (even to criticize them), imagine journalists working to center the democratic process in the story—and relegating those identity displays to a footnote.

Sure, it's hard to envision an industry pivoting away from potential profit to serve the public good, but a century ago, in the shadow of the Spanish-American War, the American Society of Newspaper Editors did just that. During the great newspaper war between William Randolph Hearst and Joseph Pulitzer in the 1890s, their rival newspapers, the *New York Journal* and the *New York World*, earned them massive fortunes for their exaggerated and deceptive accounts of Spanish atrocities against the people of Cuba. This "yellow journalism" not only made these men very rich but also ignited the passions of the American public, pulling the United States into the Spanish-American War. In the decades that followed, journalism was at a crossroads. The market for sensationalism, rumor, and celebrity news was growing. But there was also a professional recognition that the health of American democracy depended on a responsible, ethical press, one that recognized that "its opportunities as a chronicle are indissolubly linked [to] its obligations as teacher and interpreter."[8] It was in this spirit that the American Society of Newspaper Editors authored their Canons of Journalism, emphasizing members' professional obligation to "considerations of [the] public welfare" and "fidelity to the public interest."[9] The canons included a dedication to sincerity, truthfulness, accuracy, impartiality, and decency, as well as a duty to avoid "deliberate pandering to vicious instincts." While the professional association sought to formalize these professional norms, they also understood the limits of their authority, writing, "Lacking authority to enforce its canons the journalism here represented can but express the hope that deliberate pandering to vicious instincts will encounter effective public disapproval or yield to the influence of a preponderant professional condemnation."[10]

In response to conflict-framed, personality-centered, mega-identity-performance-rewarding political journalism, we need both "effective public disapproval" and "the influence of a preponderant professional condemnation." I offer this book as a springboard to both.

Two additional changes to the journalism industry would serve the goals of democracy-centered reporting: expanding community-centered local news and increasing funding for public media. We saw in chapter 6 how the devastation of local news in the United States has indirectly primed political mega-identities through a predominant focus on national over local news. Investing in editorially independent community newspapers is thus a way to anchor Americans within their geographic communities, increase the salience of local issues, and facilitate interaction through shared community goals and activities.[11]

In a recent edition of my local independent community paper, *The Retrospect*, the front page featured the headline "Anti-ragebait, Pro-community." The publishers wrote,

> If you, like me, are not happy with online conversations about important civic topics, I suggest the antidote is to subscribe to thoughtfully produced media like this newspaper. . . . The only thing that engages

more clicks and time than funny animal videos and voyeurism into celebrity lives is stoking anger among everyday citizens and family members. . . . These headlines serve only the masters of profit who add more gold to their hoard, the price paid for a culture war among friends and family.[12]

When we think of ourselves as members of a shared geographic community—concerned about the local fire department and the welfare of our neighbors, celebrating the achievements of our town's promising high school students and sports teams—we share tangible aspects of life in common with one another. And when we activate our community identities, our political mega-identities become diluted, perhaps even disconfirmed through meaningful interactions with category-violating members of partisan in- and out-groups.

Democracy-centered journalism will also require our ongoing investment and support. In a study of over 30 countries, journalism scholars Timothy Neff and Victor Pickard examined various measures of democratic health along with details about the countries' funding and support for public media. The countries with the strongest, healthiest democracies were those whose governments had made secure, long-term investments into public media infrastructure. Neff and Pickard suggest that a deliberate reinvestment in a robust American public media infrastructure would elevate the interests of democracy over commercial profits and increase democratic health. Without corporate pressures, independent public media is better equipped to hold public officials to account, interrogate elites at the center of power, and cover democratic processes and institutions in a manner that is informative rather than political-identity-igniting.[13] This would help to remedy some of the other related crises as well, including the "diminishing supply of reliable news and information and proliferating misinformation and low-quality news media."[14]

Solutions in Social Media

We know that certain social media logics and algorithms reward and incentivize moral emotional content rooted in identity and identity threat.[15] We also know that some features (like Facebook's angry emoji) are more likely to drive these dynamics than others. Some of the things we know about how social media contribute to identity-driven wrongness we learned from academic research, and some of it we learned from industry insiders, like whistle-blower Frances Haugen.[16] The opacity of many social media platforms' algorithms, internal research, priorities, and decision-making processes make it challenging for us to address how or why these platforms tap into and reinforce our political mega-identities. So, rather than making recommendations about specific ways in which social media ought to change how their platforms operate, my major recommendations are the same ones scholars and lawmakers have landed on for years: increased transparency requirements regarding algorithmic content rankings and ad targeting and making more data available to social science researchers to understand these trends.

Historically, the worst offender in this space in terms of the opacity of its algorithms, reluctance to share data, and the general runaround given to researchers has been Meta—the parent company of Facebook, Instagram, and WhatsApp. Someday, someone will write a book about the hurdles that Meta constructs to stop academic researchers from getting adequate access to its data; about how, instead of granting researchers access to anonymized data adequate to study these processes at scale, the company offers "research collaborations" and "visiting research" positions that tie the hands of academic researchers; about how Facebook bought the analytical tool CrowdTangle, which researchers used to analyze popular Facebook content, and how, after pushing back against critical findings published using CrowdTangle, Facebook began shutting it down in 2022.[17] In that book will be stories about Meta's disingenuous excuses for shutting down research activities of scholars like those at NYU's Ad Observatory studying microtargeting of political ads on Facebook,[18] as well as Meta's failure to fulfill its basic obligation to Social Science One, a consortium where academics and Facebook researchers were supposed to come together to answer crucial questions.[19] That last tale will chronicle academics' years-long wait for access to an anonymized Facebook data set that, once received by over 100 academic researchers, excluded about half of all US Facebook users. Perhaps it will even include a quote from Stanford Law professor Nate Persily, who had worked tirelessly for years to develop these relationships and establish the consortium. Persily described the data disaster to the *Washington Post* as "a friggin' outrage and a fundamental breach of promises Facebook made to the research community. It also demonstrates why we need government regulation to force social media companies to develop secure data sharing programs with outside independent researchers."[20] That tale will probably also include insights from CrowdTangle cofounder Brandon Silverman, who tweeted in 2022, "There is a lot of phenomenal research being done and brilliant people leading it, but they don't have the data & access they need. That's where we need to make the most progress. . . . We need more regulation to make it easier and in some cases, mandatory, for platforms to share more data."[21] But, until someone writes that book, this paragraph in *this* book will have to do.

The need for transparency is not just to scratch the itch of researchers interested in understanding how social media logics affect user identity, attitudes, beliefs, and behavior. Such research would subsequently empower individuals and entities to effectively produce and disseminate "counterspeech"— that is, messaging that contradicts, corrects, or disrupts messages in the information environment.[22] Without an adequate understanding of how a given piece of content ends up prominently displayed in a person's timeline or newsfeed, it is impossible to offer that same person counterspeech. Transparency in algorithms and in ad targeting criteria would allow other entities to create and appropriately target content to counter the dominant narrative, emotional appeals, and moral certainty a given audience is exposed to. It could also be designed to disrupt identity-reinforcing content that repeatedly taps into and reinforces a user's political mega-identity. But again, none of this is possible without a binding commitment on the part of the platforms—or a *requirement* of the platforms—to increase transparency and data accessibility.

Which leads me to the final point regarding the need for transparency, both in social media platforms' decision-making processes, algorithms, and content policies and in the form of anonymized data made available to researchers. Such transparency and data access would allow scholars to offer evidence-based insights that could empower lawmakers to pursue regulatory pathways rooted in empirical evidence. Without this, lawmakers run the risk of addressing the wrong problems—or addressing no problems at all.

Solutions from Regular People (you, me, us)

Tackling individual-level solutions to identity-driven wrongness is a risky business. Certain citizen-based "solutions" might look promising at first glance but run the risk of violating the nonnegotiable commitments I outlined earlier regarding democratic rights and representation. It might be tempting, for instance, to see "political polarization" as the core problem in need of a solution. But if one racially and religiously homogeneous political party works to curtail the democratic rights and representation of members of other ethnic and religious groups, "depolarization" is not the answer. If one party is pushing to reduce the representation and voice of members of ethnic and minority groups who tend to align with the opposing political party, then are efforts to push back against those antidemocratic forces normatively bad? Probably not. In this case, then, "polarization" is the wrong concern. Daniel Kreiss and Shannon McGregor urge us to think of the current political culture not in terms of polarization but in terms of "radicalization" of the Republican Party, involving "a widespread embrace of anti-democratic Christian nationalism, white nativism, an increasing willingness to tolerate violence, an embrace of disinformation as a political tactic, and the rejection of multi-ethnic democracy."[23]

The problematic dynamics discussed throughout this book have been—and continue to be—more concentrated on America's political right, where racial, religious, and cultural homogenization serve the distillation machinery especially well. This is crucial. Identity-driven wrongness thrives as America's cultural cleavages widen. It is fueled when aligned racial, religious, and cultural identities cultivate our needs for comprehension, control, and community. And our political and media apparatus is motivated to oblige through the perpetuation and purification of a distinct reality (and falsehoods) that serves these needs.

Reshuffling the Deck

The identity distillation machinery benefits from aligned, predictable, oversimplified expressions of social identity. This is why politicians feed into the culture war and why partisan groups push to make local politics about national issues such as critical race theory. It's why moralized emotional content rooted in identity goes viral on social media and why partisan cable news covers the stories most likely to outrage their partisan audiences. So, how do we, as cogs in this machinery, complicate social identity considerations and disrupt these dynamics? How do we reshuffle the deck without compromising our commitments to the nonnegotiables listed earlier?

First, we must remember that although Americans are socially sorted, most of us are not in perfect issue alignment with the political side that our race, ethnicity, religion, geography, or even our political party might suggest. For example, after the repeal of *Roe v. Wade*, the Supreme Court decision that had protected a woman's right to an abortion, the conservative Kansas legislature put the future of the state's abortion law directly in the hands of voters through a referendum. The expectation was that reliably conservative Kansas voters would support allowing the legislature to advance stricter abortion laws in the state. But the results showed that expectation was wrong. Voters rejected the measure by 18 percentage points.[24] Existing abortion law in Kansas was already quite strict, including limits on abortions after 22 weeks of pregnancy and a requirement that ultrasounds be performed before abortions can be obtained. But, to wager that Kansas voters would approve of a constitutional amendment stating that there is *no right to abortion*? That ignores the fact that voters are not as unidimensional as our political mega-identities would imply.

Put it this way: a white, Christian, rural-dwelling ice fisherman from Minnesota might identify culturally with folks on the political right, but his positions on everyday issues are probably more moderate. The assumption that people who check certain social or cultural boxes also necessarily hold extreme views only fuels the distillation engine.[25] As Mason writes, the United States is "a nation that may agree on many things but is bitterly divided nonetheless."[26] We must, therefore, allow for and encourage disconfirming instances—allow people the opportunity to reshuffle the deck. We can do this by offering a seat at the table where we can witness the aspects of everyday life that we do share—not to compromise on the fundamentals of democratic rights but to dilute mega-identities through communication and openness.

I'm reminded of the 2016 *Saturday Night Live* sketch "Black Jeopardy," featuring Tom Hanks playing the character of Doug, a white Trump supporter.

As Doug and the Black contestants respond to clues about kitchen junk drawers, scratch-off tickets, and their shared love of Tyler Perry films, they realize just how many aspects of life they share. This continues until the Final Jeopardy round, where the clue is the one nationalized cultural issue that is, in fact, dividing Black and white Americans: "Lives that Matter." (Note the correct answer was "What is Black," but we are left to assume that Doug will inevitably respond "What is Blue.") The "Black Jeopardy" sketch embodies what Buddhist author Pema Chodron refers to as the practice of "Just Like Me." Despite cultural, religious, and political cleavages, Chodron reminds us of some basic aspects of the human experience that we all share, including that "every living being desires happiness and doesn't want to suffer."[27] The same is true of Doug. Doug desires happiness and does not want to suffer. Like the rest of us, he's figuring it out as he goes.

Engaging with—or simply being around—people from an out-group can complicate the identity distillation machinery, which then alters how our needs for comprehension, control, and community are articulated. Neutral interactions with members of our out-group encourage us to see the things we have in common with people from the other side.[28] Even just witnessing (not even participating in) warm interactions between members of opposing groups can reduce our own feelings of animosity toward the out-group,[29] including when those interactions occur between political leaders of opposing parties.[30] Such experiences can reduce our sense of social distance from out-group members, suppress our political mega-identity salience, and quiet our sense of political identity threat.

Diluting our mega-identities will also require that we work hard to resist the siren song of moralized emotional content online—posts that enrage or inspire us based on our primal characteristics. This is harder than it sounds. It requires orienting ourselves to our newsfeeds and timelines with "identity disruption" as an explicit goal. As an emotionally reactive social media user myself, I find this challenging. I have taken to seeking out and sharing more political-identity-disrupting content online. Video clips of pets, sports, or art foster connections with people, are still emotionally evocative, but don't encourage a moralized partisan response.

We can also disrupt identity distillation by not curating our representations of self when we present them to the world—in person or online. There may be pressure to "perform" in keeping with the side we're on, but it is always possible to push back against that pressure. Imagine a yard sign with the following message: "In this house we: believe in regulated gun ownership, believe humans affect climate change, support reproductive health, and believe Jesus is the son of God." I suppose that wouldn't fit neatly on a sign, but you get my point. People who don't fit their side's stereotype may stay quiet for fear of violating their side's norms. But what if these nuanced folks opted instead to throw a wrench in the works, bolstered by the notion that their self-disclosure is of service to democratic and epistemic health?

Take my dear friend David. David is a former college football player who is six feet six. He and his wife drive a giant GMC Yukon Denali. David wears his Oakley sunglasses atop his baseball hat, goes deep-sea fishing, and shows up at our house in a cotton-candy-pink tank top adorned with a rainbow pride flag. When he's not in his gay pride shirt, people make assumptions about who David is and what he believes. They imagine that he holds certain views about race and sexuality. But rather than going along with their imagined sense of who he *probably* is, he challenges them and asks them why they made assumptions about him. David has decided to act as a disrupter.

The Benefits of Giving the Benefit of the Doubt

Given the alignment of sociodemographic and cultural identities on the right, it may be unlikely for our right-leaning friends to want to engage in these identity-disruptive behaviors. But recall that identity dynamics are responsive. Political mega-identities become salient when we feel they are under threat. When one team's members disrupt their presentations of self, reshuffle the deck, offer seats at the table, and diversify their perceptions of their out-group, it will reduce the identity threat perceived by the other side, thereby reducing the other side's political identity salience . . . and round it goes.

When partisan actors seek to destabilize democracy, it is not easy to articulate ways to safeguard democracy without explicitly invoking—and thus reinforcing—partisan identity. One way of pushing back against politically asymmetrical attacks on American democracy is to highlight the daylight that exists between the political and media elites benefiting from identity-driven wrongness and the people whose interests (and identity) they claim to represent. This was the method of choice of the January 6 Congressional Committee during their hearings in the House of Representatives. The committee made a distinction between the political elites who knowingly sold the Big Lie to the American people, on the one hand, and the regular Americans who came to the nation's Capitol on January 6, 2021, on the other.

The committee created a contrast between violent militia groups like the Proud Boys and the Oath Keepers, who were seeking to exploit a moment of political chaos, and the regular people who had been told by President Trump that there would be a "big protest in D.C. on January 6th" and they should "be there" since it "will be wild." In one of the hearings, the committee heard testimony from Stephen Ayres, a Trump supporter and rioter who entered the Capitol during the insurrection. Ayres discussed the importance of Trump's message in encouraging his trip to Washington: "I followed . . . President Trump, you know, on all the websites, you know. He basically put out . . . come

to the Stop the Steal rally, you know, and I felt like I needed to be down here."
Committee chair Bennie Thompson described Trump's cynical exploitation of
supporters like Ayres that day, saying, "The president's goal was to stay in
power for a second term despite losing the election. The assembled crowd was
one of the tools to achieve that goal."[31] By emphasizing the distinction between
the regular Americans who trusted the president and the powerbrokers on the
right who cynically sought to exploit them, the committee invited viewers and
journalists to complicate their understanding of political mega-identity.

One of the central roles that we can all play in combatting wrongness comes
when we encounter family or friends who confidently believe information that
contradicts evidence and expert consensus. When our loved ones believe in
conspiracy theories or misinformation, it feels frustrating—even heartbreaking.
But, remembering that the roots of wrongness often reside in confusion, pow-
erlessness, and a need for social connection might help us find the emotional
fortitude (and perhaps even compassion) to draw us closer to that person rather
than retreat. Given that belief in conspiracy theories stems from needs for comprehension, control, and community, offering our friendship and solidarity as
a means to satisfy those needs might reduce the appeal of the conspiracy theory. Offering our friendship and connection (rather than mockery and derision)
might also interrupt the very dynamics that fuel mega-identity reinforcing belief systems.

Of course, depending on the nature of the misinformation beliefs held by
our friends and family, they might include sentiments that are hateful and harmful. Offering compassion and friendship only makes sense if you are able to
offer that kind of emotional energy without causing undue harm to yourself,
your loved ones, or your psychological health. But if the relationship was—and
is—important, perhaps engaging with them, reminding them they are loved

and respected, and tapping into aspects of your shared history or identity un-related to their "wrongness" will build trust and connection. Over time, that trust and connection might reduce the appeal of—and need for—political mega-identity-reinforcing falsehoods.

Intellectual Humility

The dynamics of identity-driven wrongness benefit from the fact that they are self-reinforcing. It is through our identity-laden observations of the world that we remind ourselves again and again who we are and what we know to be true. But imagine if we slowed down that engine on our own—by reducing the influence of our preexisting knowledge and beliefs on our observations, and conversely, by allowing disconfirming observations to inform and update our knowledge and beliefs. When we practice and value intellectual humility (IH), we do both. Recognizing the limits of our own knowledge encourages us to allow identity-conflicting evidence to update our beliefs. It also reminds us to not hold on so tightly to the things we already know as we observe the world, because, after all, we might be wrong.

IH can be learned. It can be practiced.[32] It can be modeled. And it can be valued. For example, social psychologist Jonah Andrew Koetke and his colleagues implemented a "fallibility salience" intervention that successfully increased IH. They asked people three seemingly simple questions that had three counterintuitive correct answers. After they revealed the correct answers to participants (which most had gotten wrong), the researchers had the participants reflect on "why it is okay to recognize that their knowledge and beliefs may be inaccurate."[33] This simple reflection by the participants increased their IH. Better yet, it also increased the kinds of skepticism and investigative behaviors that reduce belief in misinformation.

Children as young as middle schoolers have demonstrated an increase in IH when exposed to teaching methods that emphasize individual-level improvements and normalize making mistakes.[34] Shifting classrooms from answer-oriented to question-oriented knowledge can encourage IH as well.[35] Imagine a school assignment that asks students to articulate what they believe, and then what kinds of evidence they would need to point to in order to show that their belief is *incorrect*. Or an assignment that asks them to state someone *else's* point of view on a topic, bolstered by evidence. Or an essay about the limits of what they can know on a given topic—and how fallibility is OK. Over the years, my two children have written countless persuasive essays designed to convince the reader of something. They have yet to write a single essay exploring how they might be wrong.

Encouraging people to embrace their own fallibility will certainly be challenging. It is uncomfortable to consider the limits of one's own knowledge—especially on the cultural right, where tolerance for ambiguity is lower and where intuition and emotion (what we already know and feel) may be privileged over evidence and data.[36] But we know IH is associated with endless positive pro-social outcomes, including empathy, gratitude, altruism, and curiosity.[37] We can decide that this is a virtue that we want to value in our world; that we want to watch performed on our televisions by thoughtful experts, journalists, and lawmakers; that we want to reward in everyday life, at the ballot box, and in the social media algorithm; that we ourselves want to model in our conversations with others. We can seek out and reward those who perform IH, who acknowledge the limits of what they know, and who model epistemic fallibility. When such individuals are criticized as wishy-washy or indecisive, we can use our platforms to remind others that the act of updating knowledge in the face of new information is a virtue, not a vice.

Reframing How and Why We Use Political Media

This last suggestion—to reward performances of IH by political and media elites—is part of a much-needed transformation in how and why we consume political media. By understanding the mechanisms contributing to identity distillation and identity-driven wrongness, it becomes apparent that political and media entities are operating in anticipation of our identity-driven emotional engagement. Whether it's MSNBC covering Ted Cruz talking about baby books in a nomination hearing, Tucker Carlson pushing great replacement theory, or just a headline that frames an issue as a partisan battle, the political culture producers are giving us what they think we want.

But now that we have awakened ourselves to the agency that we have in this equation, we can deliberately alter their calculus by choosing not to reward that content and by calling it out when we see it. This might even mean deleting our own emotionally reactive social media posts (like retweets of content that, in the moment, really riled us up). We're human. We respond to moralized emotional content, but through mindful actions we can deliberately work to minimize or undo how those emotional responses feed the identity distillation apparatus. And rather than encouraging or selecting political news framed as a battle between Democrats and Republicans, we can choose to consume media content that places democracy and human rights at its center, as characters in a battle with destabilizing or authoritarian forces. These stories would satisfy the press's need for conflict and drama but without explicitly priming us to view the world through the lens of our political mega-identities.

Conclusion

I wrestled for months over this final chapter on solutions to identity-driven wrongness. After numerous false starts, my husband P. J. tried to put my mind at ease. "Just explaining how and why these dynamics operate the way they do is a step towards a solution," he said. I hope he is right. This political moment feels chaotic. It feels like America's political and cultural worlds are drowning in random lies and hate. However, my reader friend, I hope you see that they are not random. They are all quite explicable, in fact. And when things are explicable, they are predictable. And when they are predictable, they are often controllable.

When I used to think about how media and political elites benefited from the distillation of our social identities, I would get angry. But after writing this book, I see anger as part of the identity distillation apparatus. Over time, instead of anger, I began to feel sorrow, coupled by a commitment to help people understand the dynamics of identity-driven wrongness. I am now convinced that every person—every journalist, every public official, every media and technology executive, and every one of us—has the capacity to disrupt this process. Each of us has the capacity to awaken our hearts and become purposeful and deliberate as we (a) enact our social identities, (b) allow our observations to update our knowledge and beliefs, and (c) reframe how and why we use political media. Our needs for comprehension, control, and community may be here to stay, but how these are enacted—and the motivations that drive how they take shape—are very much up to us.

But, of course, I could always be wrong.

Acknowledgments

When I started talking with friends and colleagues about the idea for this book, I was fortunate to find many cheerleaders of my idea to "go big." My goal was to offer up a public-facing book that would translate vast empirical work from communication, political science, sociology, and psychology to help folks make sense of our mediated political world, understand the threats to American democratic health, and consider why so many of us are so wrong. Friends and scholars such as Shannon McGregor, Regina Lawrence, Kathleen Hall Jamieson, Mike Wagner, Emily Falk, Jennifer Mercieca, Daniel Kreiss, Lily Mason, Tresa Undem, Cathlin Sullivan, and Jess Feezell all made me feel like these ideas were smart and helpful. From the beginning, my editor, Laura Davulis, lifted me up. In fact, when my agent Mark Gottlieb sent her the proposal, she responded immediately by complimenting my *Vox* article "I Was a Conspiracy Theorist, Too," which she had read and recalled from months prior. Laura, you may not know it, but I have kept that praise in my pocket to keep me going, so thank you.

I am grateful for the generosity of early readers, including Amanda Cronkhite, Matthew Carlson, Julie Wronski, and Daniel Kreiss, who spent significant time offering supportive—and critical—feedback on early drafts. Their comments and those of the anonymous reviewers helped make this book so much better. In the early days of my empirical work on epistemic motivations, ideology, and misinformation, both Christopher Federico and Erin Cassese were kind enough to offer critical feedback. Many of these ideas crystallized as Joanne Miller and I developed our joint chapter on political communication written for the *Oxford Handbook of Political Psychology*. Huge thanks to Gordon Pennycook and David Rand, who were willing to go on the record and share their thoughts on the misinformation problem, and to journalist Judd Legum, who kindly gave me permission to include one of his images in the book.

The survey data explored here come from a wonderful collaboration with Amy Bleakley and Jessica B. Langbaum, who were kind enough to bring me into a project funded by the National Institute on Aging completed during the COVID-19 pandemic in 2020 and 2021. Some of the research included in this book was made possible by Grant No. 3R01AG063954-02S1 from the National Institute of Aging. The contents of this book do not necessarily represent the official views of the NIA.

As part of that project, I had the great fortune of working with Erin Maloney to study how different ways of knowing related to belief in misinformation and political attitudes. That work features prominently in chapter 5.

The communication department at the University of Delaware is such a supportive community, with excellent colleagues like Amy Bleakley, Scott Caplan, John Crowley, Jenny Lambe, Lindsay Hoffman, and Paul Brewer. This book wouldn't have been possible without the support of department chair Kami Silk, who makes sure that I am making the right choices for myself as a scholar, a teacher, a person, and a mom.

My graduate research team was an invaluable resource throughout this process, not only for their tireless enthusiasm and research assistance but also for giving me a wonderful sense of community. Special thanks to Huma Rasheed, with whom I studied the link among conflict orientation, political attitudes, and masking behaviors, and to Brooke Molokach, whose expertise in the literature on intellectual humility has shaped my work. Brooke was also the fearless research assistant who dared help me copyedit the final manuscript. But it seems the task was rewarding: she reacted with glee as she made the same comment to me that I have written on so many student papers in the past: "Danna, Is this even a sentence?"

Thank you to the rigorous scholars from around the world whose vast research has made this project possible. I hope you find your work accurately represented in these pages. Any errors are mine and mine alone. Thank you also to Ezra Rodriguez for their help with visualizations throughout the book.

Behind the scenes are the people I love, who keep me from flying off into outer space. Jae, Stephen, Susan, Heide, Cathlin, Grace, Liz, Karen, and my entire Gallagher family, your love and friendship keep me tethered. Mimi and Poppi, thank you for always giving me a home to return to, for your continued intellectual curiosity, and for your enthusiasm for whatever it is I'm working on. Kylee, I can't wait to read your first book.

To PJ, my awesome partner—you have never once made me feel like anything less than the smartest person you've ever met. And since you're a tough reviewer, careful writer, and brilliant thinker, your confidence in me helps me talk back to my nay-saying self-critic. Thank you for always reshuffling the deck, keeping me intellectually honest and grounded, making sure I eat breakfast and do yoga, and reminding me to speak to myself and *of* myself with kindness.

Baxter and Edie, I am so grateful for the lessons you teach me about life, priorities, love, and compassion. You are two shining lights. I am so proud to know you and feel so lucky to have you as my guides.

And to Mike Young and Michelle Kennedy, I love you and miss you every day.

Thanks, friends.

Love,
DANNA

Notes

Prologue

1. Mason, L. (2018). *Uncivil agreement: How politics became our identity*. University of Chicago Press.
2. Mason, *Uncivil agreement*.
3. Mason, *Uncivil agreement*.
4. Mason, *Uncivil agreement*.
5. Young, D., Maloney, E., Bleakley, A., & Langbaum, J. B. (2022). "I feel it in my gut": Epistemic motivations, political beliefs, and misperceptions of COVID-19 and the 2020 US presidential election. *Journal of Social and Political Psychology*, 10(2), 643–656. Also see Oliver, J. E., & Wood, T. J. (2018). *Enchanted America: How intuition and reason divide our politics*. University of Chicago Press.
6. Kreiss, D., Lawrence, R. G., & McGregor, S. C. (2020). Political identity ownership: Symbolic contests to represent members of the public. *Social Media + Society*, 6(2), 2056305120926495.
7. Vaidhyanathan, S. (2018). *Antisocial media: How Facebook disconnects us and undermines democracy*. Oxford University Press.

1. People Like Us Believe These Things

1. Tillman, Z. (2021, January 21). Everything we fucking trained for: The capitol mob, in their own words. *Buzzfeed News*, https://www.buzzfeednews.com/article/zoetillman /captiol-rioters-charged-social-media-posts-violence.
2. Naylor, B. (2021, February 10). Read Trump's Jan. 6 Speech, A Key Part of Impeachment Trial. *National Public Radio*, https://www.npr.org/2021/02/10/966396848 /read-trumps-jan-6-speech-a-key-part-of-impeachment-trial.
3. Nyhan, B., & Reifler, J. (2010). When corrections fail: The persistence of political misperceptions. *Political Behavior*, 32(2), 303–330, p. 305.
4. Tan, A. S., Lee, C. J., & Chae, J. (2015). Exposure to health (mis) information: Lagged effects on young adults' health behaviors and potential pathways. *Journal of Communication*, 65, 674–698, p. 675. doi:10.1111/jcom.12163. For a review, see Vraga, E. K., & Bode, L.

(2020). Defining misinformation and understanding its bounded nature: Using expertise and evidence for describing misinformation. *Political Communication*, 37(1), 136–144.

5. Evanega, S., Lynas, M., Adams, J., Smolenyak, K., & Insights, C. G. (2020). Coronavirus misinformation: Quantifying sources and themes in the COVID-19 "infodemic." *JMIR Preprints*, 19(10).

6. Uscinski, J. E., Enders, A. M., Klofstad, C., Seelig, M., Funchion, J., Everett, C., . . . & Murthi, M. (2020). Why do people believe COVID-19 conspiracy theories? *Harvard Kennedy School Misinformation Review*, 1(3).

7. Hornik, R., Kikut, A., Jesch, E., Woko, C., Siegel, L., & Kim, K. (2021). Association of COVID-19 misinformation with face mask wearing and social distancing in a nationally representative US sample. *Health Communication*, 36(1), 6–14.

8. Uscinski, J. E., Enders, A. M., Klofstad, C., Seelig, M., Funchion, J., Everett, C., . . . & Murthi, M. (2020). Why do people believe COVID-19 conspiracy theories? *Harvard Kennedy School Misinformation Review*, 1(3). Hornik et al., Association of COVID-19 misinformation. Howard, M. C. (2022). Are face masks a partisan issue during the COVID-19 pandemic? Differentiating political ideology and political party affiliation. *International Journal of Psychology*, 57(1), 153–160.

9. Allcott, H., Boxell, L., Conway, J., Gentzkow, M., Thaler, M., & Yang, D. (2020). Polarization and public health: Partisan differences in social distancing during the coronavirus pandemic. *Journal of Public Economics*, 191, 104254. Gadarian, S. K., Goodman, S. W., & Pepinsky, T. B. (2021). Partisanship, health behavior, and policy attitudes in the early stages of the COVID-19 pandemic. *PLoS ONE*, 16(4), e0249596. Grossman, G., Kim, S., Rexer, J. M., & Thirumurthy, H. (2020). Political partisanship influences behavioral responses to governors' recommendations for COVID-19 prevention in the United States. *Proceedings of the National Academy of Sciences*, 117(39), 24144–24153. Frankovic, K. (2020, October 3). How Trump and Biden supporters differ on face masks. *YouGov*, https://today.yougov.com/topics/politics/articles-reports/2020/10/03/how-trump-and-biden-supporters-differ-face-masks.

10. Jones, B. (2020, May 26). Coronavirus death toll is heavily concentrated in Democratic congressional districts. *Pew Research Center*, https://www.pewresearch.org/fact-tank/2020/05/26/coronavirus-death-toll-is-heavily-concentrated-in-democratic-congressional-districts/.

11. Chen, H. F., & Karim, S. A. (2022). Relationship between political partisanship and COVID-19 deaths: Future implications for public health. *Journal of Public Health (Oxford, England)*, 44(3), 716–723.

12. Ivory, D., Leatherby, L., & Gebeloff, R. (2021, April 17). Least vaccinated U.S. counties have something in common: Trump voters. *The New York Times*, https://www.nytimes.com/interactive/2021/04/17/us/vaccine-hesitancy-politics.html.

13. McGreal, C. (2020, October 3). "It's a hoax. There's no pandemic": Trump's base stays loyal as president fights Covid. *The Guardian*, https://www.theguardian.com/us-news/2020/oct/03/donald-trump-base-stays-loyal-president-fights-covid-19. Perper, R.

(2020, June 20). Residents of Palm Beach County erupted at a county commissioners meeting. *Business Insider India*, https://www.businessinsider.in/international/news /residents-of-palm-beach-florida-erupted-at-a-town-meeting-after-masks-were-made -mandatory-twitter-users-were-quick-to-compare-the-intense-backlash-to-an-episode -of-parks-and-recreation-/articleshow/76619472.cms.

14. Guynn, J. (2020, October 2). Trump's COVID-19 diagnosis is not slowing virulent anti-mask movement on Facebook. *USA Today*, https://www.usatoday.com/story/tech /2020/10/02/facebook-anti-face-mask-groups-trump-covid-19/3597593001/.

15. Goodman, J., & Carmichael, F. (2020, May 30). Coronavirus: Bill Gates "microchip" conspiracy theory and other vaccine claims fact-checked. *BBC News*, https://www.bbc .com/news/52847648. Rosa-Aquino, P. (2021, June 9). Hot new conspiracy theory: Vaccines turn you into a magnet. *Intelligencer*, https://nymag.com/intelligencer/2021 /06/hot-new-conspiracy-theory-vaccines-turns-you-into-a-magnet.html.

16. Kaiser Family Foundation (2021, November 8). COVID-19 misinformation is ubiquitous: 78% of the public believes or is unsure about at least one false statement, and nearly a third believe at least four of eight false statements tested, https://www.kff .org/coronavirus-covid-19/press-release/covid-19-misinformation-is-ubiquitous-78-of -the-public-believes-or-is-unsure-about-at-least-one-false-statement-and-nearly-at-third -believe-at-least-four-of-eight-false-statements-tested/.

17. Nteta, T. (2021, December 28). One year later, new UMass Amherst poll finds continued national political division over the Jan. 6 attack on the U.S. capitol. *University of Massachusetts Amherst*, https://www.umass.edu/news/article/one-year-later-new -umass-amherst-poll-finds-continued-national-political-division-over.

18. Pfleger, P. (2021, October 22). While COVID still rages, anti-vaccine activists will gather for a big conference. NPR. *Morning Edition*, https://www.npr.org/2021/10/22 /1048162253/while-covid-still-rages-anti-vaccine-activists-will-gather-for-a-big -conference.

19. Pfleger, While COVID still rages.

20. West, J. D., & Bergstrom, C. T. (2021). Misinformation in and about science. *Proceedings of the National Academy of Sciences*, 118(15), e1912444117.

21. Lee, J., Kim, J. W., & Yun Lee, H. (2022). Unlocking conspiracy belief Systems: How fact-checking label on Twitter counters conspiratorial MMR vaccine misinformation. *Health Communication*, 1–13. Carnahan, D., & Bergan, D. E. (2021). Correcting the misinformed: The effectiveness of fact-checking messages in changing false beliefs. *Political Communication*, 39(2), 166–183. Papakyriakopoulos, O., Serrano, J. C. M., & Hegelich, S. (2020). The spread of COVID-19 conspiracy theories on social media and the effect of content moderation. *Harvard Kennedy School (HKS) Misinformation Review*, 18, https://doi.org/10.37016/mr-2020-034. Pennycook, G., McPhetres, J., Zhang, Y., Lu, J. G., & Rand, D. G. (2020). Fighting COVID-19 misinformation on social media: Experimental evidence for a scalable accuracy-nudge intervention. *Psychological Science*, 31(7), 770–780.

22. Kupferschmidt, K. (2022, March 23). Detecting bullshit: Studying the spread of misinformation should become a top scientific priority, says biologist Carl Bergstrom. *Science*, https://www.science.org/content/article/studying-fighting-misinformation -top-scientific-priority-biologist-argues.

23. Tillman, Everything we fucking trained for.

2. How Do We Know What We Know?

1. Popper, K. R. (1962). *Conjectures and refutations*. Basic Books.

2. Hanson, N. R. (1958). *Patterns of discovery*. Cambridge University Press.

3. Gillham, N. W. (2001). Sir Francis Galton and the birth of eugenics. *Annual Review of Genetics*, 35(1), 83–101.

4. Rury, J. L. (1988). Race, region, and education: An analysis of Black and White scores on the 1917 Army Alpha Intelligence Test. *The Journal of Negro Education*, 57(1), 51–65.

5. Klayman, J. (1995). Varieties of confirmation bias. *Psychology of Learning and Motivation*, 32, 385–418.

6. Nickerson, R. S. (1998). Confirmation bias: A ubiquitous phenomenon in many guises. *Review of General Psychology*, 2(2), 175–220, p. 175.

7. See Kruglanski, A. W., & Ajzen, I. (1983). Bias and error in human judgment. *European Journal of Social Psychology*, 13, 1–44. Kunda, Z. (1990). The case for motivated reasoning. *Psychological Bulletin*, 108(3), 480–498.

8. Douglas, K. M., Sutton, R. M., & Cichocka, A. (2017). The psychology of conspiracy theories. *Current Directions in Psychological Science*, 26(6), 538–542.

9. Van Prooijen, J.-W., & Douglas, K. M. (2018). Belief in conspiracy theories: Basic principles of an emerging research domain. *European Journal of Social Psychology*, 48(7), 897–908.

10. Freelon, D., & Wells, C. (2020). Disinformation as political communication. *Political Communication*, 37(2), 145–156.

11. Bago, B., Rand, D. G., & Pennycook, G. (2020). Fake news, fast and slow: Deliberation reduces belief in false (but not true) news headlines. *Journal of Experimental Psychology: General*, 149(8), 1608–1613, https://doi.org/10.1037/xge0000729.

12. Cacioppo, J. T., & Petty, R. E. (1982). The need for cognition. *Journal of Personality and Social Psychology*, 42(1), 116–131.

13. Leding, J. K., & Antonio, L. (2019). Need for cognition and discrepancy detection in the misinformation effect. *Journal of Cognitive Psychology*, 31(4), 409–415.

14. Frederick, S. (2005). Cognitive reflection and decision making. *Journal of Economic Perspectives*, 19(4), 25–42.

15. Frederick, S. (2005). Cognitive reflection and decision making, p. 27.

16. Pennycook, G., & Rand, D. G. (2019). Lazy, not biased: Susceptibility to partisan fake news is better explained by lack of reasoning than by motivated reasoning. *Cognition*, 188, 39–50.

17. Mosleh, M., Pennycook, G., Arechar, A. A., & Rand, D. G. (2021). Cognitive reflection correlates with behavior on Twitter. *Nature Communications*, 12(1), 1–10.

18. Evans, N. J., Rae, B., Bushmakin, M., Rubin, M., & Brown, S. D. (2017). Need for closure is associated with urgency in perceptual decision-making. *Memory & Cognition*, 45(7), 1193–1205. De Dreu, C. K., Koole, S. L., & Oldersma, F. L. (1999). On the seizing and freezing of negotiator inferences: Need for cognitive closure moderates the use of heuristics in negotiation. *Personality and Social Psychology Bulletin*, 25(3), 348–362.

19. Pica, G., Pierro, A., Bélanger, J. J., & Kruglanski, A. W. (2014). The role of need for cognitive closure in retrieval-induced forgetting and misinformation effects in eyewitness memory. *Social Cognition*, 32(4), 337–359.

20. Becker, E. (1997). *The denial of death*. Simon and Schuster.

21. Pyszczynski, T., Solomon, S., & Greenberg, J. (2015). Thirty years of terror management theory: From genesis to revelation. In *Advances in Experimental Social Psychology* (Vol. 52, pp. 1–70). Academic Press.

22. Pyszczynski, Solomon, & Greenberg, Thirty years of terror management theory.

23. Varki, A., & Brower, D. (2013). *Denial: Self-deception, false beliefs, and the origins of the human mind*. Hachette UK, p. 18.

24. James, A., & Wells, A. (2002). Death beliefs, superstitious beliefs and health anxiety. *British Journal of Clinical Psychology*, 41(1), 43–53. Wong, S. H. (2012). Does superstition help? A study of the role of superstitions and death beliefs on death anxiety amongst Chinese undergraduates in Hong Kong. *OMEGA-Journal of Death and Dying*, 65(1), 55–70.

25. Weinstein, N. D. (1989). Optimistic biases about personal risks. *Science*, 246(4935), 1232–1233.

26. Coyne, J. A. (2016). *Faith versus fact: Why science and religion are incompatible*. Penguin.

27. Arrowood, R. B., Coleman, T. J., III, Swanson, S. B., Hood, R. W., Jr., & Cox, C. R. (2018). Death, quest, and self-esteem: Re-examining the role of self-esteem and religion following mortality salience. *Religion, Brain & Behavior*, 8(1), 69–76. Genia, V. (1996). I, E, quest, and fundamentalism as predictors of psychological and spiritual well-being. *Journal for the Scientific Study of Religion*, 35(1), 56–64.

28. Moulding, R., & Kyrios, M. (2007). Desire for control, sense of control and obsessive-compulsive symptoms. *Cognitive Therapy and Research*, 31(6), 759–772. Moulding, R., & Kyrios, M. (2006). Anxiety disorders and control related beliefs: The exemplar of obsessive–compulsive disorder (OCD). *Clinical Psychology Review*, 26(5), 573–583. See also Stein, D. J. (2002). Obsessive-compulsive disorder. *The Lancet*, 360(9330), 397–405.

29. Southwell, B. (2023, March 9). Personal correspondence.

30. Smedley, A., & Smedley, B. D. (2005). Race as biology is fiction, racism as a social problem is real: Anthropological and historical perspectives on the social construction of race. *American Psychologist*, 60(1), 16–26.

31. Kuo, R., & Marwick, A. (2021). Critical disinformation studies: History, power, and politics. *Harvard Kennedy School Misinformation Review*, 2(4), 1–11.

32. PRRI. (2022, February 24). The persistence of QAnon in the post-Trump era: An analysis of who believes the conspiracies PRRI.org. https://www.prri.org/research/the-persistence -of-qanon-in-the-post-trump-era-an-analysis-of-who-believes-the-conspiracies/.

33. Douglas, K. M., Uscinski, J. E., Sutton, R. M., Cichocka, A., Nefes, T., Ang, C. S., & Deravi, F. (2019). Understanding conspiracy theories. *Political Psychology*, 40, 3–35, p. 4.

34. Van Prooijen, J.-W. (2018). *The psychology of conspiracy theories.* Routledge.

35. Roose, K. (2021, September 3). What is QAnon, the viral pro-Trump conspiracy theory? *The New York Times.*

36. Kornfield, M. (2021, November 2). Why hundreds of QAnon supporters showed up in Dallas, expecting JFK Jr's return. *The Washington Post*, https://www.washingtonpost .com/nation/2021/11/02/qanon-jfk-jr-dallas/.

37. Holt, J. (2021, February 10). StopTheSteal: Timeline of social media and extremist activities leading to 1/6 insurrection. *Just Security*, 10.

38. Kahn, C. (2020, November 18). Half of Republicans say Biden won because of a "rigged" election: Reuters/Ipsos poll. *Reuters*, https://www.Reuters.com/article/us-usa -election-poll/half-ofrepublicans-say-biden-won-because-of-a-rigged-election-reuters -ipsos-pollidUSKBN27Y1AJ.

39. Pennycook, G., & Rand, D. G. (2021). Examining false beliefs about voter fraud in the wake of the 2020 presidential election. *The Harvard Kennedy School Misinformation Review*, https://doi.org/10.37016/mr-2020-51.

40. Hurley, L. (2021, March 8). U.S. Supreme Court dumps last of Trump's election appeals. *Reuters*, https://www.reuters.com/article/us-usa-court-election/u-s-supreme -court-dumps-last-of-trumps-election-appeals-idUSKBN2B01LE. Nteta, T. (2021, December 28). One year later, new Umass Amherst poll finds continued national political division over the Jan. 6 attack on the U.S. Capitol. *University of Massachusetts Amherst*, https://www.umass.edu/news/article/one-year-later-new-umass-amherst -poll-finds-continued-national-political-division-over.

41. Thorson, E. (2016). Belief echoes: The persistent effects of corrected misinformation. *Political Communication*, 33(3), 460–480, p. 460.

42. Montanaro, D. (2021, November 1). Most Americans trust elections are fair, but sharp divides exist, a new poll finds. *NPR*, https://www.npr.org/2021/11/01/1050291610 /most-americans-trust-elections-are-fair-but-sharp-divides-exist-a-new-poll-finds.

43. Vermeule, C. A., & Sunstein, C. R. (2009). *Journal of Political Philosophy*, 17(2), 202–227, p. 204.

44. Romer, D., & Jamieson, K. H. (2020). Conspiracy theories as barriers to controlling the spread of COVID-19 in the US. *Social Science & Medicine*, 263, 113356. Khazan, O. (2020, October 9). How a bizarre claim about masks has lived on for months. *The Atlantic.*

45. McEvoy, J. (2021, June 3). Microchips, magnets, and shedding: Here are 5 (debunked) Covid vaccine conspiracy theories spreading online. *Forbes.*

46. McEvoy, Microchips, magnets, and shedding.

47. Van Prooijen, J.-W., Douglas, K., & De Inocencio, C. (2018). Connecting the dots: Illusory pattern perception predicts beliefs in conspiracies and the supernatural. *European Journal of Social Psychology*, 48, 320–335, https://doi.org/10.1002/ejsp.2331.

48. Umam, A. N., Muluk, H., & Milla, M. N. (2018). The need for cognitive closure and belief in conspiracy theories: An exploration of the role of religious fundamentalism in cognition. In A. A. Ariyanto, H. Muluk, P. Newcombe, F. P. Piercy, E. K. Poerwandari, & S. H. R. Suradijono (Eds.), *Diversity in unity: Perspectives from psychology and behavioral sciences* (pp. 629–637). Routledge / Taylor & Francis Group.

49. Douglas, K. M., Sutton, R. M., Callan, M. J., Dawtry, R. J., & Harvey, A. J. (2016). Someone is pulling the strings: Hypersensitive agency detection and belief in conspiracy theories. *Thinking and Reasoning*, 22, 57–77, https://doi.org/10.1080/13546783 .2015.1051586.

50. Van Prooijen & Douglas, Belief in conspiracy theories, p. 901.

51. Douglas et al., Someone is pulling the strings.

52. Van Prooijen, J.-W. (2017). Why education predicts decreased belief in conspiracy theories. *Applied Cognitive Psychology*, 31(1), 50–58.

53. Van Prooijen, J.-W., & Acker, M. (2015). The influence of control on belief in conspiracy theories: Conceptual and applied extensions. *Applied Cognitive Psychology*, 29(5), 753–761, https://doi.org/10.1002/acp.3161.

54. Van Prooijen & Acker, The influence of control, p. 755.

55. Van Prooijen, J. W., & Van Vugt, M. (2018). Conspiracy theories: Evolved functions and psychological mechanisms. *Perspectives on Psychological Science*, 13(6), 770–788. See also Weeks, B. E. (2015). Emotions, partisanship, and misperceptions: How anger and anxiety moderate the effect of partisan bias on susceptibility to political misinformation. *Journal of Communication*, 65(4), 699–719.

56. Brader, T., Marcus, G. E., & Miller, K. (2011). Emotion and public opinion. In G. C. Edwards III, L. R. Jacobs, & R. Y. Shapiro (Eds.), *The Oxford handbook of American public opinion and the media* (pp. 384–401). Oxford University Press.

57. Valentino, N. A., Brader, T., Groenendyk, E. W., Gregorowicz, K., & Hutchings, V. L. (2011). Election night's alright for fighting: The role of emotions in political participation. *The Journal of Politics*, 73(1), 156–170. Lerner, J. S., & Keltner, D. (2001). Fear, anger, and risk. *Journal of Personality and Social Psychology*, 81(1), 146.

58. Pipes, D. (1997). *Conspiracy: How the paranoid style flourishes and where it comes from*. Simon & Schuster.

59. Uscinski, J. E., & Parent, J. M. (2014). *American conspiracy theories*. Oxford University Press.

60. Uscinski & Parent, *American conspiracy theories.* Miller, J. M., Farhart, C. E., & Saunders, K. L. (2021, April). Losers' conspiracy: Elections and conspiratorial thinking. In *New York Area Political Psychology Meeting, May* (Vol. 8, p. 1017).

61. Uscinski, J. E. (2020). *Conspiracy theories: A primer*. Rowman & Littlefield.

62. Quoted in Novetsky, R., Bonja, R., & Young, A. (2022, May 16). The racist theory behind so many mass shootings. *The New York Times Daily Podcast*, https://www.nytimes.com /2022/05/16/podcasts/the-daily/buffalo-shooting-replacement-theory.html.

63. Leman, P., & Cinnirella, M. (2007). A major event has a major cause: Evidence for the role of heuristics in reasoning about conspiracy theories. *Social Psychological Review*, 9, 18–28.

64. Uscinski, J. E. (2018). *Conspiracy theories and the people who believe them*. Oxford University Press.

65. Van Prooijen, J.-W. (2018). *The psychology of conspiracy theories*. Routledge, p. 84.

66. Miller, J. M. (2020). Psychological, political, and situational factors combine to boost COVID-19 conspiracy theory beliefs. *Canadian Journal of Political Science / Revue canadienne de science politique*, 53(2), 327–334.

67. Ahmed, W., Vidal-Alaball, J., Downing, J., & Seguí, F. L. (2020). COVID-19 and the 5G conspiracy theory: Social network analysis of Twitter data. *Journal of Medical Internet Research*, 22(5), e19458.

68. Graeupner, D., & Coman, A. (2017). The dark side of meaning-making: How social exclusion leads to superstitious thinking. *Journal of Experimental Social Psychology*, 69, 218–222, https://doi.org/10.1016/j.jesp.2016.10.003.

69. Ball, P., & Maxmen, A. (2020). The epic battle against coronavirus misinformation and conspiracy theories. *Nature*, 581(7809), 371–375.

70. Van Prooijen & Van Vugt, Conspiracy theories.

71. Van Prooijen, *The psychology of conspiracy theories*, p. 63.

72. Petersen, M. B. (2020). The evolutionary psychology of mass mobilization: How disinformation and demagogues coordinate rather than manipulate. *Current Opinion in Psychology*, 35, 71–75.

73. Petersen, The evolutionary psychology of mass mobilization, p. 9.

74. Kim, Y. (2022). How conspiracy theories can stimulate political engagement. *Journal of Elections, Public Opinion and Parties*, 32(1), 1–21.

75. Goertzel, T. (1994). Belief in conspiracy theories. *Political Psychology*, 15(4), 731–742.

76. Miller, J. M., Saunders, K. L., & Farhart, C. E. (2016). Conspiracy endorsement as motivated reasoning: The moderating roles of political knowledge and trust. *American Journal of Political Science*, 60(4), 824–844. Pierre, J. M. (2020). Mistrust and misinformation: A two-component, socio-epistemic model of belief in conspiracy theories. *Journal of Social and Political Psychology*, 8(2), 617–641.

77. Freeman, D., Waite, F., Rosebrock, L., Petit, A., Causier, C., East, A., . . . & Lambe, S. (2022). Coronavirus conspiracy beliefs, mistrust, and compliance with government guidelines in England. *Psychological Medicine*, 52(2), 251–263.

78. Zuckerman, E. (2021). *Mistrust: Why losing faith in institutions provides the tools to transform them*. W. W. Norton & Company, p. 70.

79. Pew Research Center. (2021). Public trust in government: 1958–2021. Pewresearch.org. https://www.pewresearch.org/politics/2022/06/06/public-trust-in-government -1958-2022/.

80. Brenan, M. (2021). *Americans' trust in media dips to second lowest on record*. Gallup.

81. Rosenblum, N. L., & Muirhead, R. (2019). *A lot of people are saying: The new conspiracism and the assault on democracy*. Princeton University Press, p. 124.

82. Funk, C., Hefferon, M., Kennedy, B., & Johnson, C. (2019, August 2). *Trust and mistrust in Americans' views of scientific experts*. Pew Research Center. Parker, K. (2019). *The growing partisan divide in views of higher education*. Pew Research Center, 19. Gottfried, J., & Liedke, J. (2021). *Partisan divides in media trust widen, driven by a decline among Republicans*. Pew Research Center. Babington, C. (2021, September 9). Partisan views affect trust in government. *Pew Research Center*, https://www.pewtrusts.org/en/trust/archive/summer-2021/partisan-views-affect-trust-in-government.

83. Van der Linden, S., Panagopoulos, C., Azevedo, F., & Jost, J. T. (2021). The paranoid style in American politics revisited: An ideological asymmetry in conspiratorial thinking. *Political Psychology*, 42(1), 23–51.

84. Imhoff, R., Zimmer, F., Klein, O., António, J. H., Babinska, M., Bangerter, A., . . . & van Prooijen, J.-W. (2022). Conspiracy mentality and political orientation across 26 countries. *Nature Human Behaviour*, 6, 392–403. Van Prooijen, J.-W., Krouwel, A. P., & Pollet, T. V. (2015). Political extremism predicts belief in conspiracy theories. *Social Psychological and Personality Science*, 6(5), 570–578.

85. Van der Linden et al., The paranoid style in American politics revisited.

86. Van der Linden et al., The paranoid style in American politics revisited.

87. Enders, A., Farhart, C., Miller, J., Uscinski, J., Saunders, K., & Drochon, H. (2022). Are Republicans and Conservatives more likely to believe conspiracy theories? *Political Behavior*, 1–24.

88. Pasek, J., Stark, T. H., Krosnick, J. A., & Tompson, T. (2015). What motivates a conspiracy theory? Birther beliefs, partisanship, liberal-conservative ideology, and anti-Black attitudes. *Electoral Studies*, 40, 482–489.

89. Brulle, R. J., Carmichael, J., & Jenkins, J. C. (2012). Shifting public opinion on climate change: An empirical assessment of factors influencing concern over climate change in the U.S., 2002–2010. *Climate Change*, 114, 169–188.

90. Guess, A., Nagler, J., & Tucker, J. (2019). Less than you think: Prevalence and predictors of fake news dissemination on Facebook. *Science Advances*, 5(1), eaau4586.

91. Garrett, R. K., & Bond, R. M. (2021). Conservatives' susceptibility to political misperceptions. *Science Advances*, 7(23), eabf1234, p. 1.

92. Allcott, H., & Gentzkow, M. (2017). Social media and fake news in the 2016 election. *Journal of Economic Perspectives*, 31(2), 211–236. DiResta, R., Shaffer, K., Ruppel, B., Sullivan, D., Matney, R., Fox, R., . . . & Johnson, B. (2019). The tactics & tropes of the Internet Research Agency. U.S. Senate Documents, https://digitalcommons.unl.edu/senatedocs/2/.

93. Freelon, D., Bossetta, M., Wells, C., Lukito, J., Xia, Y., & Adams, K. (2020). Black trolls matter: Racial and ideological asymmetries in social media disinformation. *Social Science Computer Review*, 0894439320914853.

94. Rosenblum & Muirhead, *A lot of people are saying*.

3. How Did We Get So Far Apart?

1. Mason, L. (2018). *Uncivil agreement: How politics became our identity*. University of Chicago Press.

2. Mason, *Uncivil agreement*.

3. Fiorina, M. P., & Abrams, S. J. (2008). Political polarization in the American public. *Annual Review of Political Science*, 11, 563–588. Mason, *Uncivil agreement*. Levendusky, M. (2009). *The partisan sort: How liberals became democrats and conservatives became republicans*. University of Chicago Press.

4. Mason, *Uncivil agreement*. Levitsky, S., & Ziblatt, D. (2018). *How democracies die*. Broadway Books.

5. Mason, *Uncivil agreement*. Selway, J. S. (2011). Cross-cuttingness, cleavage structures and civil war onset. *British Journal of Political Science*, 41(1), 111–138, https://doi.org/10.1017/S0007123410000311.

6. APSA-American Political Science Association. (1950). Towards a more responsible two-party system. Supplement to the *American Political Science Review*.

7. APSA-American Political Science Association, Towards a more responsible two-party system, p. 99.

8. Grant, K. N. (2020). *The great migration and the Democratic Party: Black voters and the realignment of American politics in the 20th century*. Temple University Press. Wilkerson, I. (2020). *The warmth of other suns: The epic story of America's great migration*. Penguin UK.

9. Rosenfeld, S. (2017). *The polarizers: Postwar architects of our partisan era*. University of Chicago Press.

10. Hare, C., Poole, K. T., & Rosenthal, H. (2014, February 13). Polarization in Congress has risen sharply. Where is it going next? *The Washington Post*, 13.

11. DeSilver, D. (2022). The polarized Congress of today has roots that go back decades. *Pew Research Center*, https://www.pewresearch.org/fact-tank/2022/03/10/the-polarization-in-todays-congress-has-roots-that-go-back-decades/.

12. Gayner, J. B. (1995). *The contract with America: Implementing new ideas in the US*. The Heritage Foundation, https://www.heritage.org/political-process/report/the-contract-america-implementing-new-ideas-the-us.

13. Andris, C., Lee, D., Hamilton, M. J., Martino, M., Gunning, C. E., & Selden, J. A. (2015). The rise of partisanship and super-cooperators in the US House of Representatives. *PLoS ONE*, 10(4), e0123507.

14. Andris et al., The rise of partisanship.

15. Binder, S. A. (2004). *Stalemate: Causes and consequences of legislative gridlock*. Brookings Institution Press.

16. Fiorina, M. P., & Abrams, S. J. (2008). Political polarization in the American public. *Annual Review of Political Science*, 11, 563–588.
17. Fiorina, M. P., Abrams, S. J., & Pope, J. C. (2010). *Culture war: The myth of a polarized America*. Longman.
18. Abramowitz, A., & Webster, S. (2015, April). All politics is national: The rise of negative partisanship and the nationalization of US House and Senate elections in the 21st century. *Annual Meeting of the Midwest Political Science Association Conference*. Chicago, Illinois, April 16–19, 2015.
19. Levendusky, M. S., & Malhotra, N. (2016). (Mis)perceptions of partisan polarization in the American public. *Public Opinion Quarterly*, 80(S1), 378–391.
20. Iyengar, S., Lelkes, Y., Levendusky, M., Malhotra, N., & Westwood, S. J. (2019). The origins and consequences of affective polarization in the United States. *Annual Review of Political Science*, 22, 129–146.
21. Webster, S. W., & Abramowitz, A. I. (2017). The ideological foundations of affective polarization in the US electorate. *American Politics Research*, 45(4), 621–647.
22. Pew Research Center. (2019, October 10). Partisan antipathy: More intense, more personal, pewresearch.org/politics/2019/10/10/partisan-antipathy-more-intense -more-personal/.
23. Pew Research Center. (2014, June 12). Political polarization and personal life, https://www.pewresearch.org/politics/2014/06/12/section-3-political-polarization -and-personal-life/.
24. McCartney, W. B., Orellana, J., & Zhang, C. (2021). Sort selling: Political polarization and residential choice. *Working Papers, Federal Reserve Bank of Philadelphia*.
25. Landy, J. F., Rottman, J., Batres, C., & Leimgruber, K. L. (2021). Disgusting Demo-crats and repulsive Republicans: Members of political outgroups are considered physically gross. *Personality and Social Psychology Bulletin*, 01461672211065923.
26. Rogowski, J. C., & Sutherland, J. L. (2016). How ideology fuels affective polarization. *Political Behavior*, 38(2), 485–508.
27. Iyengar, S., Lelkes, Y., Levendusky, M., Malhotra, N., & Westwood, S. J. (2019). The origins and consequences of affective polarization in the United States. *Annual Review of Political Science*, 22, 129–146.
28. Iyengar et al., The origins and consequences of affective polarization.
29. Iyengar et al., The origins and consequences of affective polarization.
30. Druckman, J. N., Klar, S., Krupnikov, Y., Levendusky, M., & Ryan, J. B. (2022). (Mis)estimating affective polarization. *The Journal of Politics*, 84(2), 1106–1117.
31. Kingzette, J., Druckman, J. N., Klar, S., Krupnikov, Y., Levendusky, M., & Ryan, J. B. (2021). How affective polarization undermines support for democratic norms. *Public Opinion Quarterly*, 85(2), 663–677.
32. Broockman, D. E., Kalla, J. L., & Westwood, S. J. (2020). Does affective polarization undermine democratic norms or accountability? Maybe not. *American Journal of Political Science*, https://doi.org/10.1111/ajps.12719.

33. Pew Research Center. (2014, June 12). Political polarization and personal life, https://www.pewresearch.org/politics/2014/06/12/section-3-political-polarization -and-personal-life/.
34. Dunn, A., Kiley, J., Scheller, A., Baronavski, C., & Doherty, C. (2020, December 17). Voters say those on the other side "don't get" them. Here's what they want them to know. *Pew Research Center*, https://www.pewresearch.org/politics/2020/12/17/voters-say -those-on-the-other-side-dont-get-them-heres-what-they-want-them-to-know/.
35. Finkel, E. J., Bail, C. A., Cikara, M., Ditto, P. H., Iyengar, S., Klar, S., . . . & Druckman, J. N. (2020). Political sectarianism in America. *Science*, 370(6516), 533–536.
36. Klein, E. (2020). *Why we're polarized*. Simon and Schuster.
37. Pew Research Center (2020, September 10). Voters' Attitudes About Race and Gender Are Even More Divided Than in 2016. Pewresearch.org. https://www.pewresearch.org /politics/2020/09/10/voters-attitudes-about-race-and-gender-are-even-more -divided-than-in-2016/.
38. Sides, J., Tesler, M., & Vavreck, L. (2019). *Identity crisis*. Princeton University Press, p. 9.
39. Norris, P., & Inglehart, R. (2019). *Cultural backlash: Trump, Brexit, and authoritarian populism*. Cambridge University Press.
40. Phillips, A. (2017, June 16). "They're rapists." President Trump's campaign launch speech two years later, annotated. *The Washington Post*, https://www.washingtonpost .com/news/the-fix/wp/2017/06/16/theyre-rapists-presidents-trump-campaign -launch-speech-two-years-later-annotated/.
41. Falcone, M. (2011, March 28). Donald Trump steps up calls for Obama to release birth certificate. *ABC News*, https://abcnews.go.com/Politics/donald-trump-embraces -birther/story?id=13240431.
42. Prokop, A. (2016, September 16). Trump fanned a conspiracy about Obama's birthplace for years. Now he pretends Clinton started it. *Vox*, https://www.vox.com /2016/9/16/12938066/donald-trump-obama-birth-certificate-birther.
43. Tesler, M. (2016, September 19). Birtherism was why so many Republicans liked Trump in the first place. *Washington Post/Monkey Cage*.
44. Mudde, C., & Kaltwasser, C. R. (2017). *Populism: A very short introduction*. Oxford University Press.
45. Mudde, C. (2004). The populist zeitgeist. *Government and Opposition*, 39(4), 541–563.
46. Jagers, J., & Walgrave, S. (2007). Populism as political communication style: An empirical study of political parties' discourse in Belgium. *European Journal of Political Research*, 46(3), 319–345.
47. Jagers & Walgrave, Populism as political communication style.
48. Norris & Inglehart, *Cultural backlash*.
49. Norris & Inglehart, *Cultural backlash*.
50. Norris & Inglehart, *Cultural backlash*.
51. Inglehart & Norris, Trump, Brexit, and the rise of populism, p. 5.

52. Huang, J., Jacoby, S., Strickland, M., & Lai, K. (2016, November 8). Election 2016: Exit polls. *New York Times*, https://www.nytimes.com/interactive/2016/11/08/us/politics/election-exit-polls.html?_r=0.
53. Mason, L., Wronski, J., & Kane, J. V. (2021). Activating animus: The uniquely social roots of Trump support. *American Political Science Review*, 115(4), 1508–1516, pp. 1511, 1516.
54. Pew Research Center. (2020, September 10). Voters' attitudes about race and gender are even more divided than in 2016, https://www.pewresearch.org/politics/2020/09/10/voters-attitudes-about-race-and-gender-are-even-more-divided-than-in-2016/.
55. Pew Research Center. (2019, May 14). Attitudes on same-sex marriage, https://www.pewresearch.org/religion/fact-sheet/changing-attitudes-on-gay-marriage/.
56. Brown, A. (2022, February 11). Deep partisan divide on whether greater acceptance of transgender people is good for society. *Pew Research Center*, https://www.pewresearch.org/fact-tank/2022/02/11/deep-partisan-divide-on-whether-greater-acceptance-of-transgender-people-is-good-for-society/.
57. Gallup. (n.d.) Abortion trends by party identification, https://news.gallup.com/poll/246278/abortion-trends-party.aspx.
58. Layman, G. (2001). *The great divide: Religious and cultural conflict in American party politics.* Columbia University Press.
59. Balmer, R. H. (2021). *Bad faith: Race and the rise of the religious right.* William B. Eerdmans Publishing Company.
60. Balmer, *Bad faith.*
61. Brenan, M. (2022, October 18). Americans' trust in media remains near record low. *Gallup*, https://news.gallup.com/poll/403166/americans-trust-media-remains-near-record-low.aspx.
62. Doherty, C., & Kiley, J. (2019, July 29). Americans have become much less positive about tech companies' impact on the US. *Pew Research Center*, https://www.pewresearch.org/fact-tank/2019/07/29/americans-have-become-much-less-positive-about-tech-companies-impact-on-the-u-s/.
63. UChicago News (2022, January 8). Trust in science is becoming more polarized, survey finds. UChicago News, https://news.uchicago.edu/story/trust-science-becoming-more-polarized-survey-finds.
64. Cohn, N. (2021, September 8). How educational differences are widening America's political rift. *The New York Times*.
65. Pew Research Center. (2016, April 26). A wider ideological gap between more and less educated adults. *Pew Research Center: US Politics and Policy*, https://www.pewresearch.org/politics/2016/04/26/a-wider-ideological-gap-between-more-and-less-educated-adults/.
66. Pew Research Center. (2018, March 20). Trends in party affiliation among demographic groups, https://www.pewresearch.org/politics/2018/03/20/1-trends-in-party-affiliation-among-demographic-groups/.

67. Badger, E. (2019, May 21). How the rural-urban divide became America's political fault line. *The New York Times*.
68. Hmielowski, J. D., Heffron, E., Ma, Y., & Munroe, M. A. (2021). You've lost that trusting feeling: Diminishing trust in the news media in rural versus urban US communities. *The Social Science Journal*, 1–15.
69. Galston, W., & Mann, T. (2010). Republicans slide right: The parties aren't equally to blame for Washington's schism. *Brookings Institution*, https://www.brookings.edu/opinions/republicans-slide-right-the-parties-arent-equally-to-blame-for-washingtons-schism/.
70. Grossmann, M., & Hopkins, D. A. (2016). *Asymmetric politics: Ideological Republicans and group interest Democrats*. Oxford University Press.
71. Grossmann, M., & Hopkins, D. A. (2015). Ideological Republicans and group interest Democrats: The asymmetry of American party politics. *Perspectives on Politics*, 13(1), 119–139.
72. Leonard, N. E., Lipsitz, K., Bizyaeva, A., Franci, A., & Lelkes, Y. (2021). The nonlinear feedback dynamics of asymmetric political polarization. *Proceedings of the National Academy of Sciences*, 118(50), 1–11.
73. Mann, T., & Ornstein, N. (2012, April 27). Let's just say it: The Republicans are the problem. *The Washington Post*, https://www.washingtonpost.com/opinions/lets-just-say-it-the-republicans-are-the-problem/2012/04/27/gIQAxCVUIT_story.html.
74. Mann & Ornstein, Let's just say it.
75. Levitsky, S., & Ziblatt, D. (2018). *How democracies die*. Broadway Books, p. 53.
76. Pew Research Center. (2018, March 20). Trends in party affiliation among demographic groups, https://www.pewresearch.org/politics/2018/03/20/1-trends-in-party-affiliation-among-demographic-groups/.
77. Ray, J., & McElwee, S. (2018). The urban/suburban/rural divide in the 2018 midterms. *Data for Progress*, https://wthh.dataforprogress.org/blog/the-urban-suburban-rural-divide-in-the-2018-midterms.
78. Klein, *Why we're polarized*, p. 231.

4. What Does My Team Think?

1. Onorato, R. S., & Turner, J. C. (2004). Fluidity in the self-concept: The shift from personal to social identity. *European Journal of Social Psychology*, 34(3), 257–278, p. 258.
2. Reimer, N. K., Schmid, K., Hewstone, M., & Al Ramiah, A. (2020). Self-categorization and social identification: Making sense of us and them. In D. Chadee (Ed.), *Theories in social psychology* (2nd ed.). Wiley-Blackwell, p. 3.
3. Allport, G. W. (1954). *The nature of prejudice*. Addison-Wesley, p. 20.
4. Tajfel, H. (1969). Cognitive aspects of prejudice. *Journal of Biosocial Science*, 1(S1), 173–191, p. 177.
5. Reimer et al., Self-categorization and social identification, p. 3.
6. Gerard, H. B. (1963). Emotional uncertainty and social comparison. *The Journal of Abnormal and Social Psychology*, 66(6), 568–573, https://doi.org/10.1037

/h0045226. Tajfel, H., Turner, J. C., Austin, W. G., & Worchel, S. (1979). An integrative theory of intergroup conflict. *Organizational Identity: A Reader*, 56(65), 9780203505984-16.

7. Turner, J. C., & Oakes, P. J. (1986). The significance of the social identity concept for social psychology with reference to individualism, interactionism and social influence. *British Journal of Social Psychology*, 25(3), 237–252, p. 239.

8. Berger, P. L., Berger, P. L., & Luckmann, T. (1966). *The social construction of reality: A treatise in the sociology of knowledge.* Anchor, p. 51.

9. Van Bavel, J. J., & Packer, D. J. (2021). *The power of us: Harnessing our shared identities to improve performance, increase cooperation, and promote social harmony.* Little, Brown Spark, p. 25.

10. Haidt, J. (2012). *The righteous mind: Why good people are divided by politics and religion.* Vintage, p. 224.

11. Oyserman, D., Coon, H. M., & Kemmelmeier, M. (2002). Rethinking individualism and collectivism: Evaluation of theoretical assumptions and meta-analyses. *Psychological Bulletin*, 128(1), 3–72, https://doi.org/10.1037/0033-2909.128.1.3.

12. Jetten, J., Postmes, T., & McAuliffe, B. J. (2002). "We're all individuals": Group norms of individualism and collectivism, levels of identification and identity threat. *European Journal of Social Psychology*, 32(2), 189–207, https://doi.org/10.1002/ejsp.65.

13. Tajfel et al., An integrative theory of intergroup conflict, p. 36.

14. Rubin, M., & Hewstone, M. (2004). Social identity, system justification, and social dominance: Commentary on Reicher, Jost et al., and Sidanius et al. *Political Psychology*, 25(6), 823–844.

15. Trepte, S., & Loy, L. S. (2017). Social identity theory and self-categorization theory. In *The International Encyclopedia of Media Effects* (1–13). The Wiley-Blackwell ICA.

16. Tajfel et al., An integrative theory of intergroup conflict, p. 36.

17. Jost, J. T. (2020). *A theory of system justification.* Harvard University Press.

18. Tajfel, H. (1970). Experiments in intergroup discrimination. *Scientific American*, 223(5), 96–103, p. 98.

19. Oakes, P. J. (1987). The salience of social categories. In J. C. Turner, M. A. Hogg, P. J. Oakes, S. D. Rieche, and M. S. Wetherell (Eds.), *Rediscovering the social group: A self-categorization Theory* (pp. 117–141). Oxford: Blackwell.

20. Hornsey, M. J. (2008). Social identity theory and self-categorization theory: A historical review. *Social and Personality Psychology Compass*, 2(1), 204–222.

21. Hogg, M. A., Terry, D. J., & White, K. M. (1995). A tale of two theories: A critical comparison of identity theory with social identity theory. *Social Psychology Quarterly*, 58(4), 255–269, p. 261.

22. Hogg, M. A., & Reid, S. A. (2006). Social identity, self-categorization, and the communication of group norms. *Communication Theory*, 16(1), 7–30, p. 11.

23. Van Bavel & Packer, *The power of us*, p. 41.

24. Hackel, L. M., Coppin, G., Wohl, M. J., & Van Bavel, J. J. (2018). From groups to grits: Social identity shapes evaluations of food pleasantness. *Journal of Experimental Social Psychology*, 74, 270–280.

25. Van Bavel & Packer, *The power of us*.

26. Van Bavel & Packer, *The power of us*, p. 41.

27. Mason, L. (2018). *Uncivil agreement: How politics became our identity*. University of Chicago Press.

28. Hetherington, M., & Weiler, J. (2018). *Prius or pickup? How the answers to four simple questions explain America's great divide*. Houghton Mifflin. Young, D. G. (2020). *Irony and outrage: The polarized landscape of rage, fear, and laughter in the United States*. Oxford University Press

29. Klein, E. (2020). *Why we're polarized*. Simon and Schuster, p. 136

30. Huddy, L., Bankert, A., & Davies, C. (2018). Expressive versus instrumental partisanship in multiparty European systems. *Political Psychology*, 39, 173–199.

31. Green, D., Palmquist, B., & Schickler, E. (2008). *Partisan hearts and minds*. Yale University Press.

32. Green, Palmquist, & Schickler, *Partisan hearts and minds*.

33. Levendusky, M. (2009). *The partisan sort: How liberals became democrats and conservatives became republicans*. University of Chicago Press.

34. Huddy, L., Mason, L., & Aarøe, L. (2015). Expressive partisanship: Campaign involvement, political emotion, and partisan identity. *American Political Science Review*, 109(1), 1–17. Huddy, L., & Bankert, A. (2017). Political partisanship as a social identity. *Oxford research encyclopedia of politics*.

35. Huddy, Mason, & Aarøe, Expressive partisanship.

36. Mason, L., & Wronski, J. (2018). One tribe to bind them all: How our social group attachments strengthen partisanship. *Political Psychology*, 39, 257–277.

37. Mason & Wronski, One tribe to bind them all.

38. Bartels, L. (2002). Beyond the running tally: Partisan bias in political perceptions. *Political Behavior*, 24(2), 117–150. Gerber, A. S., & Huber, G. A. (2010). Partisanship, political control, and economic assessments. *American Journal of Political Science*, 54(1), 153–173. Tilley, J., & Hobolt, S. B. (2011). Is the government to blame? An experimental test of how partisanship shapes perceptions of performance and responsibility. *The Journal of Politics*, 73(2), 316–330. Bisgaard, M. (2015). Bias will find a way: Economic perceptions, attributions of blame, and partisan-motivated reasoning during crisis. *The Journal of Politics*, 77(3), 849–860.

39. Sigelman, L., & Sigelman, C. K. (1984). Judgments of the Carter-Reagan debate: The eyes of the beholders. *Public Opinion Quarterly*, 48(3), 624–628. Rouner, D., & Perloff, R. M. (1988). Selective perception of outcome of first 1984 presidential debate. *Journalism Quarterly*, 65(1), 141–147.

40. Feldman, L. (2011). Partisan differences in opinionated news perceptions: A test of the hostile media effect. *Political Behavior*, 33(3), 407–432.

41. Webster, S. W. (2020). *American rage: How anger shapes our politics*. Cambridge University Press. Huddy, L., Mason, L., & Aarøe, L. (2015). Expressive partisanship: Campaign involvement, political emotion, and partisan identity. *American Political Science Review*, 109(1), 1–17.

42. Webster, *American rage*. Lazarus, R. S. (1991). Progress on a cognitive-motivational-relational theory of emotion. *American Psychologist*, 46(8), 819–834. Sherif, M., & Cantril, H. (1947). *The psychology of ego-involvements: Social attitudes and identifications*. John Wiley and Sons.

43. Mason, *Uncivil agreement*.

44. Mason, L. (2016). A cross-cutting calm: How social sorting drives affective polarization. *Public Opinion Quarterly*, 80(S1), 351–377.

45. Abramowitz, A. I., & Webster, S. W. (2018). Negative partisanship: Why Americans dislike parties but behave like rabid partisans. *Political Psychology*, 39, 119–135. Abramowitz, A. (2010). *The disappearing center: Engaged citizens, polarization, and American democracy*. Yale University Press.

46. Martherus, J. L., Martinez, A. G., Piff, P. K., & Theodoridis, A. G. (2021). Party animals? Extreme partisan polarization and dehumanization. *Political Behavior*, 43(2), 517–540.

47. Cassese, E. C. (2021). Partisan dehumanization in American politics. *Political Behavior*, 43(1), 29–50.

48. Low, medium, and high identity salience were based roughly on the bottom, middle, and highest thirds. COVID data (ages 18–49: *N* Democrats = 119, *N* Republicans = 119; ages 50+: *N* Democrats = 506, *N* Republicans = 421). National survey data were obtained by SSRS (October 20–November 2, 2020) and included oversamples of racial and ethnic minority groups. Analyses were conducted on weighted data (weighted within each age group) to match general population demographics.

49. Low, medium, and high identity salience were based roughly on the bottom, middle, and highest thirds. Election misperception data (ages 18–49: *N* Democrats = 172, *N* Republicans = 94; ages 50+: *N* Democrats = 497, *N* Republicans = 443). National survey data were obtained by SSRS (November 26–December 4, 2020) and included oversamples of racial and ethnic minority groups. Analyses were conducted on weighted data (weighted within each age group) to match general population demographics.

50. CNN. (2021, September 12). How believing the Big Lie has become central to being a Republican, http://cdn.cnn.com/cnn/2021/images/09/12/rel5c.-.partisanship.pdf.

51. Hetherington, M. J. (2008). Turned off or turned on? How polarization affects political engagement. *Red and Blue Nation*, 2, 1–33.

52. Iyengar, S., & Krupenkin, M. (2018). The strengthening of partisan affect. *Political Psychology*, 39, 201–218.

53. Iyengar & Krupenkin, The strengthening of partisan affect.

54. Kalmoe, N. P., & Mason, L. (2022). *Radical American partisanship: Mapping violent hostility, its causes, and the consequences for democracy*. University of Chicago Press.

55. Levitsky, S., & Ziblatt, D. (2018). *How democracies die*. Broadway Books, p. 102.

56. Levitsky & Ziblatt, *How democracies die*, pp. 8–9.
57. Levitsky & Ziblatt, *How democracies die*, p. 170.
58. Levitsky & Ziblatt, *How democracies die*, p. 22.
59. Enyedi, Z. (2016). Populist polarization and party system institutionalization: The role of party politics in de-democratization. *Problems of Post-communism*, 63(4), 210–220. De la Torre, C., & Ortiz Lemos, A. (2016). Populist polarization and the slow death of democracy in Ecuador. *Democratization*, 23(2), 221–241. Ezrow, L., Tavits, M., & Homola, J. (2014). Voter polarization, strength of partisanship, and support for extremist parties. *Comparative Political Studies*, 47(11), 1558–1583.

5. What Guides My Team, Intuition or Evidence?

1. Vickers, N. [@nathanvickers]. (2021, August 5). One parent speaking out against masks and vaccines: "I have a bachelor's degree in logic, a master's in motherhood, and I'm board certified in American freedom." *Twitter*, https://twitter.com/nathanvickers/status/1423334872777699330.
2. Epstein, S., Pacini, R., Denes-Raj, V., & Heier, H. (1996). Individual differences in intuitive–experiential and analytical–rational thinking styles. *Journal of Personality and Social Psychology*, 71(2), 390–405, p. 401, http://dx.doi.org.udel.idm.oclc.org/10.1037/0022-3514.71.2.390.
3. Petty, R. E., & Cacioppo, J. T. (1986). *The elaboration likelihood model of persuasion: Central and peripheral routes to attitude change.* Springer. Chaiken, S. (1980). Heuristic versus systematic information processing and the use of source versus message cues in persuasion. *Journal of Personality and Social Psychology*, 39(5), 752–766, https://doi.org/10.1037/0022-3514.39.5.752.
4. Kahneman, D. (2011). *Thinking, fast and slow*. Macmillan.
5. Alós-Ferrer, C., Garagnani, M., & Hügelschäfer, S. (2016). Cognitive reflection, decision biases, and response times. *Frontiers in Psychology*, 7, 1402.
6. Arceneaux, K., & Vander Wielen, R. J. (2017). *Taming intuition: How reflection minimizes partisan reasoning and promotes democratic accountability.* Cambridge University Press.
7. Garrett, R. K., & Weeks, B. E. (2017). Epistemic beliefs' role in promoting misperceptions and conspiracist ideation. *PLoS ONE*, 12(9), e0184733.
8. Garrett & Weeks, Epistemic beliefs' role, p. 5.
9. Stanovich, K. E., & West, R. F. (2007). Natural myside bias is independent of cognitive ability. *Thinking & Reasoning*, 13(3), 225–247. Baron, J. (1993). Why teach thinking?–An essay. *Applied Psychology*, 42, 191–237, https://doi.org/10.1111/j.1464-0597.1993.tb00731.x; Stanovich, K. E., & West, R. F. (1997). Reasoning independently of prior belief and individual differences in actively open-minded thinking. *Journal of Educational Psychology*, 89(2), 342–357. Svedholm-Häkkinen, A. M., & Lindeman, M. (2018). Actively open-minded thinking: Development of a shortened scale and disentangling attitudes towards knowledge and people. *Thinking & Reasoning*, 24(1), 21–40.

10. Bronstein, M. V., Pennycook, G., Bear, A., Rand, D. G., ..., T. D. (2019). Belief in fake news is associated with delusionality, dogmatism, r..., ...damentalism, and reduced analytic thinking. *Journal of Applied Research in M...1 Cognition*, 8(1), 108–117, https://doi.org/10.1037/h0101832.

11. Frederick, S. (2005). Cognitive reflection and decision making. *J...* *of Economic Perspectives*, 19(4), 25–42.

12. Bronstein et al., Belief in fake news.

13. Rand, D. & Pennycook, G. (2021, October 22). Personal communication [...interview].

14. Pennycook, G., Ross, R. M., Koehler, D. J., & Fugelsang, J. A. (2016). Ath...and agnostics are more reflective than religious believers: Four empirical studies a. meta-analysis. *PLoS ONE*, 11(4), e0153039. Pennycook, G., Cheyne, J. A., Se.., Koehler, D. J., & Fugelsang, J. A. (2012). Analytic cognitive style predicts religiou. and paranormal belief. *Cognition*, 123(3), 335–346. Pennycook, G., Cheyne, J. A., Koehler, D. J., & Fugelsang, J. A. (2020). On the belief that beliefs should change according to evidence: Implications for conspiratorial, moral, paranormal, political, religious, and science beliefs. *Judgment and Decision Making*, 15(4), 476–498.

15. Rand & Pennycook, personal communication.

16. Bronstein et al., Belief in fake news, pp. 8–9.

17. Finkel, E. J., Bail, C. A., Cikara, M., Ditto, P. H., Iyengar, S., Klar, S., . . . & Druckman, J. N. (2020). Political sectarianism in America. *Science*, 370(6516), 533–536.

18. Hibbing, J. R., Smith, K. B., & Alford, J. R. (2013). *Predisposed: Liberals, conservatives, and the biology of political differences*. Routledge.

19. Jost, J. T., Glaser, J., Kruglanski, A. W., & Sulloway, F. J. (2003). Political conservatism as motivated social cognition. *Psychological Bulletin*, 129(3), 339–375. Jost, J. T., & Krochik, M. (2014). Ideological differences in epistemic motivation: Implications for attitude structure, depth of information processing, susceptibility to persuasion, and stereotyping. In A. J. Elliot, *Advances in Motivation Science*, Vol. 1 (181–231). Elsevier Academic Press.

20. Jost, J. T. (2017). Ideological asymmetries and the essence of political psychology. *Political Psychology*, 38(2), 167–208. Federico, C. M., & Ekstrom, P. D. (2018). The political self: How identity aligns preferences with epistemic needs. *Psychological Science*, 29(6), 901–913. Jost, J. T., Federico, C. M., & Napier, J. L. (2013). Political ideologies and their social psychological functions. In M. Freeden, L. T. Sargent, & M. Stears (Eds.), *Handbook of political ideologies* (pp. 232–250). Oxford University Press. Jost, J. T., Sterling, J., & Stern, C. (2017). Getting closure on conservatism, or the politics of epistemic and existential motivation. In C. Kopetz & A. Fishbach (Eds.), *The motivation-cognition interface; from the lab to the real world: A Festschrift in honor of Arie W. Kruglanski*. Psychology Press.

21. Deppe, K. D., Gonzalez, F. J., Neiman, J., Pahlke, J., Smith, K., & Hibbing, J. R. (2015). Reflective liberals and intuitive conservatives: A look at the Cognitive Reflection Test and ideology. *Judgment and Decision Making*, 10(4), 314–331.

22. Ruisch, B. C. ... , C. (2020). The confident conservative: Ideological differences in judgment decision-making confidence. *Journal of Experimental Psychology: General*, 27–544.

23. Van der Lan ... S., Panagopoulos, C., Azevedo, F., & Jost, J. T. (2021). The paranoid style in politics revisited: An ideological asymmetry in conspiratorial thinking. *Politi ... ology*, 42(1), 23–51, https://doi.org/10.1111/pops.12681. Young, D. G. ... oney, E. K., Bleakley, A., & Langbaum, J. B. (2022). "I feel it in my gut": Ep ... ic motivations, political beliefs, and misperceptions of COVID-19 and the 2020 U ... esidential election. *Journal of Social and Political Psychology*, 10(2), 643–656, p://doi.org/10.23668/psycharchives.6523.

24. ... scinski, J. E., Enders, A. M., Klofstad, C., Seelig, M., Funchion, J., Everett, C., . . . & Murthi, M. (2020). Why do people believe COVID-19 conspiracy theories? *Harvard Kennedy School Misinformation Review*, 1(3), https://doi.org/10.37016/mr-2020 -015. Havey, N. F. (2020). Partisan public health: How does political ideology influence support for COVID-19 related misinformation? *Journal of Computational Social Science*, 3(2), 319–342.

25. DeVerna, M. R., Guess, A. M., Berinsky, A. J., Tucker, J. A., & Jost, J. T. (2022). Rumors in retweet: Ideological asymmetry in the failure to correct misinformation. *Personality and Social Psychology Bulletin*, 01461672221114222.

26. Enders, A., Farhart, C., Miller, J., Uscinski, J., Saunders, K., & Drochon, H. (2022). Are Republicans and Conservatives more likely to believe conspiracy theories? *Political Behavior*, (July 22), 1–24.

27. Deppe, K. D., Gonzalez, F. J., Neiman, J., Pahlke, J., Smith, K., & Hibbing, J. R. (2015). Reflective liberals and intuitive conservatives: A look at the Cognitive Reflection Test and ideology. *Judgment and Decision Making*, 10(4), 314–331. Saribay, S. A., & Yilmaz, O. (2017). Analytic cognitive style and cognitive ability differentially predict religiosity and social conservatism. *Personality and Individual Differences*, 114, 24–29. Yilmaz, O., & Saribay, S. A. (2017). The relationship between cognitive style and political orientation depends on the measures used. *Judgment and Decision Making*, 12(2), 140–147.

28. Hare, C., & Poole, K. T. (2014). The polarization of contemporary American politics. *Polity*, 46(3), 411–429.

29. Layman, G. (2001). *The great divide: Religious and cultural conflict in American party politics*. Columbia University Press.

30. Oliver, J. E., & Wood, T. J. (2018). *Enchanted America: How intuition and reason divide our politics*. University of Chicago Press.

31. Oliver & Wood, *Enchanted America*, p. 92.

32. Oliver & Wood, *Enchanted America*, p. 114.

33. Tripodi, F. B. (2022). *The propagandists' playbook: How conservative elites manipulate search and threaten democracy*. Yale University Press, p. 19.

34. Tripodi, *The propagandists' playbook*, p. 19.

35. Federico, C. M., & Ekstrom, P. D. (2018). The political s... preferences with epistemic needs. *Psychological Science*, 29 identity aligns 913.

36. Bakker, B. N., Lelkes, Y., & Malka, A. (2021). Rethinking the ... reported personality traits and political preferences. *American Po... cience Review*, een self- 115(4), 1482–1498.

37. Bakker, Lelkes, & Malka, Rethinking the link between, p. 1496.

38. Arceneaux, K., & Vander Wielen, R. J. (2017). *Taming intuition: How re...n minimizes partisan reasoning and promotes democratic accountability*. Cambridge Uni...ty Press.

39. Young et al., "I feel it in my gut."

40. Valuing intuition and emotion and valuing evidence and data were measured us...items from Garrett and Weeks (2017). Respondents were asked to what extent they agreed or disagreed with the following: "I trust my gut to tell me what's true and what's no..." "I trust my initial feelings about the facts." "My initial impressions are almost always right." "I can usually feel when a claim is true or false even if I can't explain how I know." Items were averaged to create an "epistemic feelings" score (ages 18–49: mean (M) = 4.62, standard deviation (SD) = 1.11, α = .80; ages 50+: M = 4.80, SD = 1.03, α = .79). Respondents were also asked to what extent they agreed or disagreed (on a scale of 1 to 7) with the following statements: "Evidence is more important than whether something feels true." "A hunch needs to be confirmed with data." "I trust the facts, not my instincts, to tell me what is true." "I need to be able to justify my beliefs with evidence." Items were averaged to create an "epistemic evidence" score (ages 18–49: M = 4.96, SD = 1.15, α = .77; ages 50+: M = 5.50, SD = .98, α = .71).

41. National survey data were obtained by SSRS from November 26 to December 4, 2020, and included oversamples of racial and ethnic minority groups. Analyses were conducted on weighted data (weighted within each age group) to match general population demographics (ages 18–49: $N = 404$; ages 50+: $N = 1311$).

42. The full analysis is found in Young et al., "I feel it in my gut."

43. Oliver & Wood, *Enchanted America*, p. 88.

44. Pirro, A. L., & Taggart, P. (2022). Populists in power and conspiracy theories. *Party Politics*, 13540688221077071.

45. Oliver & Wood, *Enchanted America*, p. 115.

46. Mudde, C. (2004). The populist zeitgeist. *Government and Opposition*, 39(4), 541–563. Fieschi, C. (2019). *Populocracy: The tyranny of authenticity and the rise of populism*. Agenda Publishing, pp. 89–116. Jagers, J., & Walgrave, S. (2007). Populism as political communication style: An empirical study of political parties' discourse in Belgium. *European Journal of Political Research*, 46(3), 319–345.

47. Betz, H. G., & Johnson, C. (2004). Against the current—stemming the tide: The nostalgic ideology of the contemporary radical populist right. *Journal of Political Ideologies*, 9(3), 311–327. Mede, N. G., & Schäfer, M. S. (2020). Science-related populism: Conceptualizing populist demands toward science. *Public Understanding of Science*, 29(5), 473–491.

48. Mercieca, J... *Demagogue for president: The rhetorical genius of Donald Trump.* Texas A&... ...rsity Press.

49. Rucker, ...ey, J., & Paletta, D. (2018, November 27). Trump slams Fed chair, ...te change and threatens to cancel Putin meeting in wide-ranging question... The Post. *The Washington Post*, p. 27.

50. Bump,... ...2018, March 13). Objective information has less of a place in an intuition-...sidency. *The Washington Post*, https://www.washingtonpost.com/news .../wp/2018/03/13/objective-information-has-less-of-a-place-in-an-intuition -b...d-presidency/.

51. ...mp, Objective information has less of a place.

52. Garret & Weeks, Epistemic beliefs' role.

53. Arceneaux, K., & Vander Wielen, R. J. (2017). *Taming intuition: How reflection minimizes partisan reasoning and promotes democratic accountability.* Cambridge University Press.

54. Evans, J. S. B., & Stanovich, K. E. (2013). Dual-process theories of higher cognition: Advancing the debate. *Perspectives on Psychological Science*, 8(3), 223–241, p. 229.

55. Epstein, S. (1994). Integration of the cognitive and the psychodynamic unconscious. *American Psychologist*, 49(8), 709–724, p. 715.

56. Haselton, M. G., Bryant, G. A., Wilke, A., Frederick, D. A., Galperin, A., Frankenhuis, W. E., & Moore, T. (2009). Adaptive rationality: An evolutionary perspective on cognitive bias. *Social Cognition*, 27(5), 733–763, p. 736.

57. Greene, J., & Haidt, J. (2002). How (and where) does moral judgment work? *Trends in Cognitive Sciences*, 6(12), 517–523.

58. Van Bavel, J. J., FeldmanHall, O., & Mende-Siedlecki, P. (2015). The neuroscience of moral cognition: From dual processes to dynamic systems. *Current Opinion in Psychology*, 6, 167–172. Van Bavel, J. J., Jenny Xiao, Y., & Cunningham, W. A. (2012). Evaluation is a dynamic process: Moving beyond dual system models. *Social and Personality Psychology Compass*, 6(6), 438–454.

59. Bakker, B. N., Lelkes, Y., & Malka, A. (2021). Reconsidering the link between self-reported personality traits and political preferences. *American Political Science Review*, 115(4), 1482–1498.

60. Evans, J. S. B., & Stanovich, K. E. (2013). Dual-process theories of higher cognition: Advancing the debate. *Perspectives on Psychological Science*, 8(3), 223–241, p. 229.

61. Bakker, B. N., Lelkes, Y., & Malka, A. (2021). Reconsidering the link between self-reported personality traits and political preferences. *American Political Science Review*, 115(4), 1482–1498.

62. Rosenblum, N. L., & Muirhead, R. (2020). *A lot of people are saying.* Princeton University Press.

63. Dwyer, C., & Aubrey, A. (2020, April 3). CDC now recommends Americans consider wearing cloth face coverings in public. *NPR*, https://www.npr.org/sections/coronavirus -live-updates/2020/04/03/826219824/president-trump-says-cdc-now-recommends -americans-wear-cloth-masks-in-public.

64. Carlson, T. (2021, July 27). Tucker Carlson: New mask guidelines are about politics and control. *Fox News*, https://www.foxnews.com/opinion/tucker-carlson-new-mask -guidelines-politics-control.

65. Young, D. G., Rasheed, H., Bleakley, A., & Langbaum, J. B. (2022). The politics of mask-wearing: Political preferences, reactance, and conflict aversion during COVID. *Social Science & Medicine*, 298, 114836.

66. McLamore, Q., Syropoulos, S., Leidner, B., Hirschberger, G., Young, K., Zein, R. A., . . . & Burrows, B. (2022). Trust in scientific information mediates associations between conservatism and coronavirus responses in the US, but few other nations. *Scientific Reports*, 12(1), 1–15.

67. Young et al., The politics of mask-wearing.

68. Parker-Pope, T. (2021, April 22). Do we still need to keep wearing masks outdoors? *The New York Times*, https://www.nytimes.com/2021/04/22/well/live/covid-masks -outdoors.html.

69. Green, E. (2021, May 4). The liberals who can't quit lockdown. *The Atlantic*.

70. Leary, M. R., Diebels, K. J., Davisson, E. K., Jongman-Sereno, K. P., Isherwood, J. C., Raimi, K. T., . . . & Hoyle, R. H. (2017). Cognitive and interpersonal features of intellectual humility. *Personality and Social Psychology Bulletin*, 43(6), 793–813, p. 793.

71. Leary et al., Cognitive and interpersonal features, p. 795.

72. Svedholm-Häkkinen, A. M., & Lindeman, M. (2018). Actively open-minded thinking: Development of a shortened scale and disentangling attitudes towards knowledge and people. *Thinking & Reasoning*, 24(1), 21–40.

73. Koetke, J., Schumann, K., & Porter, T. (2021). Intellectual humility predicts scrutiny of COVID-19 misinformation. *Social Psychological and Personality Science*, 1948550620988242.

74. Huynh, H. P., & Senger, A. R. (2021). A little shot of humility: Intellectual humility predicts vaccination attitudes and intention to vaccinate against COVID-19. *Journal of Applied Social Psychology*, 51(4), 449–460.

75. Bowes, S. M., & Tasimi, A. (2022). Clarifying the relations between intellectual humility and pseudoscience beliefs, conspiratorial ideation, and susceptibility to fake news. *Journal of Research in Personality*, 98, 104220.

76. Grant, A. (2021). *Think again: The power of knowing what you don't know*. Penguin, p. 54.

6. Exemplify Us

1. Barbaro, M. (2022, March 17). The confirmation hearing of Ketanji Brown Jackson. *The Daily* (podcast), *The New York Times*, https://www.nytimes.com/2022/03/23 /podcasts/the-daily/ketanji-brown-jackson-supreme-court-hearings.html.

2. Cameron, D. (2017, April 7). Confirmations for the sitting Supreme Court justices were not nearly as partisan as Judge Gorsuch's. *The Washington Post*, https://www .washingtonpost.com/graphics/politics/scotus-confirmation-votes/.

3. Lauter, D. (2022, March 25). Essential politics: Supreme Court nomination hearings—long awful—have gotten worse. Here's why. *The Washington Post*, https://www.latimes.com /politics/newsletter/2022-03-25/ketanji-brown-jackson-hearings-essential-politics.

4. Bolton, E. (2022, March 22). Graham gets combative with Jackson: "What faith are you, by the way?" *The Hill*, https://thehill.com/homenews/senate/599208-graham-gets -combative-with-jackson-what-faith-are-you-by-the-way/.

5. Sawchuk, S. (2021, May 18). What is critical race theory, and why is it under attack? *Education Week*, https://www. edweek. org/leadership/what-is-critical-race-theory -and-why-is-it-under-attack/2021/05.

6. Kaur, H. (2022, March 24). What the children's books Ted Cruz referenced at Ketanji Brown Jackson's confirmation hearing really say. *CNN*, https://www.cnn.com/2022 /03/24/us/ted-cruz-books-ketanji-brown-jackson-cec/index.html.

7. Barbaro, The confirmation hearing of Ketanji Brown Jackson.

8. Grossmann, M., & Hopkins, D. A. (2016). *Asymmetric politics: Ideological Republicans and group interest Democrats*. Oxford University Press.

9. Grossmann & Hopkins, *Asymmetric politics*.

10. Kreiss, D., Lawrence, R. G., & McGregor, S. C. (2020). Political identity ownership: Symbolic contests to represent members of the public. *Social Media + Society*, 6(2), p. 3, https://doi.org/10.17615/kcmk-3r63.

11. Egan, P. J. (2013). *Partisan priorities: How issue ownership drives and distorts American politics*. Cambridge University Press.

12. Kreiss, Lawrence, & McGregor, Political identity ownership, p. 3.

13. Sprunt, B., & Jingnan, H. (2020, March 24). Hawley's attacks on Ketanji Brown Jackson fuel a surge in online conspiracy chatter. *National Public Radio*.

14. Bump, P. (2022, March 29). It's overly simple to tie all political rhetoric about sexual abuse to QAnon. *The Washington Post*.

15. Lippmann, W., & Curtis, M. (2017). *Public opinion*. Routledge, p. 13.

16. Raju, M. [mkraju]. (2022, March 22). Just asked Durbin about his very testy exchange with Sen. Graham at hearing . . . *Twitter*, https://twitter.com/mkraju/status /1506313915805974529.

17. Bennett, W. L. (2016). *News: The politics of illusion*. University of Chicago Press.

18. Bennett, *News: The politics of illusion*.

19. Iyengar, S. (1994). *Is anyone responsible? How television frames political issues*. University of Chicago Press.

20. Iyengar, S., *Is anyone responsible?*, p. 15.

21. Blumler, J., & Gurevitch, M. (1995). *The crisis of public communication*. Routledge.

22. Boorstin, D. (1971). From news-gathering to news-making: A flood of pseudo-events. In Schramm, W. & Roberts, D. (Eds.), *The process and effects of mass communication* (pp. 116–150). University of Illinois Press.

23. Strömbäck, J. (2008). Four phases of mediatization: An analysis of the mediatization of politics. *International Journal of Press/Politics*, 13, 228–246.

24. Edelman, M. (1988). *Constructing the political spectacle*. University of Chicago Press.

25. Strömbäck, Four phases of mediatization.

26. Hallin, D. C. (1992). Sound bite news: Television coverage of elections, 1968–1988. *Journal of Communication*, 42(2), 5–24.

27. Moyers, B. (1989, November 22). The public mind: Illusions of news. *Public Broadcasting Service*, https://billmoyers.com/content/illusions-news/.

28. Phillips, J. (2022). Affective polarization: Over time, through the generations, and during the lifespan. *Political Behavior*, 44(3), 1–26.

29. Pew Research Center. (2022). Public trust in government: 1958–2022, https://www .pewresearch.org/politics/2022/06/06/public-trust-in-government-1958-2022/.

30. Mutz, D. C. (2015). *In-your-face politics*. Princeton University Press.

31. Mutz, *In-your-face politics*.

32. Bennett, *News: The politics of illusion*, p. 55.

33. Dunaway, J., & Lawrence, R. G. (2015). What predicts the game frame? Media ownership, electoral context, and campaign news. *Political Communication*, 32(1), 43–60, https://doi.org/10.1080/10584609.2014.880975. Lawrence, R. G. (2000). Game-framing the issues: Tracking the strategy frame in public policy news. *Political Communication*, 17(2), 93–114, https://doi.org/10.1080 /105846000198422. Valkenburg, P. M., Semetko, H. A., & de Vreese, C. H. (1999). The effects of news frames on readers' thoughts and recall. *Communication Research*, 26(5), 550–569, https://doi.org/10.1177/009365099026005002.

34. Young, D. G., Hoffman, L. H., & Roth, D. (2019). "Showdowns," "duels," and "nail-biters": How aggressive strategic game frames in campaign coverage fuel public perceptions of incivility. In Boatright, R. G., Shaffer, T. J., Sobieraj, S., & Young, D. G. (Eds.), *A Crisis of Civility?* (pp. 83–94). Routledge.

35. Iyengar, S., Norpoth, H., & Hahn, K. S. (2004). Consumer demand for election news: The horserace sells. *The Journal of Politics*, 66(1), 157–175.

36. Han, J., & Federico, C. M. (2018). The polarizing effect of news framing: Comparing the mediating roles of motivated reasoning, self-stereotyping, and intergroup animus. *Journal of Communication*, 68(4), 685–711.

37. Letukas, L. (2014). *Primetime pundits: How cable news covers social issues*. Lexington Books.

38. Mutz, *In-your-face politics*. Pekary, A. (2021, January 22). CNN Public Editor: It's time to end the panel discussion format. *Columbia Journalism Review*, https://www.cjr.org /public_editor/cnn-public-editor-its-time-to-end-the-panel-discussion-format.php.

39. CNN. (2018, January 12). CNN panel debates if President Trump is a racist, https:// www.youtube.com/watch?v=CxDT9m5d8yI.

40. CNN. (2018, July 24). Panel gets heated over race and Trump's immigration rhetoric, https://www.youtube.com/watch?v=r8_eI-stGQc.

41. Proctor, S. (2020, November 3). CNN panel explodes after Trump makes unfounded claims about mail in ballots in Pennsylvania. *Yahoo News*, https://www.yahoo.com/video

/cnn-panel-explodes-trump-unfounded-claims-mail-ballots-pennsylvania-091240961
.html.

42. Han, J., & Wackman, D. B. (2017). Partisan self-stereotyping: Testing the salience
hypothesis in a prediction of political polarization. *International Journal of Communication*, 11(23), 603–625.

43. Sharockman, A. (2015, January 29). PunditFact checks in on the cable news channels.
Politifact, https://www.politifact.com/article/2015/jan/29/punditfact-checks-cable-
news-channels/.

44. Young, D. G. (2018). Tackling the "rhetorical disadvantage of science": Putting
ourselves back in the story. *Political Communication*, 35(1), 135–139, p. 138.

45. Postman, N. (2005). *Amusing ourselves to death: Public discourse in the age of show
business*. Penguin, p. 90.

46. Scully, R. (2022, March 24). Five of the most memorable moments from Jackson's
confirmation hearings. *The Hill*, https://thehill.com/homenews/senate/599643-top-5
-combative-exchanges-from-ketanji-brown-jacksons-confirmation-hearings.

47. I ran each search four times: once for any mention of "Supreme Court" and then three
separate searches for stories that included both "Supreme Court" and "Lindsey
Graham," "Supreme Court" and "Ted Cruz," and "Supreme Court" and "Cory
Booker" OR "Corey Booker." All searches took place within the period March 21–25,
2022.

48. Berry, J. M., & Sobieraj, S. (2013). *The outrage industry: Political opinion media and
the new incivility*. Oxford University Press.

49. Leonard, N. E., Lipsitz, K., Bizyaeva, A., Franci, A., & Lelkes, Y. (2021). The nonlinear
feedback dynamics of asymmetric political polarization. *Proceedings of the National
Academy of Sciences*, 118(50), 1–11. Grossmann, M., & Hopkins, D. A. (2015).
Ideological Republicans and group interest Democrats: The asymmetry of American
party politics. *Perspectives on Politics*, 13(1), 119–139.

50. Vance, J. D. (2016). *Hillbilly elegy*. HarperCollins.

51. Gabriel, T. (2017, January 12). In Iowa, Trump voters are unfazed by controversies. *The
New York Times*.

52. Quoted in Ecarma, C. (2021, July 6). Sad: J.D. Vance desperately tries to disown anti-Trump
tweets. *Vanity Fair*, https://www.vanityfair.com/news/2021/07/jd-vance-anti-trump
-tweets.

53. Ecarma, Sad: J.D. Vance.

54. Mayorquin, O. (2022, March 28). Ohio Senate race: What to know about JD Vance,
venture capitalist running for office. *USA Today*, https://www.usatoday.com/story
/news/politics/2022/03/28/midterms-2022-jd-vance-senate-candidate-ohio
/7042631001/.

55. Reichman, H. (2021, December 14). "The professors are the enemy": Right-wing
attacks on academic freedom have real repercussions. *Chronicle of Higher Education*,
https://www.chronicle.com/article/the-professors-are-the-enemy.

56. Mangold-Lenett, S. (2021, July 24). J.D. Vance calls for pro-family policy to revitalize the American dream. *Cincinnati Republic*, http://www.cincinnatirepublic.com/vance -pro-family-policy/.

57. CNN. (2022, February 27). State of the union, https://www.cnn.com/videos/politics /2022/02/27/romney-on-gop.cnn.

58. Bennett, W. L. (1990). Toward a theory of press-state. *Journal of Communication*, 40(2), 103–127, p. 106.

59. Bennett, Toward a theory of press-state, p. 125.

60. Wagner, M. W., & Gruszczynski, M. (2018). Who gets covered? Ideological extremity and news coverage of members of the US Congress, 1993 to 2013. *Journalism & Mass Communication Quarterly*, 95(3), 670–690. Also see Padgett, J., Dunaway, J. L., & Darr, J. P. (2019). As seen on TV? How gatekeeping makes the US House seem more extreme. *Journal of Communication*, 69(6), 696–719.

61. Wagner & Gruszczynski, Who gets covered?, p. 671.

62. Wagner & Gruszczynski, Who gets covered?, p. 684.

63. Ornstein, N. (2014, June 19). Yes, polarization is asymmetric—and conservatives are worse. *The Atlantic*, 19.

64. Pickard, V. (2015). *America's battle for media democracy: The triumph of corporate libertarianism and the future of media reform*. Cambridge University Press.

65. Betz, H. G., & Johnson, C. (2004). Against the current—stemming the tide: The nostalgic ideology of the contemporary radical populist right. *Journal of Political Ideologies*, 9(3), 311–327. Meyer, T. (2006). Populismus und Medien. In F. Decker (Ed.), *Populismus. Gefahr für die Demokratie oder nützliches Korrektiv?* (pp. 81–96). VS.

66. Mudde, C. (2004). The populist zeitgeist. *Government and Opposition*, 39(4), 541–563, p. 554.

67. Carlson, M., Robinson, S., & Lewis, S. C. (2021). *News after Trump: Journalism's crisis of relevance in a changed media culture*. Oxford University Press, p. 13.

68. Karpf, D. (2017). Digital politics after Trump. *Annals of the International Communication Association*, 41(2), 198–207, p. 200.

69. Bond, P. (2016, February 29). Leslie Moonves on Donald Trump: "It may not be good for America, but it's damn good for CBS." *The Hollywood Reporter*, 29.

70. DeSantis, R. (2021, July 30). Governor DeSantis issues an executive order ensuring parents' freedom to choose. *Flgov.com*, https://www.flgov.com/2021/07/30/governor -desantis-issues-an-executive-order-ensuring-parents-freedom-to-choose/. Team DeSantis [@teamrondesantis]. (2022, January 2). "When you're over the target, they're going to come after you . . ." *Twitter*, https://twitter.com/teamrondesantis/status /1479633602874908672.

71. Joyella, M. (2021, February 4). Marjorie Taylor Greene tells Congress the news media is "just as guilty as QAnon." *Forbes*, https://www.forbes.com/sites/markjoyella/2021 /02/04/marjorie-taylor-greene-tells-congress-the-news-media-is-just-as-guilty-as -qanon/?sh=3d76c8364201. Alba, D. (2022, January 2). Twitter permanently

suspends Marjorie Taylor Greene's account. *The New York Times*, https://www
.nytimes.com/2022/01/02/technology/marjorie-taylor-greene-twitter.html.

72. Izadi, E. (2021, February 5). The media can't ignore Margorie Taylor Greene. Can they figure out how to cover her? *The Washington Post*.

73. Contorno, S. (2021, August 13). Inside Fox News, DeSantis is "the future of the party." And he's taking advantage. *Tampa Bay Times*.

74. Sievert, J., & McKee, S. C. (2019). Nationalization in US Senate and gubernatorial elections. *American Politics Research*, 47(5), 1055–1080, p. 1055.

75. Hopkins, D. J. (2018). *The increasingly United States: How and why American political behavior nationalized*. University of Chicago Press, p. 3.

76. Sievert & McKee, Nationalization in US Senate and gubernatorial elections, p. 1055. Hopkins, *The increasingly United States*, p. 3.

77. Hopkins, *The increasingly United States*, p. 3

78. Prior, M. (2007). *Post-broadcast democracy: How media choice increases inequality in political involvement and polarizes elections*. Cambridge University Press. Trussler, M. (2021). Get information or get in formation: The effects of high-information environments on legislative elections. *British Journal of Political Science*, 51(4), 1529–1549.

79. Hopkins, *The increasingly United States*, p. 11.

80. Gerber, E. R., & Hopkins, D. J. (2011). When mayors matter: Estimating the impact of mayoral partisanship on city policy. *American Journal of Political Science*, 55(2), 326–339.

81. Hopkins, *The increasingly United States*, p. 11.

82. Abernathy, P. M. (2018). *The expanding news desert*. Center for Innovation and Sustainability in Local Media, School of Media and Journalism, University of North Carolina at Chapel Hill.

83. Abernathy, *The expanding news desert*.

84. Hare, K. (2021, November 30). More than 100 local newsrooms closed during the coronavirus pandemic. *Poynter*, https://www.poynter.org/locally/2021/the-coronavirus -has-closed-more-than-100-local-newsrooms-across-america-and-counting/.

85. Darr, J. P., Hitt, M. P., & Dunaway, J. L. (2018). Newspaper closures polarize voting behavior. *Journal of Communication*, 68(6), 1007–1028.

86. Godfrey, E. (2021, October 5). What we lost when Gannett came to town. *The Atlantic*, https://www.theatlantic.com/politics/archive/2021/10/gannett-local-newspaper -hawk-eye-iowa/619847/.

87. Godfrey, What we lost when Gannett came to town.

88. Darr, J. P., Hitt, M. P., & Dunaway, J. L. (2021). *Home style opinion: How local newspapers can slow polarization*. Cambridge University Press, p. 1.

89. Darr, Hitt, & Dunaway, *Home style opinion*, p. 1.

90. Gentzkow, M., & Shapiro, J. M. (2010). What drives media slant? Evidence from US daily newspapers. *Econometrica*, 78(1), 35–71. Toff, B., & Mathews, N. (2021). Is social media killing local news? An examination of engagement and ownership patterns in US community news on Facebook. *Digital Journalism*, 1–20.

91. Martin, G., & McCrain, J. (2019). Local news and national politics. *American Political Science Review*, 113(2), 372–384, https://doi.org/10.1017/S0003055418000965.
92. Shearer, E., & Tomasik, E. (2022, October 13). After increasing in 2020, layoffs at large U.S. newspapers and digital news sites declined in 2021. *Pew Research Center*, https://www.pewresearch.org/fact-tank/2022/10/13/after-increasing-in-2020 -layoffs-at-large-u-s-newspapers-and-digital-news-sites-declined-in-2021/.
93. Farhi, P. (2017, May 8). Here's what happened the last time Sinclair bought a big-city station. *The Washington Post*, https://www.washingtonpost.com/lifestyle/style/heres-what -happened-the-last-time-sinclair-bought-a-big-city-station/2017/05/08/92433126-33f7 -11e7-b4ee-434b6d506b37_story.html?utm_term=.3188bcfdd784.Google.
94. Martin, G. J., & McCrain, J. (2019). Local news and national politics. *American Political Science Review*, 113(2), 372–384.
95. Hindman, M. (2011). *Less of the same*. FCC, p. 27.
96. Bengani, P. (2019). Hundreds of "pink slime" local news outlets are distributing algorithmic stories and conservative talking points. *Tow Center for Digital Journalism*, https://www.cjr.org/tow_center_reports/hundreds-of-pink-slime-local-news-outlets -are-distributing-algorithmic-stories-conservative-talking-points.php.
97. Tarkov, A. (2012, June 30). Journatic worker takes "This American Life" inside outsourced journalism. *Poynter*, https://www.poynter.org/reporting-editing/2012 /journatic-staffer-takes-this-american-life-inside-outsourced-journalism/.
98. Tarkov, Journatic worker takes "This American Life."
99. Bengani, P. (2021, October 14). The Metric Media network runs more than 1,200 local news sites. Here are some of the non-profits funding them. *Columbia Journalism Review*, https://www.cjr.org/tow_center_reports/metric-media-lobbyists-funding.php. Kennedy, D. (2021, November 3). Follow the money: Right wing funding of "pink slime" websites tracked in new study. *WGBH*, https://www.wgbh.org/news/commentary/2021/11/03 /follow-the-money-right-wing-funding-of-pink-slime-websites-tracked-in-new-study.
100. Uberti, D. (2019, July 24). Democrats are launching "news" outlets to turn swing-state voters against Trump. *Vice News*, https://www.vice.com/en/article/j5wwa3/ democrats-are-launching-news-outlets-to-turn-swing-state-voters-against-trump.
101. Uberti, Democrats are launching "news" outlets.
102. Peterson, E., & Allamong, M. B. (2021). The influence of unknown media on public opinion: Evidence from local and foreign news sources. *American Political Science Review*, 116(2), 719–733.
103. Peterson & Allamong, The influence of unknown media.
104. Fazio, L. K., Brashier, N. M., Payne, B. K., & Marsh, E. J. (2015). Knowledge does not protect against illusory truth. *Journal of Experimental Psychology: General*, 144(5), 993–1002, https://doi.org/10.1037/xge0000098. Fazio, L. K., Rand, D. G., & Pennycook, G. (2019). Repetition increases perceived truth equally for plausible and implausible statements. *Psychonomic Bulletin & Review*, 26(5), 1705–1710, https:// doi.org/10.3758/s13423-019-01651-4.

105. Legum, J., Zekeria, T., & Crosby, R. (2021, November 8). Right wing operatives deploy massive network of fake local news sites to weaponize CRT. *Popular Information*, https://popular.info/p/right-wing-operatives-deploy-massive?s=r.

106. Legum, Zekeria, & Crosby, Right wing operatives.

107. Grumbach, J. (2022). *Laboratories against democracy: How national parties transformed state politics* (Vol. 182). Princeton University Press, p. 13.

108. Pickard, V. (2019). *Democracy without journalism? Confronting the misinformation society*. Oxford University Press, p. 5.

109. Helmore, E. (2019, July 17). The Squad: Progressive Democrats reveal how they got their name. *The Guardian*.

110. Quoted in Cummings, W. (2019, July 14). Trump tells congresswomen to "go back" to the "crime infested places from which they came." *USA Today*.

111. Moore, M. (2022, March 17). AOC, far-left pols urge Biden to bypass Congress on energy, immigration and more. *New York Post*.

112. Hagle, C. (2019, April 12). Six weeks of Fox's Alexandria Ocasio-Cortez obsession: "Totalitarian, ignorant, scary, and waging a 'war on cows.'" *Media Matters*, p. 12.

113. Esposito, E. (2021). Introduction: Critical perspectives on gender, politics and violence. *Journal of Language Aggression and Conflict*, 9(1), 1–20.

114. Relman, E., & Hickey, W. (2021, September 4). AOC is on the ballot: 44% of Americans report seeing a political ad mentioning Alexandria Ocasio-Cortez, alternately a socialist villain and a progressive champion. *Business Insider*.

115. Vote-USA.org, (2020, April 7). Marjorie Green Congressional Campaign Ad. *YouTube*, https://www.youtube.com/watch?v=2oP99HiZ_iA.

116. Bowman, B. (2020, July 1). Lauren Boebert ran against AOC and the "squad," and beat Rep. Scott Tipton in the process. *Rollcall.com*, https://rollcall.com/2020/07/01/lauren-boebert-ran-against-aoc-and-the-squad-and-beat-rep-scott-tipton-in-the-process/.

117. Boebert, L. (2020, June 2). Lauren Boebert For Congress—Say No to Scott Tipton 30. *YouTube*, https://www.youtube.com/watch?v=T0yYeOWmU30.

118. Klein, E. (2020). *Why we're polarized*. Simon and Schuster, p. xix.

119. Leibovich, M. (2019, February 25). How Lindsey Graham went from Trump skeptic to Trump sidekick. *New York Times Magazine*, 25.

7. Separate Us

1. Ajzen, I., & Fishbein, M. (2000). Attitudes and the attitude-behavior relation: Reasoned and automatic processes. *European Review of Social Psychology*, 11(1), 1–33.

2. Gitlin, T. (1978). Media sociology: The dominant paradigm. *Theory and Society*, 6(2), 205–253, p. 216.

3. Wheeler, S. C., DeMarree, K. G., & Petty, R. E. (2014). Understanding prime-to-behavior effects: Insights from the active-self account. *Social Cognition*, 32, 109–123.

4. Peterson, T. (1956). *Magazines in the twentieth century*. University of Illinois Press, p. 66.

5. Turow, J. (1997). *Breaking up America: Advertisers and the new media world.* University of Chicago Press.

6. Pearson, R. (2005). The writer/producer in American television. In Hammond & Mazdon (Eds.), The contemporary television series (pp. 11–26). Edinburgh University Press.

7. Lazarsfeld, P. F., & Merton, R. K. (2000). Organized social action. In P. Marris & S. Thornham (Eds.), *Media studies: A reader.* Edinburgh University Press, p. 249. (Original work published 1948)

8. Katz, E., Blumler, J. G., & Gurevitch, M. (1973). Uses and gratifications research. *The Public Opinion Quarterly,* 37(4), 509–523.

9. Signorielli, N., & Morgan, M. (2009). Cultivation analysis-research and practice. In M. B. Salwen & D. W. Stacks Jr. (Eds.), *An integrated approach to communication theory and Research* (2nd ed., pp. 106–121). Erlbaum.

10. Gerbner, G., Gross, L., Morgan, M., & Signorielli, N. (1980). The mainstreaming of America: Violence profile no. 11. *Journal of Communication,* 30(3), 10–29, p. 15, https://doi.org/10.1111/j.1460-2466.1980.tb01987.x.

11. Morgan, M., & Shanahan, J. (2010). The state of cultivation. *Journal of Broadcasting & Electronic Media,* 54(2), 337–355.

12. Roskos-Ewoldsen, B., Davies, J., & Roskos-Ewoldsen, D. R. (2004). Implications of the mental models approach for cultivation theory. *Communications,* 9, 345–363. Morgan & Shanahan, The state of cultivation.

13. Lippman, J. R., Ward, L. M., & Seabrook, R. C. (2014). Isn't it romantic? Differential associations between romantic screen media genres and romantic beliefs. *Psychology of Popular Media Culture,* 3(3), 128–140.

14. Roskos-Ewoldsen, D. R., Roskos-Ewoldsen, B., & Carpentier, F. R. D. (2002). Media priming: A synthesis. In J. Bryand, D. Zillmann, & M. B. Oliver (Eds.), *Media effects* (pp. 107–130). Routledge.

15. Mastro, D., Behm-Morawitz, E., & Ortiz, M. (2007). The cultivation of social perceptions of Latinos: A mental models approach. *Media Psychology,* 9(2), 347–365. Callanan, V. J., & Rosenberger, J. S. (2011). Media and public perceptions of the police: Examining the impact of race and personal experience. *Policing & Society,* 21(2), 167–189.

16. Mastro, D., Behm-Morawitz, E., & Ortiz, M. (2007). The cultivation of social percep-tions of Latinos: A mental models approach. *Media Psychology,* 9(2), 347–365.

17. Callanan & Rosenberger, Media and public perceptions of the police.

18. Vallone, R., Ross, L., & Lepper, M. (1985). The hostile media phenomenon: Biased perception and perceptions of media bias in coverage of the Beirut massacre. *Journal of Personality and Social Psychology,* 49, 577–585.

19. Coe, K., Tewksbury, D., Bond, B. J., Drogos, K. L., Porter, R. W., Yahn, A., & Zhang, Y. (2008). Hostile news: Partisan use and perceptions of cable news programming. *Journal of Communication,* 58(2), 201–219.

20. Prior, M. (2007). *Post-broadcast democracy: How media choice increases inequality in political involvement and polarizes elections.* Cambridge University Press.

21. Stroud, N. J. (2011). *Niche news: The politics of news choice.* Oxford University Press on Demand.
22. Stroud, *Niche news.*
23. Arceneaux, K., & Johnson, M. (2013). *Changing minds or changing channels? Partisan news in an age of choice.* University of Chicago Press. Guess, A. M., Lyons, B., Nyhan, B., & Reifler, J. (2018). *Avoiding the echo chamber about echo chambers: Why selective exposure to like-minded political news is less prevalent than you think.* The Knight Foundation.
24. Prior, M. (2013). Media and political polarization. *Annual Review of Political Science,* 16, 101–127.
25. Prior, Media and political polarization.
26. Wollebæk, D., Karlsen, R., Steen-Johnsen, K., & Enjolras, B. (2019). Anger, fear, and echo chambers: The emotional basis for online behavior. *Social Media + Society,* 5(2), 2056305119829859.
27. Levendusky, M. (2013). *How partisan media polarize America.* University of Chicago Press.
28. Levendusky, M. S. (2013). Why do partisan media polarize viewers? *American Journal of Political Science,* 57(3), 611–623, p. 613.
29. Davis, N. T., & Dunaway, J. L. (2016). Party polarization, media choice, and mass partisan-ideological sorting. *Public Opinion Quarterly,* 80(S1), 272–297. Levendusky, M. (2009). *The partisan sort: How liberals became Democrats and conservatives became Republicans.* University of Chicago Press.
30. Levendusky, M. (2014, February 3). Are Fox and MSNBC polarizing America? *The Washington Post,* https://www.washingtonpost.com/news/monkey-cage/wp/2014/02/03/are-fox-and-msnbc-polarizing-america/.
31. Young, D. G. (2020). *Irony and outrage: The polarized landscape of rage, fear, and laughter in the United States.* Oxford University Press.
32. Kelly, J. P. (2019). Television by the numbers: The challenges of audience measurement in the age of big data. *Convergence,* 25(1), 113–132.
33. Karpf, D. (2017). Digital politics after Trump. *Annals of the International Communication Association,* 41(2), 198–207, p. 200.
34. Confessore, N. (2022, April 30). How Tucker Carlson reshaped Fox News—and became Trump's heir. *The New York Times,* https://www.nytimes.com/2022/04/30/us/tucker-carlson-fox-news.html.
35. Slater, M. D. (2007). Reinforcing spirals: The mutual influence of media selectivity and media effects and their impact on individual behavior and social identity. *Communication Theory,* 17(3), 281–303.
36. Slater, M. D. (2015). Reinforcing spirals model: Conceptualizing the relationship between media content exposure and the development and maintenance of attitudes. *Media Psychology,* 18(3), 370–395, p. 373.
37. Long, J. A., Eveland, W. P., Jr., & Slater, M. D. (2019). Partisan media selectivity and partisan identity threat: The role of social and geographic context. *Mass Communication and Society,* 22(2), 145–170.

38. Slater, Reinforcing spirals model, p. 387.

39. Haidt, J. (2012). *The righteous mind: Why good people are divided by politics and religion*. Vintage.

40. Berry, J. M., Glaser, J. M., & Schildkraut, D. J. (2021). Race and gender on Fox and MSNBC. In *The Forum* (Vol. 18, No. 3, pp. 297–317). De Gruyter.

41. US Census. (2021). *Race and Hispanic origin*, https://www.census.gov/quickfacts /fact/table/US/PST045221.

42. Barr, J. (2021, June 24). Critical race theory is the hottest topic on Fox News. And it's only getting hotter. *The Washington Post*.

43. Barr, Critical race theory is the hottest topic on Fox News.

44. Smith, G., & Searles, K. (2014). Who let the (attack) dogs out? New evidence for partisan media effects. *Public Opinion Quarterly*, 78(1), 71–99, https://doi.org/10 .1093/poq/nft082. Levendusky, *How partisan media polarize America*.

45. Jamieson, K. H., & Cappella, J. N. (2008). *Echo chamber: Rush Limbaugh and the conservative media establishment*. Oxford University Press. Mason, L. (2018). *Uncivil agreement: How politics became our identity*. University of Chicago Press.

46. Jost, J. T. (2017). Asymmetries abound: Ideological differences in emotion, partisanship, motivated reasoning, social network structure, and political trust. *Journal of Consumer Psychology*, 27(4), 546–553, https://doi.org/10.1016/j.jcps.2017.08 .004.

47. Hmielowski, J. D., Hutchens, M. J., & Beam, M. A. (2020). Asymmetry of partisan media effects? Examining the reinforcing process of conservative and liberal media with political beliefs. *Political Communication*, 37(6), 852–868, p. 863.

48. Feldman, L., Myers, T. A., Hmielowski, J. D., & Leiserowitz, A. (2014). The mutual reinforcement of media selectivity and effects: Testing the reinforcing spirals framework in the context of global warming. *Journal of Communication*, 64(4), 590–611. Davis, N. T. (2018). Perceptions of elites and (asymmetric) sorting. *Research & Politics*, 5(2), 2, https://doi.org/10.1177/2053168018777099.

49. Lin, M. C., Haridakis, P. M., & Hanson, G. (2016). The role of political identity and media selection on perceptions of hostile media bias during the 2012 presidential campaign. *Journal of Broadcasting & Electronic Media*, 60(3), 425–447.

50. Reid, S. A. (2012). A self-categorization explanation for the hostile media effect. *Journal of Communication*, 62(3), 381–399. Feldman, L. (2011). Partisan differences in opinionated news perceptions: A test of the hostile media effect. *Political Behavior*, 33(3), 407–432.

51. Levendusky, *How partisan media polarize America*.

52. Lee, S., & Cho, J. (2022). When CNN praises Trump: Effects of content and source on hostile media perception. *SAGE Open*, 12(1), 21582440221079890.

53. Hampton, R., & Martinelli, M. (2020, November 7). Here's the moment Fox News called the election for Biden. *Slate*, https://slate.com/news-and-politics/2020/11/fox -news-biden-winner-presidential-election.html.

54. See Bump, P. (2021, February 11). A year of election misinformation from Trump, visualized. *The Washington Post*, Critical race theory is the hottest topic on Fox News. And it's only getting hotter.

55. Folkenflik, D. (2020, June 13). Conflict flared at Fox News after Biden's victory in 2020, former Fox editor says. *NPR*, https://www.npr.org/2022/06/13 /1104825880/conflict-flared-at-fox-news-after-bidens-victory-in-2020-former -fox-editor-says.

56. Barr, J. (2020, December 27). Why these Fox News loyalists have changed the channel to Newsmax. *The Washington Post*, https://www.washingtonpost.com/media/2020 /12/27/fox-news-viewers-switch-to-newsmax/.

57. Stelter, B. (2020, December 8). Newsmax TV scores a ratings win over Fox News for the first time ever. *CNN*, https://www.cnn.com/2020/12/08/media/newsmax-fox-news -ratings/index.html.

58. Barr, Why these Fox News loyalists.

59. Grynbaum, M. (2021, May 28). Fox News intensifies its pro-Trump politics as dissenters depart. *The New York Times*, https://www.nytimes.com/2021/05/28 /business/media/trump-fox-news.html.

60. Wemple, E. (2020, December 5). Bogus "suitcase" story rolls away from Fox News. *The Washington Post*, https://www.washingtonpost.com/opinions/2020/12/05 /bogus-suitcase-story-rolls-away-fox-news/.

61. Baker, S. (2021, January 7). Republicans and Fox News personalities are fanning the flames of an evidence-free theory that antifa helped storm the Capitol with Trump supporters. *Business Insider*, https://www.businessinsider.com/capitol-siege-antifa -false-theory-republicans-fox-news-2021-1.

62. Folkenflik, D. (2021, November 22). 2 Fox News commentators resign over Tucker Carlson series on the Jan 6 siege. *NPR*, https://www.npr.org/2021/11/21 /1052837157/fox-resignations-tucker-carlson-patriot-purge-documentary.

63. Grynbaum, M. (2022, March 27). Chris Wallace says life at Fox News became "unsus-tainable." *The New York Times*, https://nytimes.com/2022/03/27/business/media /chris-wallace-cnn-fox-news.html.

64. Gardiner, G. (2019). *Legal epistemology*. Oxford Bibliographies.

65. Spencer, S. (2020, November 25). Baseless conspiracy theory targets another election technology company. *FactCheck.org*, https://www.factcheck.org/2020/11/baseless -conspiracy-theory-targets-another-election-technology-company/.

66. Klein, C. (2022, March 9). Fox News won't be getting out of a $2.7 billion lawsuit over its rigged voting machine claims. *Vanity Fair*, https://www.vanityfair.com/news/2022 /03/fox-news-smartmatic-lawsuit.

67. Quinn, M. (2021, March 23). Sidney Powell tells court "no reasonable person" would take her voter fraud claims as fact. *CBS News*, https://www.cbsnews.com/news/sidney -powell-dominion-defamation-lawsuit-voter-fraud/.

68. Petersen, M. B. (2020). The evolutionary psychology of mass mobilization: How disinformation and demagogues coordinate rather than manipulate. *Current Opinion in Psychology*, 35, 71–75.
69. Thompson, S. A., Yourish, K., Peters, J. W. (2023, February 25). What Fox News hosts said privately vs. publicly about voter fraud. *The New York Times*, https://www.nytimes.com/interactive/2023/02/25/business/media/fox-news-dominion-tucker-carlson.html.
70. US Dominion, Inc v. Fox News Network, LLC. N21C-03-257 (2023). Brief in Support of its Motion for Summary Judgment on Liability of Fox News Network, pp. 1–2.
71. US Dominion, Inc v. Fox News Network, LLC, p. 2.
72. US Dominion, Inc v. Fox News Network, LLC, p. 23.
73. Baker, P. (2023, March 4). Inside the panic at Fox News after the 2020 election. *The New York Times*.
74. Baker, Inside the panic at Fox News after the 2020 election.
75. US Dominion, Inc v. Fox News Network, LLC, p. 155. For details of Tucker Carlson's departure, see Battaglio, S. (2023, April 24). Tucker Carlson departs Fox News, pushed out by Rupert Murdoch. *Los Angeles Times*. https://www.latimes.com/entertainment-arts/business/story/2023-04-24/tucker-carlson-is-out-at-fox-news.
76. Cited in Chase, R. (2023, February 18). Fox News hosts doubted 2020 election fraud claims off camera as they promoted them on air. *Los Angeles Times*, https://www.latimes.com/world-nation/story/2023-02-18/off-camera-fox-hosts-doubted-2020-election-fraud-claims.
77. Roscoe, A. & Folkenflick, D. (2023, January 22). Dominion Voting Systems $1.6 billion defamation suit against Fox News goes to trial. *NPR*, https://www.npr.org/2023/01/22/1150647042/dominion-voting-systems-1-6-billion-defamation-suit-against-fox-news-goes-to-tri.
78. Tripodi, F. B. (2022). *The propagandists' playbook: How conservative elites manipulate search and threaten democracy*. Yale University Press, p. 14.
79. Office of the Inspector General. (2019, December). *Review of four FISA applications and other aspects of the FBI's Crossfire Hurricane Investigation*, https://www.justice.gov/storage/120919-examination.pdf.
80. Wemple, E. (2019, December 26). Rachel Maddow rooted for the Steele dossier to be true. Then it fell apart. *The Washington Post*, https://www.washingtonpost.com/opinions/2019/12/26/rachel-maddow-rooted-steele-dossier-be-true-then-it-fell-apart/.
81. Rachel Maddow Show. (2017, March 8). The Rachel Maddow Show transcript. *MSNBC*, https://www.msnbc.com/transcripts/rachel-maddow-show/2017-03-08-msna971386.
82. Druckman, J. N., Levendusky, M. S., & McLain, A. (2018). No need to watch: How the effects of partisan media can spread via interpersonal discussions. *American Journal of Political Science*, 62(1), 99–112.

83. Song, H., & Boomgaarden, H. G. (2017). Dynamic spirals put to test: An agent-based model of reinforcing spirals between selective exposure, interpersonal networks, and attitude polarization. *Journal of Communication*, 67(2), 256–281.

84. Muddiman, A., Budak, C., Romas, B., Kim, Y., Murray, C., Burniston, M. M., . . . & Stroud, N. J. (2020, December 17). *Cable and nightly network news coverage of coronavirus.* Center for Media Engagement.

85. Jamieson, K. H., & Albarracin, D. (2020). The relation between media consumption and misinformation at the outset of the SARS-CoV-2 pandemic in the US. *The Harvard Kennedy School Misinformation Review.*

86. Romer, D., & Jamieson, K. H. (2021). Conspiratorial thinking, selective exposure to conservative media, and response to COVID-19 in the US. *Social Science & Medicine*, 291, 114480.

87. Motta, M., Stecula, D., & Farhart, C. (2020). How right-leaning media coverage of COVID-19 facilitated the spread of misinformation in the early stages of the pandemic in the US. *Canadian Journal of Political Science*, 53(2), 335–342, p. 340.

88. Simonov, A., Sacher, S. K., Dubé, J. P. H., & Biswas, S. (2020). *The persuasive effect of Fox News: Non-compliance with social distancing during the Covid-19 pandemic* (No. w27237). National Bureau of Economic Research.

89. Ball, P., & Maxmen, A. (2020). The epic battle against coronavirus misinformation and conspiracy theories. *Nature*, 581(7809), 371–375.

90. Ruiz, J. B., & Bell, R. A. (2021). Predictors of intention to vaccinate against COVID-19: Results of a nationwide survey. *Vaccine*, 39(7), 1080–1086. Motta, M., & Stecula, D. (2021). The influence of partisan media in the face of global pandemic: How news media influenced COVID-19 vaccine hesitancy. *SocArXiv*, https://doi.org/10.31235/osf.io/xj4nq.

91. Rand, D. & Pennycook, G. (2021, October 22). Personal communication [zoom interview].

92. Newman, N., Fletcher, R., Robinson, C. T., Eddy, K., & Nielsen, R. K. (2022). *Reuters digital news report 2022.* University of Oxford, Reuters Institute for the Study of Journalism, https://reutersinstitute.politics.ox.ac.uk/sites/default/files/2022-06/Digital_News-Report_2022.pdf.

93. Jurkowitz, M., Mitchell, A., Shearer, E., & Walker, M. (2020, January 24). Democrats report much higher levels of trust in a number of news sources than Republicans. *Pew Research Center*, https://www.pewresearch.org/journalism/2020/01/24/democrats-report-much-higher-levels-of-trust-in-a-number-of-news-sources-than-republicans/.

8. Curate Us

1. Haidt, J. (2022, April 11). Why the past 10 years of American life have been uniquely stupid. *The Atlantic*, https://www.theatlantic.com/magazine/archive/2022/05/social-media-democracy-trust-babel/629369/.

2. Altheide, D. L., & Snow, R. (1979). *Media logic.* SAGE.

3. Abbate, J. (2000). *Inventing the internet*. MIT Press.
4. Baran, P. (2018). Paul Baran and the origins of the internet. RAND Objective Analysis, *Effective Solutions*, http://www.rand.org/about/history/baran.html.
5. Shirky, C. (2008). *Here comes everybody: The power of organizing without organizations*. Penguin.
6. Jackson, S. J., Bailey, M., & Welles, B. F. (2020). *#HashtagActivism: Networks of race and gender justice*. MIT Press.
7. Jackson, S. (2019, December 27). Twitter made us better. *The New York Times*, https://www.nytimes.com/interactive/2019/12/27/opinion/sunday/twitter-social-media.html.
8. Bonilla, Y., & Rosa, J. (2015). #Ferguson: Digital protest, hashtag ethnography, and the racial politics of social media in the United States. *American Ethnologist*, 42(1), 4–17, p. 7.
9. Graham, R., & Smith, S. (2016). The content of our #characters: Black Twitter as counterpublic. *Sociology of Race and Ethnicity*, 2(4), 433–449.
10. Graham & Smith, Content of our #characters.
11. Freelon, D., McIlwain, C., & Clark, M. (2018). Quantifying the power and consequences of social media protest. *New Media & Society*, 20(3), 990–1011.
12. Tufekci, Z. (2017). *Twitter and tear gas: The power and fragility of networked protest*. Yale University Press.
13. Jamieson, K. H. (2020). *Cyberwar: How Russian hackers and trolls helped elect a president; what we don't, can't, and do know*. Oxford University Press.
14. Jamieson, *Cyberwar*.
15. Jamieson, *Cyberwar*.
16. Carmichael, F., & Haynes, C. (2021, August 10). Facebook removes anti-vax influencer campaign. *BBC News*, https://www.bbc.com/news/blogs-trending-58167339.
17. Johnson, C., & Marcellino, W. (2021). Reining in COVID-19 disinformation from China, Russia and elsewhere. *RAND Corporation*, https://www.rand.org/blog/2021/11/reining-in-covid-19-disinformation-from-china-russia.html.
18. Barnes, J. E. (2021, August 5). Russian disinformation targets vaccines and the Biden administration. *The New York Times*, https://www.nytimes.com/2021/08/05/us/politics/covid-vaccines-russian-disinformation.html.
19. Dovere, E. (2022, June 19). US is worried about Russia using new efforts to exploit divisions in 2022 midterms. *CNN*, https://www.cnn.com/2022/06/19/politics/us-worries-russia-exploit-divisions-2022-midterms/index.html.
20. Young, D. G., & McGregor, S. (2020, February 14). Mass propaganda used to be difficult, but Facebook made it easy. *The Washington Post*.
21. Lazarsfeld, P. F., & Merton, R. K. (2000). Organized social action. In P. Marris & S. Thornham (Eds.), *Media studies: A reader*, p. 249. (Original work published 1948). NYT Press.
22. Guess, A., Nyhan, B., Lyons, B., & Reifler, J. (2018). *Avoiding the echo chamber about echo chambers*. Knight Foundation.

23. Carrett, R. K. (2017). The "echo chamber" distraction: Disinformation campaigns are the problem, not audience fragmentation. *Journal of Applied Research in Memory and Cognition*, 6(4), 370–376, https://doi.org/10.1016/j.jarmac.2017.09.011.
24. Katz, E. (1957). The two-step flow of communication: An up-to-date report on an hypothesis. *Public Opinion Quarterly*, 21(1), 61–78.
25. Jamieson, *Cyberwar*.
26. Hao, K. (2021, September 6). Troll farms reached 140 million Americans a month on Facebook before 2020 election, internal report shows. *MIT Technology Review*, https://www.technologyreview.com/2021/09/16/1035851/facebook-troll-farms -report-us-2020-election/.
27. Reddi, M., Kuo, R., & Kreiss, D. (2021). Identity propaganda: Racial narratives and disinformation. *New Media & Society*, 14614448211029293.
28. Freelon, D., Bossetta, M., Wells, C., Lukito, J., Xia, Y., & Adams, K. (2020). Black trolls matter: Racial and ideological asymmetries in social media disinformation. *Social Science Computer Review*, https://doi.org/10.1177/0894439320914853.
29. Freelon et al., Black trolls matter, p. 14.
30. Jankowicz, N. (2020). *How to lose the information war: Russia, fake news, and the future of conflict*. Bloomsbury Publishing.
31. Tufekci, Z. (2018, August 14). How social media took us from Tahrir Square to Donald Trump. *MIT Technology Review*.
32. O'Connell, B. (2018, October 23). How does Facebook make money? *The Street*, https://www.thestreet.com/technology/how-does-facebook-make-money-14754098.
33. Meta. (2022, February 2). Meta reports fourth quarter and full year 2021 results, https://s21.q4cdn.com/399680738/files/doc_financials/2021/q4/FB-12.31 .2021-Exhibit-99.1-Final.pdf.
34. Lima, C. (2021, October 26). A whistleblower's power: Key takeaways from the Facebook papers. *The Washington Post*, 26.
35. For reports' findings and summaries, see Isaac, M. (2021, October 29). Facebook wrestles with the features it used to define social networking. *The New York Times*, https://www .nytimes.com/2021/10/25/technology/facebook-like-share-buttons.html.
36. Kantrowitz, A. (2021, November 5). The case to reform the share button, according to Facebook's own research. *OneZero*, https://onezero.medium.com/the-case-to-reform -the-share-button-according-to-facebooks-own-research-ed2073720564.
37. Merrill, J. B., & Oremus, W. (2021, October 26). Five points for anger, one for a "like": How Facebook's formula fostered rage and misinformation. *The Washington Post*.
38. Merrill & Oremus, Five points for anger.
39. Frenkel, S., & Kang, C. (2021). *An ugly truth: Inside Facebook's battle for domination*. Hachette UK, p. 63.
40. Zarouali, B., Dobber, T., De Pauw, G., & de Vreese, C. (2020). Using a personality-profiling algorithm to investigate political microtargeting: Assessing the persuasion effects of personality-tailored ads on social media. *Communication Research*, 0093650220961965.

41. Aral, S. (2021). *The hype machine: How social media disrupts our elections, our economy, and our health—and how we must adapt.* Currency.
42. Bail, C. (2021). *Breaking the social media prism.* Princeton University Press, p. 50.
43. Goffman, E. (2021). *The presentation of self in everyday life.* Anchor. (Original work published 1956)
44. Goffman, *Presentation of self in everyday life*, p. 10.
45. Vaidhyanathan, S. (2018). *Antisocial media: How Facebook disconnects us and undermines democracy.* Oxford University Press, p. 50.
46. Vaidhyanathan, *Antisocial media*, p. 50.
47. Pennycook, G., Epstein, Z., Mosleh, M., Arechar, A. A., Eckles, D., & Rand, D. G. (2021). Shifting attention to accuracy can reduce misinformation online. *Nature*, 592(7855), 590–595, p. 592.
48. Settle, J. E. (2018). *Frenemies: How social media polarizes America.* Cambridge University Press, p. 8.
49. Settle, *Frenemies*, p. 50.
50. Settle, *Frenemies*, p. 79.
51. McClain, C., Widjaya, R., Rivero, G., & Smith, A. (2021). The behaviors and attitudes of US adults on Twitter. *Pew Research Center*, https://www.pewresearch.org/internet /2021/11/15/the-behaviors-and-attitudes-of-u-s-adults-on-twitter/.
52. Molokach, B., Oittinen, E., Young, D., Bleakley, A., Langbaum, J. (November 18, 2022). "Epistemic Humility and Media Use as Predictors of Belief in Misinformation." Paper Presented at the annual meeting of the National Communication Association in New Orleans, LA, November 17–20.
53. See Nelson, J. L., & Webster, J. G. (2017, July–September). The myth of partisan selective exposure: A portrait of the online political news audience. *Social Media + Society*, 1–13. Eady, G., Nagler, J., Guess, A., Zilinsky, J., & Tucker, J. A. (2019). How many people live in political bubbles on social media? Evidence from linked survey and Twitter data. *Sage Open*, 9(1), 2158244019832705.
54. The Reuters Institute for Journalism & Fletcher, R. (2020, January 24). *The truth behind filter bubbles: Bursting some myths.* Reuters Institute.
55. Garrett, The "echo chamber" distraction, p. 370.
56. Bruns, A. (2019). *Are filter bubbles real?* John Wiley & Sons.
57. Bruns, A. (2019, July 30). Filter bubbles and echo chambers: Debunking the myths. *Medium*, https://medium.com/dmrc-at-large/are-filter-bubbles-real-3be22bd9230e.
58. Nguyen, C. T. (2020). Echo chambers and epistemic bubbles. *Episteme*, 17(2), 141–161.
59. Tufekci, How social media took us from Tahrir Square to Donald Trump, pp. 14, 18.
60. See Edelson, L., & McCoy, D. (2021, September 22). How Facebook hinders misinformation research. *Scientific American*, https://www.scientificamerican.com /article/how-facebookhinders-misinformation-research.
61. Mehta, I. (2023, February 14). Twitter's Restrictive API May Leave Researchers Out in the Cold. *Tech Crunch*, https://techcrunch.com/2023/02/14/twitters-restrictive-api -may-leave-researchers-out-in-the-cold/.

62. Gramlich, J. (2021, June 1). 10 facts About Americans and Facebook. *Pew Research Center*. https://www.pewresearch.org/fact-tank/2021/06/01/facts-about-americans -and-facebook/.

63. Silverman, B. [@brandonsilverm]. (2022, June 8). Instead of using measurements that try and capture some sort of mythological average experience . . . *Twitter*, https:// twitter.com/brandonsilverm/status/1534527964796186625.

64. Lewis-Kraus, G. (2022, June 3). How harmful is social media? *The New Yorker*, https://www.newyorker.com/culture/annals-of-inquiry/we-know-less-about-social -media-than-we-think.

65. Nelson, J. L., & Taneja, H. (2018). The small, disloyal fake news audience: The role of audience availability in fake news consumption. *New Media & Society*, 20(10), 3720–3737.

66. Enders, A. M., Uscinski, J. E., Seelig, M. I., Klofstad, C. A., Wuchty, S., Funchion, J. R., . . . & Stoler, J. (2021). The relationship between social media use and beliefs in conspiracy theories and misinformation. *Political Behavior*, 44(3), 1–24.

67. Guess, A. M. (2021). (Almost) everything in moderation: New evidence on Americans' online media diets. *American Journal of Political Science*, 65(4), 1007–1022.

68. Bekafigo, M. A., & McBride, A. (2013). Who tweets about politics? Political participation of Twitter users during the 2011 gubernatorial elections. *Social Science Computer Review*, 31(5), 625–643.

69. Garrett, R. K. (2019). Social media's contribution to political misperceptions in US presidential elections. *PLoS ONE*, 14(3), e0213500.

70. Ribeiro, M. H., Ottoni, R., West, R., Almeida, V. A., & Meira, W., Jr. (2020, January). Auditing radicalization pathways on YouTube. In M. Hildebrandt & C. Castillo (Eds.), *Proceedings of the 2020 conference on fairness, accountability, and transparency* (pp. 131–141). Association for Computing Machinery.

71. Chen, A. Y., Nyhan, B., Reifler, J., Robertson, R. E., & Wilson, C. (2022). Subscriptions and external links help drive resentful users to alternative and extremist YouTube videos. arXiv preprint arXiv:2204.10921, p. 10, https://arxiv.org/abs/2204.10921.

72. Ribeiro et al., Auditing radicalization pathways on YouTube.

73. Lewis-Kraus, How harmful is social media?

74. Bor, A., & Petersen, M. B. (2022). The psychology of online political hostility: A comprehensive, cross-national test of the mismatch hypothesis. *American Political Science Review*, 116(1), 1–18, p. 15.

75. Sydnor, E. (2019). *Disrespectful democracy: The psychology of political incivility*. Columbia University Press.

76. Rasheed, H., Brewer, P. R., & Young, D. G. (2021, May). "I hate arguments": Conflict avoidance, competitive trait anxiety, and social media political expression. Paper presented at the 2021 annual meeting of the International Communication Association. Virtual conference, May 27–31.

77. Brady, W. J., Crockett, M. J., & Van Bavel, J. J. (2020). The MAD model of moral contagion: The role of motivation, attention, and design in the spread of moralized content online. *Perspectives on Psychological Science*, 15(4), 978–1010, p. 978.

78. Brady, W. J., Wills, J. A., Jost, J. T., Tucker, J. A., & Van Bavel, J. J. (2017). Emotion shapes the diffusion of moralized content in social networks. *Proceedings of the National Academy of Sciences*, 114(28), 7313–7318.

79. Brady, W. J., Wills, J. A., Burkart, D., Jost, J. T., & Van Bavel, J. J. (2019). An ideological asymmetry in the diffusion of moralized content on social media among political leaders. *Journal of Experimental Psychology: General*, 148, 1802–1813. Brady et al., Emotion shapes the diffusion of moralized content in social networks.

80. Rufo, C. [@realchrisrufo]. (2022, July 21). No child has an innate sense of being "genderqueer," "pansexual," "two-spirit," or "gender-fluid." Adults impose these ideological constructs on children . . . *Twitter*, https://twitter.com/realchrisrufo/status /1550247931453718528.

81. Pennycook, G., & Rand, D. G. (2021). The psychology of fake news. *Trends in Cognitive Sciences*, 25(5), 388–402. Solovev, K., & Pröllochs, N. (2022, April). Moral emotions shape the virality of COVID-19 misinformation on social media. In F. Laforest, R. Troncy, E. Simperl, et al. (Eds.), *Proceedings of the ACM Web Conference 2022* (pp. 3706–3717). Association for Computing Machinery.

82. Osmundsen, M., Bor, A., Vahlstrup, P. B., Bechmann, A., & Petersen, M. B. (2021). Partisan polarization is the primary psychological motivation behind political fake news sharing on Twitter. *American Political Science Review*, 115(3), 999–1015.

83. Pennycook et al., Shifting attention to accuracy can reduce misinformation online, p. 592.

84. Ernst, N., Blassnig, S., Engesser, S., Büchel, F., & Esser, F. (2019). Populists prefer social media over talk shows: An analysis of populist messages and stylistic elements across six countries. *Social Media + Society*, 5(1), 2056305118823358. Bennett, A., & Seyis, D. (2021). The online market's invisible hand: Internet media and rising populism. *Political Studies*, 00323217211033230.

85. Ernst et al., Populists prefer social media over talk shows.

86. Brady et al., An ideological asymmetry.

87. Brady et al., An ideological asymmetry, p. 1808.

88. See Kyrychenko, Y. (2022, March 26). Big data, social media and politics: Who shares fake news on Facebook and more with Joshua Tucker. *Medium*, https://medium.com /random-forest-dsc/big-data-social-media-and-politics-how-tech-shapes-democracy -with-joshua-tucker-c4d8321b7e1b.

89. Guess, A., Nagler, J., & Tucker, J. (2019). Less than you think: Prevalence and predictors of fake news dissemination on Facebook. *Science Advances*, 5(1), eaau4586.

90. Guess, A., Nyhan, B., & Reifler, J. (2018). Selective exposure to misinformation: Evidence from the consumption of fake news during the 2016 US presidential campaign. *European Research Council*, 9(3), 1–14, p. 2.

91. Reuning, K., Whitesell, A., & Hannah, A. L. (2022). Facebook algorithm changes may have amplified local Republican parties. *Research & Politics*, 9(2), 20531680221103809.

NOTES TO PAGES 220–222

92. Jost, J. T., van der Linden, S., Panagopoulos, C., Hardin, C. (2018). Ideological asymmetries in conformity, desire for shared reality, and the spread of misinformation. *Current Opinion in Psychology*, 23, 77–83.
93. Garrett, R. K., & Bond, R. M. (2021). Conservatives' susceptibility to political misperceptions. *Science Advances*, 7(23), eabf1234.
94. Yang, Y., Davis, T., & Hindman, M. (2022). Visual Misinformation on Facebook. *Journal of Communication*. Preprint: https://doi.org/10.1093/joc/jqac051.
95. Freelon, D., Marwick, A., & Kreiss, D. (2020). False equivalencies: Online activism from left to right. *Science*, 369(6508), 1197–1201, p. 1199.
96. Benkler, Y., Faris, R., & Roberts, H. (2018). *Network propaganda: Manipulation, disinformation, and radicalization in American politics*. Oxford University Press.
97. Freelon, D. (2019, December 18). Tweeting left, right, & center: How users and attention are distributed across Twitter. *Knight Foundation*, https://knightfoundation .org/wp-content/uploads/2019/12/KF-Twitter-Report-Part1-v6.pdf.
98. Swisher, K. (2018, October 8). Zuckerberg: The Recode interview. *Recode*, https:// www.vox.com/2018/7/18/17575156/ mark-zuckerberg-interview-facebook-recode-kara-swisher.
99. Facebook (n.d.). Meta's third-party fact-checking program. Facebook.com, https:// www.facebook.com/journalismproject/programs/third-party-fact-checking.
100. Facebook (n.d.). About fact-checking on Facebook and Instagram. Facebook .com. https://www.facebook.com/business/help/2593586717571940 ?id=673052479947730.
101. Bengani, P., & Karbal, I. (2020, October 30). Five days of Facebook fact-checking. *Columbia Journalism Review*, cjr.org/analysis/five-days-of-facebook-fact-checking.php.
102. Jin, K. (2020, Dec 18). Keeping people safe and informed about the coronavirus, Facebook.com. https://about.fb.com/news/2020/12/coronavirus/#latest.
103. Jim, K. Keeping people safe and informed.
104. Facebook (2020, September 3). New steps to protect the US elections. Facebook.com, https://about.fb.com/news/2020/09/additional-steps-to-protect-the-us-elections/.
105. Levine, A. S. (2021, October 25). Inside Facebook's struggle to contain insurrectionists' posts. *Politico*, https://www.politico.com/news/2021/10/25/facebook-jan-6 -election-claims-516997.
106. Facebook Oversight Board. (2021, May). Oversight Board upholds former president Trump's suspension, finds Facebook failed to impose proper penalty. *Facebook Oversight Board*, https://oversightboard.com/news/226612455899839-oversight -board-upholds-former-president-trump-s-suspension-finds-facebook-failed-to-impose -proper-penalty/.
107. Emily K. Vraga & Leticia Bode. (2020). Defining misinformation and understanding its bounded nature: Using expertise and evidence for describing misinformation, *Political Communication*, 37(1), 136–144, https://doi.org/10.1080/10584609.2020 .1716500.

108. Mantzarlis, A. (2018, March 12). Six key points from the EU Commission's new report on disinformation. *Poynter*, https://www.poynter.org/fact-checking/2018/six-key -points-from-the-eu-commission%c2%92s-new-report-on-disinformation/.

109. Oremus, W. (2022, March 3). To fight misinformation, Twitter expands project to let users fact-check each other's tweets. *The Washington Post*, https://www.washingtonpost .com/technology/2022/03/03/twitter-birdwatch-fact-check-misinfo-test/.

110. Pennycook, G., McPhetres, J., Zhang, Y., Lu, J. G., & Rand, D. G. (2020). Fighting COVID-19 misinformation on social media: Experimental evidence for a scalable accuracy-nudge intervention. *Psychological Science*, 31(7), 770–780.

111. Fazio, L. (2020). Pausing to consider why a headline is true or false can help reduce the sharing of false news. *Harvard Kennedy School Misinformation Review*, 1(2), https:// doi.org/10.37016/mr-2020-009.

9. Disrupt Us

1. Finkel, E. J., Bail, C. A., Cikara, M., Ditto, P. H., Iyengar, S., Klar, S., . . . & Druckman, J. N. (2020). Political sectarianism in America. *Science*, 370(6516), 533–536, p. 536.

2. Althaus, S. L. (2012). What's good and bad in political communication research? Normative standards for evaluating media and citizen performance. In H. A. Semetko & M. Scammell (Eds.), *Sage handbook of political communication* (pp. 97–112). Sage Publications.

3. Election Coverage and Democracy Network. (2020). *Recommendations for media covering the 2020 U.S. presidential election*, https://mediafordemocracy.org/wp -content/uploads/2020/10/ECAD-Recommendations.pdf.

4. Viser, M. (2022, September 26). The Biden-Trump rematch, in many ways, has already begun. *The Washington Post*.

5. Cadelago, C., & McGraw, M. (2022, October 28). Biden and Trump step into a Pennsylvania Proxy War. *Politico*.

6. Todd, C., Murray, M., Kamisar, B., Bowman, B., & Marquez, A. (2022, November 2). The 2022 midterms are just another battle between America's entrenched divides. *NBC News*, https://www.nbcnews.com/meet-the-press/first-read/2022-midterms-are-just -another-battle-entrenched-divides-rcna55201.

7. Young, D. G., Hoffman, L. H., & Roth, D. (2019). "Showdowns," "duels," and "nail-biters": How aggressive strategic game frames in campaign coverage fuel public perceptions of incivility. In Boatright, R. G., Shaffer, T. J., Sobieraj, S., & Young, D. G. (Eds.), *A Crisis of Civility?* (pp. 83–94). Routledge.

8. Brown, S. (1937). Society of Newspaper Editors. *The Public Opinion Quarterly*, 1(4), 114–120, p. 114.

9. Brown, S. Society of Newspaper Editors. Saalberg, H. (1973). The canons of journal-ism: A 50-year perspective. *Journalism Quarterly*, 50(4), 731–734, p. 731.

10. Saalberg, Canons of journalism, p. 734.

11. Darr, J. P., Hitt, M. P., & Dunaway, J. L. (2021). *Home style opinion: How local newspapers can slow polarization*. Cambridge University Press.

12. The Retrospect. (2022, March 25). Anti-ragebait, pro-community.
13. Neff, T., & Pickard, V. (2021). Funding democracy: Public media and democratic health in 33 countries. *The International Journal of Press/Politics*, 19401612211060255.
14. Pickard, V. (2019). *Democracy without journalism? Confronting the misinformation society*. Oxford University Press, p. 5.
15. Brady, W. J., Crockett, M. J., & Van Bavel, J. J. (2020). The MAD model of moral contagion: The role of motivation, attention, and design in the spread of moralized content online. *Perspectives on Psychological Science*, 15(4), 978–1010. Brady, W. J., Wills, J. A., Jost, J. T., Tucker, J. A., & Van Bavel, J. J. (2017). Emotion shapes the diffusion of moralized content in social networks. *Proceedings of the National Academy of Sciences*, 114(28), 7313–7318.
16. Mac, R. (2021, October 5). Who is Frances Haugen, the Facebook whistle-blower? *The New York Times*. https://www.nytimes.com/2021/10/05/technology/who-is-frances -haugen.html.
17. Alba, D. (2022, June 23). Meta pulls support for tool used to keep misinformation in check. *Bloomberg News*. Ingram, M. (2021, August 5). Facebook shuts down research, blames user privacy rules. *Columbia Journalism Review*. Roose, K. (2021, July 15). Inside Facebook's Data Wars. *The New York Times*.
18. Edelson, L., & McCoy, D. (2021, August 10). We research misinformation on Facebook. It just disabled our accounts. *The New York Times*.
19. Timberg, C. (2021, September 10). Facebook made big mistake in data it provided to researchers, undermining academic work. *The Washington Post*.
20. Timberg, Facebook made big mistake.
21. Silverman, B. [@brandonsilverm]. (2022, June 8). But that's not where we're at right now. We're not even close. *Twitter*, https://twitter.com/brandonsilverm/status /1534527972106915840.
22. Kreiss, D., & McGregor, S. C. (2019). The "arbiters of what our voters see": Facebook and Google's struggle with policy, process, and enforcement around political advertising. *Political Communication*, 36(4), 499–522.
23. Kreiss, D., & McGregor, S. (2022). A review and provocation: On polarization and platforms. *New Media and Society*. https://doi.org/10.1177/14614448231161880.
24. Hollingsworth, H., & Hanna, J. (2022, August 24). Kansas recount confirms results in favor of abortion rights. *AP*, https://apnews.com/article/kansas-abortion-vote-recount -e874f56806a9d63b473b24580ad7ea0c.
25. Druckman, J. N., Klar, S., Krupnikov, Y., Levendusky, M., & Ryan, J. B. (2022). (Mis)estimating affective polarization. *The Journal of Politics*, 84(2), 1106–1117.
26. Mason, L. (2015). "I disrespectfully agree": The differential effects of partisan sorting on social and issue polarization. *American Journal of Political Science*, 59(1), 128–145, p. 142.
27. Michaels, L. (2016, October 22). Black Jeopardy. *Saturday Night Live*. https://www .youtube.com/watch?v=O7VaXlMvAvk. Chödrön, P. (2019). *Welcoming the unwel- come: Wholehearted living in a brokenhearted world*. Shambhala Publications, p. 27.

28. Wojcieszak, M., & Warner, B. R. (2020). Can interparty contact reduce affective polarization? A systematic test of different forms of intergroup contact. *Political Communication*, 37(6), 789–811.

29. Joyce, N., & Harwood, J. (2014). Improving intergroup attitudes through televised vicarious intergroup contact: Social cognitive processing of ingroup and outgroup information. *Communication Research*, 41(5), 627–643.

30. Huddy, L., & Yair, O. (2021). Reducing affective polarization: Warm group relations or policy compromise? *Political Psychology*, 42(2), 291–309.

31. Linton, C., Watson, K., Yilek, C., & Quinn, M. (2022, July 13). "It felt as if a mob was being organized": Jan. 6 committee lays out Trump's role related to mobilizing extremists. *CBS News*. https://www.cbsnews.com/live-updates/january-6-committee -hearing-trump-extremists/

32. Krumrei-Mancuso, E. J. (2017). Intellectual humility and prosocial values: Direct and mediated effects. *The Journal of Positive Psychology*, 12(1), 13–28.

33. Koetke, J., Schumann, K., Porter, T., & Smilo-Morgan, I. (2021). Fallibility salience increases intellectual humility: Implications for people's willingness to investigate political misinformation. *Personality and Social Psychology Bulletin*, 01461672221080979.

34. Porter, T., Molina, D. C., Lucas, M., Oberle, C., & Trzesniewski, K. (2022). Classroom environment predicts changes in expressed intellectual humility. *Contemporary Educational Psychology*, 102081.

35. Watson, L. (2020). "Knowledge is power": Barriers to intellectual humility in the classroom. In M. Alfano, M. Lynch, A. Tanesini (Eds.), *The Routledge Handbook of Philosophy of Humility* (pp. 439–450). Routledge.

36. Young, D. G., Maloney, E. K., Bleakley, A., & Langbaum, J. B. (2022). "I feel it in my gut": Epistemic motivations, political beliefs, and misperceptions of COVID-19 and the 2020 US presidential election. *Journal of Social and Political Psychology*, 10(2), 643–656.

37. Krumrei-Mancuso, E. J. (2017). Intellectual humility and prosocial values: Direct and mediated effects. *The Journal of Positive Psychology*, 12(1), 13–28. Leary, M. R., Diebels, K. J., Davisson, E. K., Jongman-Sereno, K. P., Isherwood, J. C., Raimi, K. T., . . . & Hoyle, R. H. (2017). Cognitive and interpersonal features of intellectual humility. *Personality and Social Psychology Bulletin*, 43(6), 793–813.

Index